Contents

MATH

READING

SCIENCE

Introduction

▰▰▰▰▰▰▰▰▰▰▰▰▰▰▰▰▰

Are you tired of *ordinary* ACT coaching? Does advice telling you to narrow your options, pace yourself, and plug in answer choices seem overly simplistic and not enlightening? If so, you're reading the right book.

You know there's more to achieving a 36 on the ACT than just pacing yourself and making sure you answer each question. Maybe you already know that every correct reading question is worth another point but haven't been able to get beyond missing one or two per passage. Maybe you trip over the same trigonometry questions, no matter how much you practice. Maybe you're just goal-oriented and know that a score of 30 places you in the top 5 percent of the approximately 1.5 million students who take the test each year.

If any of these scenarios sounds familiar, congratulations! You're ahead of the game already. You are the target audience of this book: students who already meet high expectations in math, English, reading, and science, and yet want to achieve the perfect score on the ACT. You know the value of a high score and its ability to earn you the higher education positions you want and deserve.

If you strive for perfection on the ACT, you've opened the right book. This book is designed to help you gain skills and strategies that go far beyond the basics. You are reading the correct preparation guide if you possess the following qualities:

1. You have a general understanding of the ACT but would like to learn some of the test's many nuances.
2. You are a solid student: one who is focused, who has worked hard all along, and who will continue to work hard.
3. You answer many of the easier questions correctly already. This book hones in on questions that the ACT writes specifically to set the great students apart from the good ones.
4. You are willing to plan and practice. The effectiveness of this book will increase exponentially if you use it methodically and practice consistently. Begin preparing several weeks, if not a few months, before your test date, and consider supplementing this book with other practice materials.
5. You are ready for a textbook that offers fresh advice and is written in a conversational voice that speaks directly to you.

WHAT CONTENT IS ON THE ACT?

You have two options when registering for the ACT. You can take the ACT or the ACT Plus Writing, which includes a forty-minute essay. Although not all schools require the writing portion, many of the most competitive ones do. Before deciding which test to take, check with your counselor about schools that require the writing section, or find the information at *ACT.org*.

What Do the Sections of the Test Look Like?

English Section—36 points

- 45 minutes to read 5 passages and complete 75 questions
- Multiple-choice format—4 answer choices for each question
- Questions that test your knowledge of sentence structure, grammar, usage, and punctuation (about 40 questions)
- Questions that test your sense of style, strategy, revision, and organization in writing (about 35 questions)

Mathematics Section—36 points

- 60 minutes to complete 60 questions
- Multiple-choice format—5 answer choices for each question
- Questions that test your knowledge of pre-algebra and elementary algebra (about 24 questions
- Questions that test your knowledge of intermediate algebra and coordinate geometry (about 18 questions)
- Questions that test your knowledge of plane geometry and, to a lesser extent, trigonometry (about 18 questions)

Reading Section—36 points

- 35 minutes to read 4 or 5 passages and answer 40 questions
- Multiple-choice format—4 answer choices per question
- Passages that cover four different content areas: prose fiction, humanities, social studies, and natural sciences
- Questions that test your ability to extract detail, draw conclusions, determine main points and tone, and define vocabulary in context

Science Reasoning Section—36 points

- 35 minutes to read 6–7 passages and answer 40 questions
- Multiple-choice format—4 answer choices per question
- Passages that cover the subject areas of biology, chemistry, Earth/space science, and physics
- Questions that test your ability to analyze charts and graphs (about 15 questions), compare data from multiple experiments (about 18 questions), and scrutinize the viewpoints of two or more students, scientists, or hypotheses (about 7 questions)

Writing Section (Optional)—12 points

- 40 minutes to read a short prompt, plan, and write an essay in response to the given prompt
- Designed to test your ability to argue a position on an issue, to write a focused—and organized—essay, to use logic and detail to support your argument, and to use language effectively

HOW ARE SCORES FIGURED?

Your composite score reflects the average of all four subject-area scores: English, mathematics, reading, and science. The number of correct responses for each category, called a "raw score," is entered into a computer, which in turn sends it through a complex formula to give you a "scaled score." Because each testing session offers a different test, the ACT company has developed a complex algorithm so that all students, no matter which test they take, end up with comparative scores for comparative performances.

Each content category also has subcategories that will appear on your score report. For example, English has three subcategories: production of writing, knowledge of language, and conventions of standard English. (For more information on subcategories, see ACT's website under the heading "Understanding Your Scores.") You will receive a percentile score for each subcategory; however, the subcategory scores and the overall score for the category have no mathematical correlation. The subcategory percentile scores exist simply to help you assess your strengths as well as areas in which you could improve.

The optional writing section (the essay) is scored separately, so if you take the ACT and write the optional essay, you'll receive a composite essay score between 2 and 12 (the sum of two readers' scores) based on a rubric that assesses 4 categories. This book addresses the ACT writing rubric in detail in Chapter 25.

Finally, you'll receive a Science, Technology, Engineering, and Math (STEM) score that represents your overall performance on mathematics and science sections combined. If you take the ACT with the optional essay you'll also receive an English Language Arts (ELA) score that represents your overall performance on the English, reading, and writing tests. You will only receive an ELA score if you take the ACT with the optional essay.

How Many Questions Can I Miss and Still Earn an Exceptional Score?

To get into the 99th percentile, which is a score of 33, you can miss anywhere from 4–7 questions on each test for English and mathematics; however, you can miss only 2–4 science or reading questions. In order to achieve a perfect score of 36 on the ACT, you do not need to answer every question correctly. "Perfect" does not have to be perfect. In order to reach the 99th percentile on the writing test, you need to score an 11 or 12. The rubric is based on 6 points. Your scaled score is obtained by doubling the points you get. Your writing scaled score is then meshed with your English score; you will receive a composite English/Writing score. For example, if you score a 33 on English and a 10 on writing, your composite English/Writing score will be a 32. In order to achieve a 36, you must earn a 12 on the writing test and a 36 on the English test.

How Should I Use This Book to Achieve the Perfect Score?

As you work your way through this book, focus on perfection. Read through each section and complete all practice questions. This book gives a solid review of the content you need to know along with specific strategies for answering different types of problems and questions. In order to achieve the perfect score, you need to know how to answer all questions. As you work through each section of the book, identify which questions cause you the most difficulty; then go back and review the sections of the book that apply directly to those areas.

Along the way, you will see test-taking tips—specific, easily remembered advice about the best ways to approach the test.

WHAT SHOULD I BRING ON TEST DAY?

1. **TEST CENTER ADMINISTRATION TICKET**—if you are testing on an established ACT test date.
2. **IDENTIFICATION.** Your administration ticket is not identification. Your administration ticket tells you which type of identification to bring, or you can go to *www.actstudent.org* if you need further assistance.
3. **SHARPENED SOFT LEAD NO. 2 PENCILS** with good erasers. You may *not* use mechanical pencils or pens (ink or felt tip).
4. **A WATCH WITHOUT AN ALARM.** Pacing yourself is critical if you expect to achieve the perfect score. Your cell phone does not count as a watch; do not bring a phone in the room. If your watch alarm or phone sounds during testing, you will be dismissed and your answer document will not be scored.
5. **GRAPHING CALCULATOR.** *ACT.org* outlines specific parameters for allowable calculators.

POISE AND PREPARATION

This book guides you through the nuances of the ACT. It helps you reach a strong understanding of the content and provides plenty of practice questions to test your understanding of the concepts. But there are some basic things you can do to prepare for the ACT, as you should for any test. You may well be familiar with these guidelines, but it never hurts to have a reminder.

1. Make sure you have registered and paid for the right test.
2. Know the test location and how to get there.
3. Get plenty of sleep the night before the test.
4. Eat a healthy breakfast.
5. Don't overload on sugar, caffeine, or energy drinks.
6. Bring a healthy snack for the break to keep you going.
7. Double check that you have all your materials.
8. Relax—this is only a test.

Some of you may read this last piece of advice and think, "Relax?! Doesn't the author know that this is the most important test of my life?! If I don't do well, I'll never get into (insert your college of choice here), and my life will be ruined!"

The authors of this book do know how you are feeling and that you may be under a tremendous amount of pressure and stress to do well on the ACT. You would not be taking the time to read this book if you were not concerned about your scores. We repeat the last bit of advice: **Relax. Stay Calm. It's only a test.**

The ACT is only one factor that colleges and universities consider when making admissions decisions. Your high school courses, grades, extracurricular activities, community service, application essays, and recommendations are put together to give a more complete picture of you as an applicant. Admissions officers realize that ACT scores are a snapshot of how you did on one test on one particular day and that they do not define you as a person. Plus, you can (almost) always retake the test and submit your best scores.

Keeping the ACT in perspective is one of the best ways to ensure that you earn the scores that you are capable of getting. Too many students allow panic to set in on the day of the test. They forget the strategies they've practiced and start making simple mistakes. Do what

TIP

Don't study or review for the ACT the night before the test. Take some time off, watch a movie, or hang out with friends. Give your brain some down time.

you can to help yourself stay calm and focused. Listen to music, take deep breaths, work out, quote lines from your favorite movie, or tell jokes to your friends. Do something to help distract you from obsessing about the test.

That said, the focus that you direct to your preparation will give you the confidence you need on test day to achieve the perfect score. As a strong student, trust your abilities. *ACT 36* will reinforce the knowledge you already have without wasting time on information you don't need to know. Use this book to hone your skills and to enhance your understanding of the ACT testing format and questioning practices. Once you have refined the skills you already possess and have identified areas in which you need more work, use the book to turn your areas of concern into areas of strength. When you have practiced and prepared diligently, you can rest the night before the test and walk into the ACT room poised for greatness—ready to achieve the perfect score.

INSIDE THE ACT 36 MIND

Throughout the book you will see boxed text like this. These boxes contain helpful insights about how the test questions are structured, how to avoid distracters that are meant to confuse you, and how to arrive at correct answers—all within a limited time frame. Pay attention to them and good luck!

ONLINE PRACTICE TEST

Access the full-length online practice test at *barronsbooks.com/tp/ACT36* or by scanning the QR Code below.*

*Be sure to have your copy of *ACT 36*, 4th edition on hand to complete the registration process.

English

Fundamentally Speaking

1

→ **PREPARATION**

→ **OVERVIEW OF THE ENGLISH SECTION**

→ **THE FIVE KEYS OF THE ENGLISH SECTION**

→ **FINDING THE CORRECT ANSWER**

→ **"DEGREE OF DIFFICULTY" CONCEPTS**

→ **SIX POINTS TO REMEMBER**

PREPARATION

The ACT English section tries to determine your formal knowledge of writing. Working through this section of the test is *not* a creative process. To get a perfect score in English, trust your skill and intuition as an editor *and* commit to memory a finite number of the rules governing English usage. Induction into the 36 Club requires thorough knowledge of the conventions, strategies, and tips provided in the following chapters.

Chapters one through six will teach you the skills you'll need to edit with confidence. Forty-five minutes is ample time to complete all 75 questions in the English section provided you've mastered the fundamentals. Believe it or not, there are even more important reasons than college admission for committing this information to memory. Master the basics of English and you'll benefit in academic and professional realms long after you've forgotten about the ACT.

TIP

Master the basics of the English language and you'll benefit long after you've forgotten about the ACT.

OVERVIEW OF THE ENGLISH SECTION

As stated, you will have 45 minutes to answer 75 questions, which adds up to about 36 seconds per question. But keep the following idea in mind:

> 36 seconds is *too much time* for 75% of the questions on this test and *not enough time* for 25% of the questions.

Here are some basic ground rules:

- **THE READING ITSELF IS EASY.** There will be five, 15-question nonfiction passages on the test, all written at about ninth grade level.
- **SINCE DEGREE OF DIFFICULTY IS RANDOM, DO THE QUICK, EASY QUESTIONS FIRST.** The ACT attempts to throw you off by intermittently presenting more time-consuming questions. Never spend so much time on a time-consuming question that you lose the opportunity for easy points somewhere else.
- **THERE IS NO GUESSING PENALTY ON THIS OR ANY ACT SECTION.** Even if a question stumps you completely, guess.

- **THE ACT ENGLISH TEST *DOES NOT* COVER SPELLING.** Although you might be asked to fix some commonly misused words (there, their, and they're, for example), you won't have to spell anything correctly.
- **THE ACT ENGLISH TEST *DOES NOT* COVER VOCABULARY.** You won't be asked to define any words, although you will be asked to replace misused words with more acceptable or precise ones.
- **YOU *WILL* BE TESTED ON PUNCTUATION, GRAMMAR, USAGE, STYLE, AND ORGANIZATION.** The topics break down as follows (approximately):

Sentence Structure..25%
Grammar and Usage....................................15%
Writing Strategy and Revision....................15%
Sense of Style..15%
Organization...15%
Punctuation..15%

THE FIVE KEYS OF THE ENGLISH SECTION

1. Economy

Do not forget this one! Whether you're answering a question about punctuation, sentence structure, style, or grammar, *less* is usually *more*.

REMEMBER

The simplest sounding option is often the correct answer.

Here are two examples:

Stew Michaels wanted to <u>form</u> a nonprofit organization to help people in Darfur and Eastern Chad.

1. **A.** NO CHANGE
   B. begin and found
   C. formulate
   D. provide the formation of

EXPLANATION: (A) "Form" (A) is the most economical choice here. "Begin and found" (B) is redundant, "formulate" (C) is used incorrectly, and "provide the formation of" (D) is unnecessarily wordy. **In general, look for the most concise form of the phrase.**

Lance, <u>and his buddy,</u> think NASCAR is righteous.

2. **F.** NO CHANGE
   G. and his buddy,
   H. and his buddy
   J. , and his buddy

Many students make huge gains *just* by adopting the principle of economy. No matter what the question asks, the simplest sounding answer is right a lot of the time.

EXPLANATION: (H) The phrase "Lance and his buddy" is a compound noun, just like "He and I." The entire phrase, as one entity, warrants the plural verb "think," so no commas are necessary. **In general, avoid heavily punctuated answers.**

2. Order

Always tackle questions in the order that maximizes your potential to score well. A 10-second question gets you the same number of points as a 2-minute question. Do the quick questions first. Mark and come back to the ones that are going to take a while.

TIP

Easy questions are worth the same number of points as difficult ones.

Here's a sample passage and two questions:

> [1] The Wheaton family shuddered; they had never seen a live brown bear. [2] Miraculously, the bear approached the family and, ignoring them, began eating peanut butter. [3] It was all John could do to keep from laughing. [4] They knew they had <u>none</u>[1] time to run for safety, so they stuck together in the tent and hoped for the best.

1. **A.** NO CHANGE
    B. ample
    C. no
    D. few

2. Which of the following sequences of sentences would make paragraph 4 most logical?

    F. 2, 3, 1, 4
    G. 1, 4, 2, 3
    H. 1, 2, 3, 4
    J. 4, 1, 2, 3

At a glance, it's clear that question 2 will take you longer than question 1, and yet they are worth the same amount toward your overall score. As a general rule, questions that include a preceding statement or question that precedes the answer choices will take longer.

3. Pacing

A variety of traps in this section rely on students—especially bright ones—working too quickly. Slow down and read as an editor would read: quickly but conscientiously. Listen to wording, be aware of the contexts of underlined portions, and never assume an answer is correct without considering every option. For many of you, slowing down will be more important than working quickly.

TIP

Don't rush so much that you make silly mistakes.

4. Intuition

Once you slow down, trust yourself! Does it sound wrong, especially when you whisper it to yourself? If so, it probably is wrong. Sometimes, an answer choice will *look* wrong. Sometimes, you can trust your sense of style, organization, or development. Consider order and pacing, but work confidently.

TIP

Remember that all the answers are right in front of you, and one of them is correct!

On the other hand, remember that some questions intend to trap students because they don't consider that casual, conversational English is often unconventional. *Intuition* refers to your knowledge of formal, written English; it is not an invitation to accept lazy, casual, or colloquial language.

5. Clarity and Logic

First, think, "Is it economical?" Then think, "Is it clear?" and "Is it logical?" As a writer, it's important to practice economy, but it's equally important to employ clarity and logic. At times, correct answers may sound overly formal to you. Many native speakers of American English, for example, pronounce the word "have" in "could have" as "of" or "uh." The result sounds like, "I could of," or, "I coulda." To your peers, you might say, "That bike *I rode on* yesterday handled *nice*!" when formal English dictates that you say, "That bike *on which I rode* yesterday handled *nicely*!" Informal or "slang" versions of phrases will never be the correct answer to an ACT English question.

FINDING THE CORRECT ANSWER

Does It Sound Right?

Your ear can help you identify errors in sentence structure, diction, parallelism, and redundancy. For example, the ACT loves to test your ability to distinguish among fragments, sentences, and run-ons. Read the following fragment out loud:

> Although I love cheese.

Your ear tells you that it's an incomplete thought. Chapter 2 addresses independent and dependent clauses, which you'll need to know thoroughly to identify sentences, fragments, and run-ons, but use your ear as back-up.

Does It Look Right?

Sometimes your ear will fool you, so you'll need your eyes, too. Remember *could of*? Consider this example:

> The Senators have decided to take there tea in the Oak Room.

This sentence sounds fine. But what *looks* funny? Did you spot the incorrect use of *there*? To spot homonym errors such as this one, you'll need your eyes, not your ears. Refer to Chapter 4 for a list of these commonly misused words.

> If you need to review words that sound the same but are spelled differently, study the list of the most common word-choice goofs in Chapter 4.

Does It Make Sense?

Logic will help you identify misplaced modifiers, adjective/adverb issues, and colloquialisms when your eyes and ears fail you. For example, ACT often plays hide-and-seek with logical relationships:

> The mountain lake surrounded by elk are usually filled with icebergs.

Now cut some dead wood:

The ~~mountain~~ lake ~~surrounded by elk~~ are ~~usually~~ filled with icebergs.

which gives you:

The lake are filled with icebergs.

You know the final sentence in the series is incorrect, but it's easy to miss this subject-verb agreement error if you're working quickly. Practice will help you get to know some of these common ACT traps.

"DEGREE OF DIFFICULTY" CONCEPTS

Within the English section, you will occasionally see "Degree of Difficulty" concepts, designed to help more advanced students sort through nuances of the test. Here is a sample:

DEGREE OF DIFFICULTY CONCEPT: LISTS

I was raised in the Southwest. Yucca plants, gravel, and <u>railroad ties covered my front yard,</u>[1] sunny days dominated; hot-air balloons occasionally <u>would float</u>[2] overhead; and an overall sense of calm stoicism dominated the ethos.

1. **A.** NO CHANGE
   B. railroad ties covered my front yard;
   C. railroad ties covered my front yard
   D. railroad ties covered my front yard and

2. **F.** NO CHANGE
   G. will float
   H. float
   J. floated

EXPLANATIONS

1. **(B)** *Semicolons* used in lists are uncommon but may be found in the test. If phrases within lists contain commas, semicolons can be used to outrank commas and indicate list elements.
2. **(D)** *Parallel structure:* All list elements begin with a noun and an "ed" verb. The phrase "would float" in question 2 throws off this pattern and needs to be replaced.

Of Note Here: *Multiple prompts in a single sentence:* When confronted with multiple items in a sentence, read the entire sentence first. Then go back and address elements one at a time. This strategy will help you slow down and will provide clues as to how context influences individual answers.

As is always
the case on
the ACT, if you
don't know the
answer, guess.

SIX POINTS TO REMEMBER

1. Five passages—15 questions per passage. 45 minutes to answer 75 questions about style, sentence structure, punctuation, organization, grammar, and usage.

2. The reading itself is easy, and the degree of difficulty of the questions is random. If you don't know the answer, guess.

3. The ACT will not test your knowledge of spelling or vocabulary. Word choice questions all have to do with usage, not spelling.

4. Remember the Five Keys

 ECONOMY. The simplest sounding answer is right a lot of the time.

 ORDER. Always tackle questions in the order that maximizes your potential to score well.

 PACING. For many of you, slowing down will be more important than working quickly.

 INTUITION. Once you slow down, trust your abilities.

 CLARITY AND LOGIC. Remember that correct answers will be clear and logical. You may need to slow down at times to notice logical relationships.

5. Remember the following:

   - Does it sound right? This technique works best with sentence structure questions.
   - Does it look right? Consider the sentence visually even when it sounds right.
   - Does it make sense? Sometimes, you'll have to sift through extra verbiage to discover logical relationships.

6. Look for "Degree of Difficulty" concepts within the English chapters, which will help you confront and master some of the more subtle elements of the test.

Punctuation: Minimize the Madness 2

- → LESS IS MORE
- → FOUR KEYS TO PUNCTUATION QUESTIONS
- → TWELVE PUNCTUATION RULES
- → SIX KEY CONCEPTS TO MINIMIZE THE PUNCTUATION MADNESS

LESS IS MORE

One of the most important rules of thumb in punctuation is simplicity. Punctuation exists to clarify your sentence, not decorate it. The less you punctuate, the better.
Consider the following example:

> The Arapahoe football team won it's first game; and hopes to enter the league with a perfect record.

TIP

Worth repeating: The less you punctuate, the better!

The previous sentence needs only one punctuation mark: a period. Might you have been tempted to replace the semicolon with a comma? Might you have paused before removing the apostrophe in "it's"? "Less is More" means removing extra punctuation when you're unsure, not adding it.

FOUR KEYS TO PUNCTUATION QUESTIONS

1. It's Mostly About the Commas

The comma is the most heavily tested punctuation mark. Use the five comma rules in this chapter to hone your understanding of comma placement, and remember to punctuate sparingly. Of the ten or so punctuation questions on the test, half will test comma use.

2. Forget About Quotes

You do not need to know how to punctuate quotations properly to do well on the ACT English test.

3. Learn To Use Four Other Punctuation Marks

Using this chapter to learn *just a few* rules governing semicolons, colons, dashes, and apostrophes can help you when another punctuation mark is being tested.

4. Intuition Is Your Last Line of Defense

Consider the following example:

> <u>Bob, and his best friend, decided</u> they would spray paint Bob's car pink and put princess decals on the hood.

Do the commas in the previous sentence make sense to you on a gut level? Probably not. At times, your intuition or "feel" may have to replace your knowledge of punctuation rules. If you don't *see, hear, or sense* a pause, you probably *do not* need a comma, colon, semicolon, or dash.

TWELVE PUNCTUATION RULES

Before you study the 12 rules you do need to know, please review five grammatical terms:

---

1. **Clause:** A group of words that contains a subject, an object, or both, plus a verb.

    Example: *"I love The Beatles."*

    In this case, *"I"* is the subject, *"love"* is the verb, and *"The Beatles"* is the object.

2. **Independent Clause:** A clause that can stand on its own as a sentence.

    Example: *"I love the Beatles."*

3. **Dependent Clause:** A clause that cannot stand on its own as a sentence. A dependent clause "depends" on the rest of the sentence to make sense.

    Examples:

    "because I love the Beatles"
    "After I loved the Beatles"
    "loving The Beatles"
    "that I loved The Beatles"

4. **Possession:** showing ownership or belonging.

    Example: *Bob's copy of "Abbey Road" remains on the shelf.*

5. **Conjunction:** a word that connects words, phrases, or clauses together.

    Example: *The Beatles went through a trippy phase,* **but** *I still picture them as fairly clean-cut.*

Commas

COMMA RULE #1

A comma separates introductory words from the main part of the sentence.

Introductory Phrase = Comma

Correct: ***After seven hours of studying***, *I raised my ACT score by five points.*

Correct: ***Over the years***, *our band has gotten better.*

Correct: ***Knowing my teacher had "a thing" about being late***, *I made sure to be on time to class.*

Upon completion of the <u>building the contractor</u> sent us the bill.

A. NO CHANGE
B. building the contractor,
C. building, the contractor
D. building the, contractor

EXPLANATION: (C) The main subject is the contractor. The clause "Upon completion of the building" only indicates the time period when the bill was sent, so it really "introduces" the main part of the sentence.

COMMA RULE #2

Use a pair of commas to "hug" words or phrases that are nonessential to the integrity of the sentence.

Nonessential? Give it a Hug.

Information can be *relevant* but still not necessary to make a sentence grammatical. If you can remove the phrase and the sentence still makes sense, it needs commas around it.

Nonessential phrases are also called "by the way" phrases or "BTW" phrases, as in, *I am freaking out now, **by the way**, because prom is coming up.*

BTW? Give It a Hug.

Correct: *Joey, **the homeless man at my subway stop**, plays "Stairway to Heaven" on a flute.*

Correct: *Steve, **who loves tennis so much he wears white shorts to school in winter**, has a tournament in Phoenix next week.*

My brother <u>Ron, an optometrist owns</u> his own practice.

A. NO CHANGE
B. Ron an optometrist owns
C. Ron, an optometrist, owns
D. Ron—an optometrist—owns

EXPLANATION: (C) *An optometrist* is a nonessential or BTW phrase and needs a comma hug.

COMMA RULE #3

A comma separates two independent clauses if one of the following words comes in between them: For, And, Nor, But, Or, Yet, So. If it helps, you can remember that the first letters of these words spell "FANBOYS."

Independent, (FANBOYS) Independent

FANBOYS

For
And
Nor
But
Or
Yet
So

Please note:
Sentences that
contain an
independent
and a dependent
clause, separated
by a FANBOYS
word, often
look much like
the previous
sentences. In
these cases,
no comma is
necessary.

Correct: *I'm thinking of going to Georgetown,* **but** *I had a great time visiting U of A.*

Correct: *Steve was the best soccer player in his region,* **so** *they invited him to try out for the national team.*

Correct: *I'll take the #2 with a Coke,* **and** *I'll have a shake, too.*

Independent (FANBOYS) Dependent = No Comma

Correct: *I'm thinking of going to Georgetown* **but** *had a great time visiting U of A.*

Correct: *I'll take the #2 with a coke* **but** *will pass on the shake.*

PRACTICE QUESTION

Mike was the first person on the scene of the <u>accident, and tried</u> to help the injured passenger.

A. NO CHANGE
B. accident and tried
C. accident and, tried
D. accident; and tried

EXPLANATION: (B) When you see a FANBOYS word, split the sentence in half. Say the first part of the sentence alone: *Mike was the first person on the scene of the accident.* Then, say the part of the sentence that comes after the FANBOYS word alone: *tried to help the injured passenger.* The second half of the sentence doesn't sound like a complete sentence, so no comma is necessary.

Independent (FANBOYS) Dependent = No Comma

DEGREE OF DIFFICULTY CONCEPT: PUNCTUATION

PRACTICE QUESTION

My mother either wanted to ride her bicycle to <u>work or she</u> wanted to work out at the jiu-jitsu gym that evening.

A. NO CHANGE
B. work; or she
C. work or, she
D. work, or she

EXPLANATION: (D) The ACT will try to trap you with language that is, for lack of a better term, a little "off." Don't allow stilted language to lead you away from what you already know: if independent clauses surround a coordinating conjunction, a comma must precede the conjunction. You are used to seeing "and" between two clauses, but don't forget that the other FANBOYS words operate by the same set of rules.

COMMA RULE #4

A comma separates words in a list or series. This is the easy one.

Correct: *For summer camp, they say I need **two pairs of pants, bug spray, sunscreen, and a llama.***

Correct: *How could you **dump me, tell Julie you love her, go to prom with her, and then tell me** you love me!*

THE ADJECTIVE TEST

If you can say the word "and" between the adjectives that modify a noun, then they need a comma in between them. (*My friend has a relaxed, happy grin every day.*)

If they don't make sense after you insert "and," omit the comma. (*While bathing in the powerful summer sun, I dream of acing the ACT.*)

Another way to determine the need for a comma is to reverse the order of the adjectives. If the new combination still makes sense, then you need a comma. (*"happy, relaxed grin"* makes as much sense as *"relaxed, happy grin." "Summer powerful sun,"* on the other hand, makes no sense.)

PRACTICE QUESTION

I found an <u>expensive, long, turquoise prom dress</u> on the discount rack.

A. NO CHANGE
B. expensive long turquoise prom dress
C. expensive long, turquoise prom dress
D. expensive, long, turquoise, prom, dress

EXPLANATION: (A) Test the adjective combinations by placing "and" between them:

- *expensive and long dress* — sounds correct
- *long and turquoise dress* — sounds correct
- *turquoise and prom dress* — sounds *incorrect*

Through this test, you've determined that "prom" is not one of the adjectives. "Prom" and "dress" make a special pair; they are a team and can't be separated, like you and your date.

Reversing the adjectives also helps here, as in the following example: "*prom, turquoise dress*" sounds incorrect.

INSIDE THE ACT 36 MIND

The ACT will never test you on the serial or "Oxford" comma. In other words, you will never be asked to determine the correctness of last comma in a list.

COMMA RULE #5

A comma is used to separate an "ing" verbal phrase at the end of a sentence when the phrase refers to the entire sentence before it. Remember this rule as "The 'Ing' Thing." Thanks to the clever student who coined this term.

Test for this rule by changing the order of the two halves of the sentence. If the meaning of the sentence doesn't change, you need a comma:

Correct: Barbara did well, considering she hadn't studied at all.

Correct: *Considering she hadn't studied at all, Barbara did well.*

The next two examples are more subtle, but they help explain the rule more clearly:

Correct: *Mr. Spare offered rewards to students <u>trying</u> to improve their test scores.*
  (The absence of a comma indicates that the "ing" word refers only to the word right before it: "students." Therefore, no comma is necessary.)

Correct: *Mr. Spare offered rewards to students, <u>trying</u> to improve their test scores.*
  (The comma clarifies the meaning of the sentence, indicating that the "ing" word does more than describe *students* but also explains *why* Mr. Spare offered rewards. Therefore, a comma is necessary.)

PRACTICE QUESTION

The seven-year-old looked away from me <u>when he lied reinforcing my suspicions.</u>

  A. NO CHANGE
  B. when he, lied reinforcing my suspicions.
  C. when he lied, reinforcing my suspicions.
  D. when he lied; reinforcing my suspicions.

EXPLANATION: (C) It is clear that the "ing" word in this case modifies the whole clause preceding it, not just the word "lied" that precedes it. So, the sentence needs a comma before "reinforcing."

INSIDE THE ACT 36 MIND

Your intuition will come into play on "Ing Thing" questions because a natural pause will almost always occur when the "ing" word refers to the whole sentence.

Rules Governing Other Punctuation Marks

SEMICOLON RULE #1

A semicolon separates two independent clauses when you *do not* see one of the following words: For, And, Nor, But, Or, Yet, So. Again, remember the acronym FANBOYS.

Independent clauses without a FANBOYS word still need more than a comma between them. A comma just isn't enough.

Independent; Independent

Correct: *I'm thinking of going to Georgetown; D.C. is an ideal place for me to begin my political career.*

Correct: *Steve was the best soccer player in his region; his knuckle-ball free kicks were nothing short of lethal.*

Correct: *I'll take the #2 with a Coke; it's got the most trans fat, which is what I'm shooting for.*

SEMICOLON RULE #2

If you see *therefore, however, also, moreover, otherwise,* or another conjunctive adverb between two independent clauses, "hug" it with a semicolon and a comma. The first letter of each of these words spells "THAMO," which will help you identify them. When placed between two independent clauses, "THAMO" words need a semicolon in front of them and a comma behind.

Independent; *however,* Independent

Correct: *I like gigantic pick-up trucks; **however**, they're not practical in New York City.*

Correct: *Cats aren't friendly and often spray the couch; **therefore**, I have decided officially to become a dog person.*

DEGREE OF DIFFICULTY CONCEPT: PUNCTUATION

PRACTICE QUESTION

There is no predicting how the weather will be in Colorado in March. I <u>will however need</u> a sweater, as it is sure to be windy.

A. NO CHANGE
B. I will, however,
C. I will; however,
D. I will: however,

EXPLANATION: (B) When conjunctive adverbs interrupt a thought in the middle of a sentence, they become "BTW" phrases and need a comma hug. Conjunctive adverbs or THAMO (therefore, however, accordingly, moreover, otherwise) all operate this way. Two exceptions are "otherwise" and "so," which *do not* need a comma when they follow a semicolon. Make sure you consider the rule; don't just scan for what looks correct.

I enjoy playing volleyball in the <u>sand; however, I love</u> volleyball so much that I would probably play in the diaper-changing room of a preschool as well.

A. NO CHANGE
B. sand; however I love
C. sand, however, I love
D. sand however I love

EXPLANATION: (A) Two independent clauses surround the THAMO in this case.

Independent; *however,* **Independent**

After the rigorous ACT test, I plan on going home and taking a <u>nap, I</u> may also find a large container of ice cream and gorge myself.

A. NO CHANGE
B. nap I,
C. nap; I
D. nap: I

EXPLANATION: (C) You know that a comma is incorrect because the underlined portion doesn't follow one of the previously mentioned comma rules. Remember that two independent clauses need a stronger buffer than just a comma. Since each clause in the sentence is independent, you need a semicolon.

Independent; Independent

INSIDE THE ACT 36 MIND

It is never correct to connect two independent clauses with a comma. This error is known as a "comma splice."

COLON RULE

A colon follows an *independent* clause and introduces ("tees up") an example, explanation, short phrase, or list. The word, phrase, or clause that *follows* the colon need not be an independent clause.

A colon connects the sentence in front of it to the information that follows. The information after the colon is always related to the information that preceded it.

Sentence: detail, list, or explanation

Correct: *There's only one city where I'd ever live: Boulder, Colorado.*

Correct: *The grumpy teacher had only three rules in her class: be on time, sit quietly, and check your creativity at the door.*

PRACTICE QUESTION

Martha has a serious <u>problem and she's fourteen and</u> doesn't know how to tie her shoes.

A. NO CHANGE
B. problem, she's fourteen and
C. problem she's fourteen and
D. problem: she's fourteen and

EXPLANATION: (D) The key word in the first half of the sentence is "problem." The second half of the sentence indicates the nature of Martha's problem, which means that a colon should follow.

PRACTICE QUESTION

Charles took the following items to <u>the beach; a football</u>, a towel, an iPod, his cell phone, and an apple.

A. NO CHANGE
B. the beach: a football
C. the beach a football
D. the beach—a football

EXPLANATION: (B) The word "following" should tell you that a list is coming. When you introduce a list, you need a colon.

DASH RULE

Use dashes to "hug" a major break or interruption in thought. You need one on either side of the break. If ACT tests you on a dash, they'll usually want you to use two, one on each side of the statement in another "hug" situation.

An author might want a major break for emphasis, or she might need to place an entire sentence within the body of another sentence, in which case no other punctuation will suffice.

Correct: *Skiing at Vail is expensive—**it cost me one hundred forty-five bucks last time I went**—but the back bowls are worth every penny.*

—Complete Sentence/Nonessential Clause—

Dashes can also be used when placing a list within a sentence:

Correct: *Three of my most difficult classes—**history, physics, and English**— are all first thing in the morning.*

Correct: *My friends—**Jill, Kim, and Sophie**—all lifeguard with me during summer vacation.*

PRACTICE QUESTION

I can't believe the heat <u>today—it is 110 degrees—I</u> need to find some shade.

A. NO CHANGE
B. today, it is 110 degrees, I
C. today; it is 110 degrees, I
D. today: it is 110 degrees, I

EXPLANATION: (A) The in-set clause is an independent clause that needs an extra "hug" from two dashes.

PRACTICE QUESTION

I used to play with Barbie dolls, <u>only when I felt lonely and</u> I would make my brother play with me.

A. NO CHANGE
B. only when I felt lonely; and
C. only when I, felt lonely, and
D. —only when I felt lonely—and

EXPLANATION: (D) The phrase "only when I felt lonely" is a BTW that definitely needs a "hug" of some kind. The answer options don't include a comma hug, so the only logical response is D.

DEGREE OF DIFFICULTY CONCEPT: PUNCTUATION

There are three primary issues on the ballot this <u>season: health care, immigration, and tax reform, so I</u> plan on making some calls for the candidate I support.

A. NO CHANGE
B. season, health care, immigration, and tax reform, so I
C. season—health care, immigration, and tax reform—so I
D. season; health care, immigration, and tax reform; so I

EXPLANATION: (C) Your knowledge of punctuation may be tested here. In this instance, a BTW phrase already has commas in it and needs to be offset by a dash at each end. Although your understanding of colons might lead you to choose "NO CHANGE" here, separating the BTW phrase takes precedence grammatically over introducing a list.

APOSTROPHE RULES

Apostrophe Rule #1

An apostrophe indicates possession:

's = singular possession

Correct: ***Danny's*** *hat says "Duke" on it.*

s' = plural + possession

Correct: *Both of my **parents'** siblings live in Rochester, New York.*

Make sure the noun actually possesses something. You may rush to place an apostrophe just because the word is plural and "feels" like it needs one. When you slow down and think, you'll easily distinguish between plurality and possession.

Incorrect: *The Daltons' and the Larsons' travelled to Charleston during the month of June.*
Correct: *The Daltons' boat and the Larsons' car washed away in the flood.*

> **INSIDE THE ACT 36 MIND**
>
> When two nouns possess the same item or idea, the second noun is given the punctuation, not the first:
>
> Correct: Joe and Anne's basement was also destroyed by the flood.

I didn't like Mr. <u>Morrisons'</u> advice about talking to girls, so I decided to talk to my hamster, Lyle, instead.

    A. NO CHANGE
    B. Morrisons
    C. Morrisons,
    D. Morrison's

EXPLANATION: (D) Because "Mr." indicates only one person, we know that the apostrophe comes before the *s*. The correct spelling is Morrison's.

We drove to the lake <u>in Angie's and Paige's</u> convertible dressed as the latest all-girl band.

    A. NO CHANGE
    B. in: Angie and Paige's
    C. in Angie and Paige's
    D. in Angie and Paiges

EXPLANATION: (C) Be careful here. The first noun in the phrase "Angie and Paige" does not receive an apostrophe. Only the noun immediately before the object that is being possessed receives that honor.

Apostrophe Rule #2

An apostrophe indicates a contraction:
The only ones you're likely to see are

> *it's (it + is)*
> *there's (there + is)*
> *they're (they + are)*
> *who's (who + is)*
> *you're (you + are)*

Correct: ***It's*** *a fact that elephants are bigger than mice.*

Correct: *My cousin,* ***who's*** *a genius on the violin, will attend Juilliard.*

If you're unsure that the apostrophe correctly indicates a contraction, pull the word apart to make sure you're "hearing" it correctly.

Example (correct)*:* <u>*They're*</u> *going to dig a deep hole in my back yard.*

You say*:* <u>*They are*</u> *going to dig a deep hole in my back yard.*

Example (incorrect): *I am going to take a ride on* <u>*they're*</u> *boat.*

You say: *I am going to take a ride on* <u>*they are*</u> *boat.*

<u>Whose</u> going to the luau with us tonight?

A. NO CHANGE
B. Who's
C. Whose,
D. Who has

EXPLANATION: (B) If you separate the word and it still makes sense, you need a contraction: *who is = who's.*

INSIDE THE ACT 36 MIND

Because it's so easy to do, ACT will often try to convince you that a question tests punctuation when really it assesses a different skill. Look at the answer options. If the answer has punctuation in some responses and not others, or punctuation moves around within a phrase, punctuation may be a distracter. Knowing the rules thoroughly is the best way to avoid this trap.

SIX KEY CONCEPTS TO MINIMIZE THE PUNCTUATION MADNESS

1. Stop! Look! Listen! Does the sentence look correct? Does it sound correct? Use your eyes, ears, and sense of logic to help you identify punctuation problems.

2. Know twelve punctuation rules, five of which are comma rules.

3. Know your FANBOYS words: *for, and, nor, but, or, yet,* and *so,* and THAMO words: *therefore, however, also, moreover,* and *otherwise,* and know how to punctuate them.

4. Don't worry about quotations.

5. Know how to identify independent and dependent clauses.

6. Know how to identify BTWs or "By the Way Phrases," and don't forget about instances when punctuation "hugs" a word or phrase.

Sound Sentences

→ **BACK TO THE BASICS: SUBJECT-VERB AGREEMENT**

→ **TENSE AGREEMENT: KEEP IT CONSISTENT**

→ **SYNTAX AND STYLE**

→ **EIGHT BASIC CONCEPTS FOR KEEPING SENTENCES SOUND**

BACK TO THE BASICS: SUBJECT-VERB AGREEMENT

Rule #1: A noun must agree in number with its verb.

> The <u>boy takes</u> the test seriously.
>
> The <u>girls take</u> the test seriously.

Often you will know instinctively when a sentence sounds, looks, or feels awkward; however, certain questions on the ACT will test your conscious understanding of errors and may trick confident readers who work too quickly. Reading efficiently is not as important in the English section as it is in other sections. Instead of focusing on pacing, train yourself to slow down and read sentences on the ACT English section *exactly as they are written* on the test. To make sure you notice subtle mistakes, read sentences twice or read them quietly to yourself. Look for relationships between words—like a noun and a verb—that are separated by extra language. In this chapter, we offer several ways that you can identify and fix common sentence errors tested on the ACT.

TIP

Train your brain to read sentences on the ACT exactly as they are written. That's the key in choosing the correct answer.

Sentence Simplification

One of the easiest ways to identify issues with subject-verb agreement is to simplify the sentence.

Incorrect: Claudia and Kevin, *who are on the speech and debate team together,* first decides to start dating after Kevin asks Claudia to Winter Formal.

To test for subject-verb agreement, remove all words or phrases that are not critical to the subject or the action.

Incorrect: **Claudia and Kevin**, ~~*who are on the speech and debate team together,*~~ first **decides** ~~to start dating after Kevin asks Claudia to Winter Formal.~~

When you simplify, it becomes obvious that the subject and verb disagree:

Claudia and Kevin decides.

ACT often inserts extra phrases intentionally to try to confuse you. Words will appear to be the main subject of the sentence when they're not, especially if you're just scanning the underlined areas for an answer.

PRACTICE QUESTION

George, encouraged by his <u>friends, are</u> finally going to get a memorial tattoo.

A. No Change
B. friends, is
C. friends are
D. friends: are

EXPLANATION: (B) As you should always do, find the main subject and verb so that you don't make a hasty error: **George,** ~~encouraged by his friends~~, **are** ~~finally~~ going ~~to get a memorial tattoo~~. **George are going** is the simplified version of the sentence, which should sound wrong.

DEGREE OF DIFFICULTY CONCEPT: SUBJECT-VERB AGREEMENT

PRACTICE QUESTION

The few times I have been, the experience of climbing with friends <u>have given</u> me the joy that comes from scouting a new route, pushing my body in new ways, and eventually displaying the scars and scrapes that the rock leaves behind on my hands.

A. NO CHANGE
B. has given
C. has gave
D. have gave

EXPLANATION: (B) Subject-verb agreement is simple, so ACT makes it more complicated through positioning. The first phrase is placed at the beginning of the sentence to throw you off, so take it out. ~~The few times I have been~~. You're left with the **experience of climbing with friends have given me the joy . . . . Experience** is singular but **have given** is plural. All of a sudden it's a simple question.

"Each Is One Body": Looks Plural, Acts Singular

Remember the phrase *Each Is One Body* to help you remember that the pronoun *each*, as well as pronouns that end in *one* and *body,* are singular and require a singular verb such as *is*. The pronouns *either* and *neither* also fall into the singles category.

Common "Plural-Sounding" Words That "Act" Singular

Pronouns	Amount	Plural sounding but still singular	Collective Nouns
each	dollars	civics	group
everyone	years	news	team
every one	decades	media	committee
everybody		mathematics	class
anyone		measles	family
anybody			
someone			
no one			
either			
neither			

PRACTICE QUESTION

Each of the <u>boys dance</u> well enough to be on a music video.

    F. NO CHANGE
    G. boy's dance
    H. boys, dance
    J. boys dances

EXPLANATION: (J) The prepositional phrase *of the boys* points to the pronoun *each* as the subject of the sentence. Remove *of the boys* and try the sentence, remembering that the pronoun *each* belongs to the Singles Club: ***Each dances well enough to be on a music video.***

Amount Words: Special Circumstances

Words indicating amount, like the word ***none***, which must be followed by the word "of," may remain plural. In this case, look to the noun at the end of the "of" phrase, which dictates the verb's status.

- **None of** <u>my friends</u> want to see the new Tom Cruise movie with me. (**friends want**)
- **A fraction of** <u>my friends</u> work retail in the mall during the summer. (**friends work**)
- **Seventy percent of** <u>the student body</u> works during the summer. (**student body works**)

Other "amount" words that require the word "of" include *part, majority, some, all, none,* and *remainder.*

TENSE AGREEMENT: KEEP IT CONSISTENT

When a passage starts in one tense, it needs to stay in one tense, usually for the entire paragraph. Consider the following examples that highlight tense consistency:

Incorrect: Joe <u>ran</u> the race and <u>wins</u>.

Correct: Joe ran the race and won.

TIP

Use the phrase "each is one body" to remember that the word *each* and pronouns that end in *-one* and *-body* are singular.

Incorrect: Caitlin <u>tries</u> to teach her mom how to text but didn't expect her to get it.

Correct: Caitlin <u>tried</u> to teach her mom how to text but didn't expect her to get it.

Exception: If it is obvious that the tense has changed, then a shift in tenses is allowed:

Correct: Bruce <u>asked</u> Georgia to go to the independent movie today and <u>will ask</u> Chuck to go to the action thriller with him tomorrow.

PRACTICE QUESTION

As soon as the last bell rang, Mr. Brooks' class <u>rushes</u> the door.

A. NO CHANGE
B. will rush
C. has been rushing
D. rushed

EXPLANATION: (D) The verb *rang* and the verb *rushes* should match. Because *rang* is in the past tense, *rushes* should be **rushed**.

Pronoun Usage: Singular or Plural?

Each Is One Body pronouns (see previous page) dominate pronoun agreement questions. ACT will use these singular pronouns to trick us, mostly because when speaking we often use plural verbs with these words. The ACT assesses how well you know formal English, so memorize your **Each, Any, and Body** pronouns and look for them.

PRACTICE QUESTIONS

Circle the correct pronoun for the following sentences.

1. Everyone took (his/their) water gun to the spring gathering, which is held on the ball fields at the end of the school year.

2. If anybody wants to go to the water park this weekend, (she/they) should give (her/their) number to Abby so she can get (her/them) a discounted rate.

ANSWERS
1. his   2.   she, her, her

Other Issues You Might Encounter

REFLEXIVE PRONOUNS

Reflexive pronouns like *myself, herself, themselves,* and *ourselves,* reflect back on the subject of the sentence; they are not used as the subject of the sentence. ACT uses reflexive pronouns as a trap because some people use them incorrectly to "sound" more proper or formal:

Incorrect: Tammy and *myself* spent the day at the go-cart track.

Correct: Tammy and *I* spent the day at the go-cart track.

Also, make sure that subjects and reflexive pronouns agree in number:

Correct: Freida and Freddy sent *themselves* postcards while on their trip to Dubai.

Correct: Flo sent *herself* flowers after she broke up with Forrest.

Correct: We sent candy to *ourselves* before we even knew we won the contest.

OTHER AGREEMENT ISSUES

The following sample questions and explanations review two other areas of pronoun agreement that could appear on the ACT test.

PRACTICE QUESTION: AGREEMENT "IN PERSON"

When the juniors come to class, we know that not all of <u>you will have your</u> homework done.

F. NO CHANGE
G. you will have you're
H. them will have their
J. you, will have your

EXPLANATION: (H) Be aware of consistent "person." This sentence should stay in the third person. Replace the underlined portion with ***them will have their*** and read the sentence again.

PRACTICE QUESTION: UNCLEAR REFERENT

When Jeremy and Justin went to the rodeo in Kansas, they met the rodeo clowns and <u>they</u> showed them how to rope.

A. NO CHANGE
B. they,
C. , they
D. Jeremy

EXPLANATION: (D) In this sentence, you should notice the ambiguity surrounding who taught whom to rope. *So,* replace ***they*** with ***Jeremy*** (option D) and see if it sounds correct. It does—D is the only option that clarifies the sentence sufficiently.

SYNTAX AND STYLE

Sentences, Fragments, and Run-ons: Part or Whole?

Knowing whether or not a sentence is truly a sentence is essential for success on the ACT English section. Practice identifying sentences, fragments, and run-ons, and keep in mind that your knowledge of punctuation will often help you identify a grammatical sentence. This book includes a chapter on punctuation for review.

Our school joined with a neighboring <u>school and developed</u>[1] a girls' lacrosse team. After two years as a team, they made it to the state playoffs <u>and the team worked hard and placed second in the state this year</u>[2] Being incredibly proud. The[3] athletic director threw the team a party the weekend after they played. Next year, the team is looking to win the state championship and maintain a standard of excellence for years <u>to come, each</u>[4] school will likely develop separate teams in the future.

1. **A.** NO CHANGE
   B. Our school, joined with a neighboring school and developed a girls' lacrosse team
   C. Our school joined with a neighboring school, and developed a girls' lacrosse team.
   D. Our school joined with a neighboring school; developing a girls' lacrosse team.

2. **F.** NO CHANGE
   G. , and the team worked hard and placed second in the state this year.
   H. . And the team worked hard, and placed second in the state this year.
   J. : and the team worked hard and placed second in the state this year.

3. **A.** NO CHANGE
   B. Being incredibly proud – the
   C. Being incredibly proud, the
   D. Being incredibly proud the

4. **F.** NO CHANGE
   G. to come: each
   H. to come. Each
   J. to come and each

NOTE

The answers and explanations for these questions will review many of the punctuation rules from Chapter 2. We cannot tell you enough how much knowing punctuation rules will help you with these kinds of questions!

EXPLANATIONS

1. **(A)** The word ***and*** connects the independent clause, ***our school joined with a neighboring school***, with the dependent clause, ***developed a girls' lacrosse team***, so no comma is necessary to make a complete sentence.

   Independent (FANBOYS) Dependent = No Comma

2. **(G)** The word ***and*** connects two independent clauses, so you must include a comma to create a complete sentence.

   Independent, (FANBOYS) Independent

3. **(C)** ***Being incredibly proud*** describes ***the athletic director*** in the subsequent independent clause; it is an introductory phrase and can't stand alone.

   Nonessential Introduction = Comma

4. **(H)** The error displayed in this sentence is a comma splice: two independent clauses "spliced" together using a comma. Comma splices are to be avoided at all times. To complete this sentence, use either a semicolon or a period plus a capital letter.

~~independent, independent~~

DEGREE OF DIFFICULTY CONCEPT: THE "ING" TRAP

PRACTICE QUESTION

It is sometimes hard to tell at a dog park whether the owners or their pets enjoy themselves more. The dogs being off-leash for once and free to behave as all dogs want to, but the owners are also able to discuss their pets with other owners and share in the bonding that happens when enthusiasts discuss their favorite topic.

A. The dogs' being
B. The dogs were
C. The dogs are
D. The dogs

EXPLANATION: (C) "ing" phrases are never used as verbs, but ACT *loves* to trap students with this common error. If you see an "ing" phrase, first assume that ACT is setting a trap for you, then check the grammar. Note that ACT also tests your understanding of tense consistency here (the difference between B and C). See page 25 for more details on verb consistency.

Modifier Agreement

A phrase that describes the noun or verb must be located *immediately next to* the noun or verb that it is describing. Otherwise, confusion ensues:

Incorrect: *The tennis player asked the swimmer to help change her tire in a short skirt.*

The previous sentence is ambiguous because the clause describing the tennis player is in the wrong location. Moving "in a short skirt" clarifies this sentence:

Correct: *The tennis player in a short skirt asked the swimmer to help change her tire.*

Here's another example:

Incorrect: *The group of freshmen boys admired the cluster of senior girls with grins on their faces.*

If you move the phrase "with grins on their faces" *next to* the phrase it modifies, the meaning of the sentence becomes clear:

Correct: *With grins on their faces, the group of freshmen boys admired the cluster of senior girls.*

The flowering trees and the yellow bushes that bloom in early spring smell like rotten meat and sour milk in the front of the school and next to the school sign cause many students to park in the back of the building in order to save their noses a little torture.

F. NO CHANGE
G. Many students park in the back of the building in order to save their nose a little torture because of the flowering trees that smell like rotten meat and the yellow bushes that smell like sour milk, bloom in early spring in front of the school and next to the school sign.
H. The flowering trees smell like rotten meat and the yellow bushes smell like sour milk, bloom in early spring in front of the school and next to the school sign cause many students to park in the back of the building in order to save their noses a little torture.
J. Blooming in early spring, the flowering trees in front of the school that smell like rotten meat and the yellow bushes next to the school sign that smell like sour milk cause many students to park in the back of the building in order to save their noses a little torture.

TIP

Remember the modifier rule: The modifying phrase should be located next to the noun or verb that it modifies.

EXPLANATION: (J) You will find one or two of these time-consuming questions on each ACT English test. Notice that each option is a rewrite of the original sentence with a different arrangement of phrases, so all you need to do is find the one that makes the most sense. The modifier rule: **the modifying phrase should be located next to the noun or verb that it modifies.** If you're short on time, consider leaving this question until after you've done all the less time-consuming ones. The sentence that reads most smoothly and that has all of its modifiers in the correct places is option J.

DEGREE OF DIFFICULTY CONCEPT: PHRASE PLACEMENT MAKES THE DIFFERENCE

The only regret I have about going to college in Colorado is that I <u>more often</u> didn't follow my friends to the mountains to ski, hike, or climb. Even though I stayed home to study, I never . . .

The best placement for the underlined portion would be:

A. where it is now.
B. after the word *follow.*
C. after the word *friends.*
D. after the word *mountains.*

EXPLANATION: (D) When asked to place a phrase properly, remember that the phrase always modifies what it immediately follows. When confronted with a question like this one, go through your choices deliberately looking for subtle distinctions. The narrator doesn't regret following his *friends* more often; instead, he regrets not following his *friends to the mountains* more often. Watch out for these minute differences in meaning.

Parallel Structure: Achieving the Perfect Balance

Incorrect use of parallel structure is common in writing. If you want to ace the ACT, learn how to identify unparallel phrases and fix them.

Incorrect: *Miss Sharp sang, danced, and was cooing as she entered the room for our first period class.*

Lists offer great potential for faulty parallelism, so naturally ACT loves to use them. Fixing parallel structure requires that you use a skill you may have learned from Sesame Street years ago: "One of these things is not like the other." When the ACT gives you a list, find the mismatched item and make it match the others:

Correct: *Miss Sharp sang, danced, and cooed as she entered the room for our first period class.*

DEGREE OF DIFFICULTY CONCEPT: PARALLEL STRUCTURE

PRACTICE QUESTIONS

I had two friends who were avid climbers, <u>one still is:</u>[1] and most weekends they would grab climbing gear, pack a light lunch, <u>and would head up</u>[2] to The Flatirons to check out a new route.

1. **A.** NO CHANGE
   B. ; one still is
   C. —one still is—
   D. , one still is;

2. **F.** NO CHANGE
   G. and be heading up
   H. and headed up
   J. and head up

The few times I have been, the experience of climbing with friends has given me the joy that comes from scouting a new route, <u>to push my body</u>[3] in new ways, and eventually displaying the bruises, scars, and <u>scrapings</u>[4] that the rock leaves behind on my hands.

3. **A.** NO CHANGE
   B. by pushing my body
   C. pushed my body
   D. pushing my body

4. **F.** NO CHANGE
   G. scrapings,
   H. scrapes
   J. scraped

EXPLANATIONS: Parallel structure, parallel structure, and parallel structure. If you still aren't comfortable with this concept, also called *parallelism,* look it up on the internet and practice until you never miss a question.

1. **(C)** The parenthetical phrase "*one still is*" must have parallel punctuation on either side. One could use parentheses, commas, or dashes in this example, but there must be the same punctuation on either side of the phrase to maintain parallelism.

2. **(J)** In this question, all elements of the list need to employ present tense verbs: the first *would* before *grab* governs all verbs in the list.

3. **(D)** Here, list elements are formed using "ing" words, as the phrase "*joy that comes from*" governs all elements of the list. To make the sentence parallel, change *to push* to *pushing.*

4. **(H)** In order to follow the pattern in *bruises* and *scars,* the next term should be *scrapes* and not *scrapings.*

Of Note Here: In both of these examples two test questions appear within the same sentence. Don't let this ACT trick throw you; work through each question methodically.

EIGHT BASIC CONCEPTS FOR KEEPING SENTENCES SOUND

1. Listen to the "sound" of the sentence. If a sentence doesn't sound right, there is probably something wrong with it.

2. Slow down and read words exactly as they appear on the page. Intuition and pacing can help you, but not if your brain instinctively "hears" a sentence or phrase incorrectly.

3. Know how to simplify a sentence to determine its subject and verb so that a deceptively simple subject-verb agreement issue doesn't fly under your radar.

4. Remember the phrase "Each is One Body." ACT often tests your knowledge of the pronoun "each" and pronouns that end with "one" and "body." These pronouns are singular.

5. "Amount" pronouns like *none, fraction,* and *percent* that require the word "of" do not determine the subject-verb agreement. In these exceptional cases, the noun at the end of the "of" phrase dictates whether or not the verb is singular or plural.

6. Know how to identify independent and dependent clauses, and learn the punctuation rules from Chapter 2.

7. Be able to identify misplaced modifiers. It must be clear which noun a pronoun modifies. It must also be clear which phrase modifies which noun or verb.

8. To identify unparallel structure, ask, "Which of these things is not like the other?" If you see an underlined list, watch out for a parallel structure question.

World of Words

4

→ **SPOTTING WORD CHOICE MISTAKES**

→ **HOW TO THINK ABOUT WORD CHOICE QUESTIONS**

→ **COLLOQUIALISMS AND SLANG**

→ **MISUSED VERBS: SUBSTITUTE ANOTHER WORD**

→ **PREPOSITIONAL IDIOMS**

→ **ADJECTIVES AND ADVERBS**

→ **COMPARATIVES AND SUPERLATIVES**

→ **INCORRECT CONJUNCTIONS: CONTINUATION OR CONTRAST?**

→ **IMPRECISE AND REDUNDANT PHRASING**

→ **EIGHT WAYS TO CHOOSE THE RIGHT WORDS**

Consider three word choice mistakes:

- "It's getting cold, so I think I'll go to my room and achieve some pants."
- "This idea is true in and out of itself."
- "For every useful website in cyberspace, there's 100 useless ones."

Did you spot all three errors? Microsoft Word only caught one. *Achieve* should be *retrieve*, *in and out of* should be *in and of*, and *there's* should be *there are*.

SPOTTING WORD CHOICE MISTAKES

See if you can identify the incorrect word in each sentence:

1. Bob and myself are thinking about founding an internet company.

   Incorrect word: _____

2. Sadie is the biggest of my two Golden Retrievers.

   Incorrect word: _____

3. My car is old, but it looks like the engine might of been replaced.

   Incorrect word: _____

4. Stan is the person that left his keys at the front desk.

   Incorrect word: _____

5. I was worried over the idea that I had acne.

   Incorrect word: _____

You should have found the following *incorrect* uses: 1. *myself*. 2. *biggest*. 3. *of*. 4. *that*. 5. *over*. If you're shooting for the perfect score, then you'll need to tighten up your knowledge of the most subtle errors in usage and diction.

TIP

Don't use the plural pronoun *their* to refer to the singular noun "everyone."

It's easy for a high-achieving student to dismiss the concept of word choice when studying for the ACT. But you'll need to study a group of colloquialisms and word-use errors so common that they often feel, look, or sound correct.

Sadie the Golden Retriever, from question 2, is the *bigger* of the two dogs. (Note: Sadie would be *biggest* if there were three or more dogs.)

In the sentence *Everyone get out their notebook,* "everyone" refers to a group of people, so you might be tempted to use the plural pronoun *their*. Formal English dictates that you use a singular pronoun with words that end in *one* such as *someone, anyone, everyone,* and *no one*: *Everyone get out his or her notebook.* (See page 24, "Looks Plural, Acts Singular.")

HOW TO THINK ABOUT WORD CHOICE QUESTIONS
DEGREE OF DIFFICULTY CONCEPT: SUBTLE DISTINCTIONS

PRACTICE QUESTION

The dog trainer was amazing. We were able to <u>demand</u> behaviors from dogs without seeming to put forth much effort at all.

A. NO CHANGE
B. coax
C. compel
D. enlist

EXPLANATION: (B) Vocabulary is a subtle science. Option A is incorrect as anyone who has attempted to make a dog do something knows that to "demand" behaviors is usually ineffective. Then option B is not correct since "Compel" means "to bring about through force or pressure," which is not useful when training an animal. Option C is incorrect as "Enlist" can mean to gain help but is not commonly used in this context. This leaves option B. "Coax" implies gradual, subtle manipulation, and the narrator wants to emphasize how effortless the process seems.

Of Note Here: Moving quickly through a test makes one susceptible to overlooking the nuances of words. However, such nuances can be the difference between high scores and very high scores, so slow down and consider meanings. As suggested on page 35, it might help to define the word yourself in context and then "plug in" a synonym.

TIP

The ACT wants you to simplify word choice more often than it wants you to formalize language. Be economical and clear, not fancy!

To reign over the World of Words, you'll need to be able to do the following:

1. Identify incorrect colloquial, idiomatic, and slang expressions and replace them with more formal language.
2. Know a small list of misused homonyms, *except* versus *accept*, for example.
3. Understand when to use an adjective and when to use an adverb.
4. Develop good instincts when it comes to keeping verb tense consistent and pronoun use proper (covered in our "Sound Sentences" chapter).
5. Know the difference between comparatives and superlatives.
6. Identify and clarify wordy, imprecise, or redundant language.

COLLOQUIALISMS AND SLANG

Formal versus Informal Tone

Identifying colloquialisms and determining whether or not they are appropriate will require you to sense tone in a passage. If the passage is formal, avoid all colloquial expressions. If the passage has an informal feel, colloquial language might be appropriate:

Here's an example of the difference:

1. **FORMAL.** As stated, the student's belligerent behavior resulted in serious harm to the desk, to wit: a broken and mangled left desk leg, lacerations to the desk top, and four conglomerations of chewing gum beneath the aforementioned desktop. Witnesses, including but not limited to one student and one classroom teacher, corroborated that the student had in fact caused the damage. In short, the desk was ***all jacked up***.

2. **INFORMAL.** I went into class and, feeling angry, began to mess with my desk. After I'd worked the leg back and forth till it popped off, I broke it into a few pieces. Then having dismantled the leg completely, I wrote angry phrases on the desktop and stuck some gum underneath. Bobby turned to me and said, "Man, that desk is ***all jacked up***." I felt much better until I realized Mr. Loupe was standing right behind me.

Here are the major hints that passage two is informal:

1. first person "I"
2. colloquial verbs such as "mess"
3. contractions
4. dialog

REMEMBER

Knowing the difference between clear, precise writing and overly "fancy" writing will serve you well on the ACT.

Be sure you can sense the difference between informal and formal writing on the English section so you can spot incorrect usage accordingly. Remember these three rules:

1. ACT prefers clear writing to formal writing.
2. Informality does not excuse imprecision.
3. If the tone is formal, colloquialisms are never correct.

MISUSED VERBS: SUBSTITUTE ANOTHER WORD

If you see an underlined verb but don't notice a tense issue, you have a word choice question. What follows is a helpful strategy in such a situation:

1. Pretend to "white out" the underlined word.
2. Read the sentence again, substituting a word that makes sense.
3. Check the answer choices for a word that matches the word you substituted.

Consider the following example:

Around a child's first birthday, his awareness of his surroundings suddenly <u>heightens</u>.

A. NO CHANGE
B. improves
C. raises
D. rises

If you "white out" the underlined portion, you get the following:

Around a child's first birthday, his awareness of his surroundings suddenly _____.

Reading back over the sentence and attempting to fill in the blank, you probably realize that the sentence calls for a verb that means "gets better":

Around a child's first birthday, his awareness of his surroundings suddenly <u>gets better</u>.

Consider the answer choices. *Heightens* (A) can mean either "intensifies" or "increases in height." *Raise* and *rise* (C and D) have similar meanings; they also mean "intensify," "increase," or "move upward." *Improves* (B) is the only word that fits the definition "gets better" and is therefore correct. Answer **(B)**.

The substitution method is an invaluable tool for word choice questions. If you sense even slight imprecision, you probably need to make a change.

PREPOSITIONAL IDIOMS

TIP

Read carefully so that you don't miss an incorrect preposition in an idiom.

Idioms are words that make sense only through common use. Some idioms are easy to identify because they have become common figurative expressions: *nailing Jell-O to a wall* or *a couple sandwiches short of a picnic*. Other idioms, such as *on the other hand,* are so embedded in our language that we use them without considering their metaphorical or even illogical nature.

Prepositional idioms are the easiest to overlook. Consider the following phrases, all of which use the word *look*:

Do you . . .

   . . . look *up* a word or look *in* a word?
   . . . look *out* for traffic or look *on* for traffic?
   . . . look *over* a document or look *inside* a document?
   . . . look *to* grandma for advice or look *at* grandma for advice?
   . . . look *into* an issue or look *inside* an issue?

You're able to identify the correct ones, but you don't know why. You just *know*, for the same reason you know that a new trend is *in*, Bob is a little *off*, and something's wrong *with* that guy. But be careful: ACT will sometimes try to add an incorrect idiom surreptitiously.

To ace this section, slow down and think like an editor. Realize that you might fail to spot a prepositional idiom because your reading skills are *too good*. Also realize that there is often no logical explanation for the use of one idiom over another.

When I met Joan, she was so <u>onto</u>[1] dance that she wore a tutu to school. Now, she thinks <u>off</u>[2] dancing as little more than something to do on a Saturday night.

1. **A.** NO CHANGE
   B. in
   C. into
   D. in for

2. **F.** NO CHANGE
   G. in
   H. on
   J. of

ANSWERS

1. **(C)**   2. **(J)**

"Lucky 13" Misused Words

ACT plays favorites when it comes to commonly misused words. In this section, we give you the ACT favorites and explain them. If you want to explore misused words even further, we offer a short list at the end of the section.

No matter what you do, memorize this "Lucky 13" List:

1. ACCEPT VERSUS EXCEPT

Accept is the verb that usually means "recognize" or "take on."
Except means *apart from* and indicates a contrast. It often appears in its noun form, *exception*.

Examples:

- "I recently *accepted* a Fulbright Scholarship to study in Munich."
- "*Except* for Harleys, I hate motorcycles."

2. EFFECT VERSUS AFFECT

Effect, for the purposes of the ACT, will always be a noun synonymous with *result*.
Affect is a verb that means *to influence*.

Examples:

- The results of the homecoming vote *affected* the freshman class enormously.
- I don't really trust that Rogaine will have the desired *effect*, so I'm going for the comb-over.

3. FEWER VERSUS LESS

Fewer refers to a number, to something you can actually count.
Less refers to an amount of something.

Thinking about cooking might help you with this distinction. You have *fewer* chocolate chips but *less* flour. You have *fewer* tomatoes but *less* tomato sauce.

> **TIP**
>
> Memorize these commonly missed words— and create your own list.

> **REMEMBER**
>
> Colloquially, it's more common to use *less* than it is to use *fewer*. For example, "There are less cars on the road." This is incorrect! Watch out for this inconspicuous error.

Examples:

- I liked the presidential candidate a little *less* after he said he would solve global warming and joblessness by hiring people to build windmills.
- *Fewer* people voted in 2000 than in 2008.

4. THEN VERSUS THAN

Then refers to time, either something is coming next or something has occurred in the past. Fittingly, it sounds like "when."

Than indicates a comparison between two things. Fittingly, it sounds like "and."

Examples:

- I did crunches, and *then* I blasted my pecs.
- It was *then* that I discovered my talent for losing things.
- It's better to have loved and lost *than* never to have loved at all.
- Horses are generally bigger and more aggressive *than* ponies, but ponies are cuddlier.

5. TO, TOO, AND TWO

To is a preposition.

Too means *also*.

Two is the spelled-out version of *2*.

Slow down on these so you don't miss an easy one!

Examples:

- Charlie got a *two* on his AP chemistry test, at which point he decided to major in English.
- Going *to* the beach is Lance's favorite pastime.
- Kelly likes the beach, *too*.

6. IT'S VERSUS ITS

It's means *it is*.

Its is possessive.

You might also encounter *theirs, ours,* or *yours,* which behave similarly when indicating possession.

Examples:

- After battling *its* rival, the lion licked *its* wounds.
- *It's* unrealistic to think things will turn out well every time you do something, but you should still assume you'll succeed.

7. FARTHER VERSUS FURTHER

Farther indicates physical distance. ("Far" indicates distance.)

Further indicates degree or level. ("Fur" increases body heat by "degree.")

Examples:

- Littleton, Colorado is *farther* from Beijing than it is from Tokyo.
- When it comes to manipulating perspective, Picasso goes *further* than Cezanne.

8. COULD/WOULD/SHOULD/MIGHT *HAVE* VERSUS COULD/WOULD/SHOULD/MIGHT *OF*

Of is never correct.

Examples:

- Incorrect: I *might of* taken the EMT class, but I didn't have enough time in the evenings.
- Correct: I *might have* taken the EMT class, but I didn't have enough time in the evenings.

9. THEIR VERSUS THEY'RE VERSUS THERE

Their indicates possession.
They're is a contraction of *they are.*
There refers to location, as in *over there.*

Examples:

- *Their* SUV now costs $120 to fill up.
- *They're* considering buying a Prius.
- The Prius dealership is over *there* by Starbuck's, where they buy *their* five-dollar lattes.

10. THAT VERSUS WHICH

That adds specific information to a subject or object and doesn't need a comma before it.
Which is used as part of a by the way (BTW) phrase and needs a comma "hug"—see Chapter 2.

Examples:

- The waterfall *that* empties into Phelps Lake starts above the tree line. (The clause *empties into Phelps Lake* defines the waterfall.)
- The waterfall, *which* empties into Phelps Lake, starts above tree line. (The clause *empties into Phelps Lake* adds (BTW) information but doesn't define the subject.)

11. THAT/WHICH VERSUS WHO

That/Which are used with inanimate objects.
Who is used with humans.

Examples:

- Incorrect: The security guard *that* works at Target is actually Marilyn Monroe's cousin.
- Correct: The security guard *who* works at Target is actually Marilyn Monroe's cousin.
- Incorrect: The pet store owner, *which* loves Milky Ways, was waiting on a shipment of toucans.
- Correct: The pet store owner, *who* loves Milky Ways, was waiting on a shipment of toucans.

12. WHO VERSUS WHOM: SUBJECT OR OBJECT?

Substitute "who" for a subject (he, she, they, we)
Substitute "whom" for an object (him, her, them, us)

- Incorrect: Whom is the favorite to win Wimbledon?
- Correct: Who is the favorite to win Wimbledon?
- Incorrect: Who do you want to win Wimbledon?
- Correct: Whom do you want to win Wimbledon?

TIP

If you're confused about when to use *who* and *whom,* remember that who refers to a subject and whom refers to an object.

Hint #1 for Who/Whom:

Make the question into a statement and then substitute either *he* or *him*. *Him* has the same ending as *whom*, and both words refer to objects. *He* and *who* refer to subjects:

- Correct: Who is the favorite to win Wimbledon? Answer: He is. Use *who*.
- Correct: Whom do you want to win Wimbledon? Answer: I want him. Use *whom*.
- Correct: The painter *who* did the mural downtown is up for a major award.

    You'd say, ". . . he did the mural downtown . . . ," so *who* is correct!

- Correct: The painter, *whom* we contacted to do the mural downtown, is up for a major award.

    You'd say, ". . . we contacted him . . . ," so *whom* is correct!

Hint #2 for Who/Whom:

Think "who → verb" and "whom → noun/pronoun." *Who* stands in for a subject, so a verb will often follow it. Likewise, *whom* will usually precede a noun or pronoun.

13. I VERSUS ME WITH A LINKING VERB SUCH AS "TO BE"

Linking verbs are like "equals signs"; they don't act on objects. Therefore, they are often bracketed by subjects:

Example: It was I who answered the phone.

- Try to restructure the sentence so it makes sense: Who answered the phone? I answered the phone. You wouldn't say *Me answered the phone*. "I" is the correct pronoun.

    Example: The guy who dressed up like Shrek and scared the kids was *he*!

- You ask: Who dressed up like Shrek? Answer: He dressed up like Shrek. You wouldn't say *Him dressed up like Shrek*. "He" is the correct pronoun.

    Example: My brother is as unhappy as *I*. (Implied verb)

- An implied "am" could be added to the end of the sentence but isn't: *My brother is as unhappy as I (am)*. "I" is the correct pronoun even if "am" is implied.

    Example: Tim is happier than he.

- Again, a verb is implied. You wouldn't say *Tim is happier than him is*. You would say: Tim is happier than he is. "He" is the correct pronoun. Another way to test this sentence is to reverse the order. You would say *He is happier than Tim*, not *Him is happier than Tim*. Comparison sentences are often reversible.

Finally, here are some commonly misused phrases you might see:

supposed to, *not* suppose to	couldn't care less, *not* could care less
used to, *not* use to	intents and purposes, *not* intensive
toward, *not* towards	purposes
no one, *not* noone	going to, *not* gonna
anyway, *not* anyways	supposedly, *not* supposably

ADJECTIVES AND ADVERBS

You know the following distinction already: adjectives modify nouns; adverbs modify verbs, adjectives, and other adverbs. You can usually spot an adverb because it contains the suffix *-ly*.

The ACT may try to tempt you into "formalizing" the sentence with an adverb. Don't be fooled.

PRACTICE QUESTION

As <u>gently</u> as my dog is, she would still protect my family in an emergency.

A. NO CHANGE
B. gentle and tender
C. gently and tenderly
D. gentle

EXPLANATION: (D) A linking verb "links" a noun with an adjective. It defines them as equal, or at least as a pair. Linking verbs are often versions of "to be": *am, is, are, was, were, be, being,* and *been.* The following sentences are short to help you see the common use of noun + linking verb + adjective.

- She is gentle.
- They are perfect.
- We seem happy.

The third word in each sentence modifies the pronoun (the first word) in the sentence. When an active verb is added, the adjectives change to adverbs.

- She is smiling gently.
- They are playing perfectly.
- We seem to be singing happily.

PRACTICE QUESTIONS

Identify and fix the adverb problems in the following sentences.

1. The man's vision returned gradually, until finally he could see clear enough to make out the horizon.

2. Even though late-night television commercials often tell you it's easy, in reality it's difficult to get rich quick.

EXPLANATIONS

1. *Clear* should be changed to *clearly*. *Clearly* describes how the man could see. *See* is a verb, so only an adverb can modify it.

2. *Quick* should be changed to *quickly*. *Get* is a verb that needs an adverb to modify it. Incidentally, even though you might be tempted to change *easy* to *easily*, don't be fooled. *It's*, a contraction of "it is," contains the linking verb "to be." The adjective *easy* is the correct choice.

Remember: *Good* is an adjective and *well* is an adverb, unless you're talking about someone's physical or emotional state.

- Tiger Woods is so *good* at golf. (*Good* modifies Tiger.)
- Tiger Woods did not play *well* in his last tournament. (*Well* modifies how Tiger plays.)
- Tiger Woods is not *well*, so he won't play in the Open Championship. (*Well* refers to Tiger's physical state.)

COMPARATIVES AND SUPERLATIVES

Use comparatives (*bigger, faster, hotter, funnier*) when comparing two things. Use comparatives with *than*, as in, "Elephants are bigger than monkeys."

Use superlatives (*biggest, fastest, hottest, funniest*) when comparing *more than two things*.

Incorrect: Of the two 100-meter runners on the track team, Tim has the *fastest* time.

Correct: Of the two 100-meter runners on the track team, Tim has the *faster* time.

Incorrect: Ryan is the *stronger* of the three discus throwers.

Correct: Ryan is the *strongest* of the three discus throwers.

INCORRECT CONJUNCTIONS: CONTINUATION OR CONTRAST?

Transition words, such as the FANBOYS words (*for, and, nor, but, or, yet, so*) plus words like *because, when, before, after, since, unless, therefore*, and *although*, will indicate either continuation or contrast. If the second clause is a *continuation* of an idea, you'll need a word such as "and," "since," or "because." If the second clause *contrasts* the original statement, expect "but," "yet," or "although."

INSIDE THE ACT 36 MIND

ACT loves to mix up transition words to catch people who are just scanning the underlines for mistakes.

I had to get to work by 7:00, but the buses weren't running until 8:00. My grandmother told me that I could borrow her Buick, <u>and</u>[1] I couldn't get it started. At 6:45, I thought to call my co-worker Randy, <u>and luckily</u>[2] he hadn't left his house yet and could come get me.

1. **A.** NO CHANGE
   B. even though
   C. but
   D. but it wouldn't start and

2. **F.** NO CHANGE
   G. which
   H. but
   J. and unfortunately

ANSWERS

1. **(C)**   2. **(F)**

IMPRECISE AND REDUNDANT PHRASING

Chapter 1 explained that the ACT favors concise, economical writing.

Assume you're facing a question about imprecision or redundancy when . . .

> . . . you don't see anything grammatically wrong in or around the underlined section.

> . . . you sense that there are too many words, phrases, or clauses in the underlined section.

> . . . you see answer choices that reword the same idea.

> . . . you see the word OMIT in the answer choices.

DEGREE OF DIFFICULTY CONCEPT: SPOTTING REDUNDANCY

We got up after a lengthy debate about anatomy. <u>Having studied, my father</u> is a doctor and well versed about the human body. Needless to say, one look at Gray's Anatomy confirmed his opinion.

A. NO CHANGE
B. My father
C. Having earned his M.D., my father
D. Owing much to his studies, my father

EXPLANATION: (B) If you can omit words and achieve the same meaning, do so. "Cutting the dead wood" will buy you a few correct answers on the ACT English test every time. A wordier answer might be tempting here, but less is always more. "My father is a doctor" implies a good deal of study, so stating explicitly that he studied or earned a degree is redundant.

REMEMBER

For more extra-challenging practice, you can go online for the Challenge Round with 50 difficult questions.

TIP

If you can remove words from a sentence without changing its meaning, do so.

A few times my father took <u>my sister and I</u>[1] to the Albuquerque Balloon Fiesta grounds before dawn to watch hundreds of hot-air balloons launch. Later on during Balloon Fiesta <u>mornings, after</u>[2] many of the balloons had landed, <u>we sometimes searched out landing sites where we thought balloonists might land away from traffic and power lines.</u>[3] Once we got really lucky and a balloon touched down in the field right next to our house.[4]

1. A. NO CHANGE
  B. my sister and me
  C. us
  D. I and my sister

2. F. NO CHANGE
  G. mornings after
  H. mornings. After
  J. mornings; after

3. A. NO CHANGE
  B. we sometimes searched out landing sites away from traffic and power lines where balloonists might land.
  C. we sometimes searched out protected spots where we thought balloonists might land.
  D. we sometimes sought landing zones where, protected from traffic and other dangers, balloonists could land.

4. For the sake of clarity, the writer is considering adding the following sentence to the paragraph:

> Most of the time, though, we simply woke up at a normal hour and took in the spectacular view afforded to us and to all of the city's residents: a sky dotted with hundreds of balloons.

This sentence should be placed
  F. before sentence 1.
  G. after sentence 1.
  H. after sentence 2.
  J. after sentence 3.

(Explanations are on the following page.)

EXPLANATIONS

1. **(B)** This question tests your understanding of how subject and object pronouns function. When a *me* or *I* personal pronoun is the object of a sentence, then use the pronoun *me*. When it is the subject of the sentence, then use *I*.

2. **(F)** Remember comma rules here. A comma is needed after *mornings* to complete the prepositional phrase, "*during Balloon Fiesta mornings.*"

3. **(C)** This is a redundancy/economy of language question. When you see four different phrasings that essentially contain the same meaning, look for the most concise version. "NO CHANGE" might tempt you, but it is not the answer. *Landing sites* by definition is a spot where *balloonists would land.*

4. **(G)** This question tests your ability to determine logical paragraph organization. Since sentence 1 says "*a few times*" the narrator went to the grounds before dawn, it follows that the next sentence should be that "*most of the time*" the narrator woke up at a normal hour to watch the hot air balloons instead.

Of Note Here: As we've stated before, don't allow the existence of multiple questions within the same short passage distract you. Work methodically, using the context to answer questions one-by-one.

EIGHT WAYS TO CHOOSE THE RIGHT WORDS

1. For the most part, the ACT tests your knowledge of formal, written English. Except in rare cases, and *especially* if you sense formality, avoid colloquialisms and slang.

2. Know the "Lucky 13" list by heart, and review the list of other common mistakes.

3. Slow down and think like an editor, especially when you see a preposition.

4. Substitute your own word when you sense an inaccuracy.

5. Keep it simple when it comes to adjectives and adverbs, and know the rules.

6. Use a comparative with two and a superlative with more than two.

7. Think, "Continuation or contrast?" when a transitional phrase is in question.

8. Remove redundant or imprecise language. Be economical without being unclear.

Thinking Like a Writer

5

→ **IMPORTANT STRATEGIES TO CONSIDER**
→ **QUESTION CATEGORIES**
→ **PRACTICE THINKING LIKE A WRITER**
→ **SIX CRITICAL CONCEPTS TO HELP YOU THINK LIKE A WRITER**

The ACT English section includes questions that test your knowledge of strategy and style: essentially your understanding of how one might communicate effectively, clearly, and accurately. Strategy and style questions account for 25 to 35 percent of the test, or about 20 to 25 questions, so you do not want to overlook them. If you have a high score already, these questions are an opportunity to set yourself apart.

Strategy and style questions require a different kind of reading than many English questions. Often you'll need to read an entire paragraph—even an entire passage—before you can answer them. If you see a question stem or bracketed numbers, the most obvious hints that one of these questions is coming, pay attention to the main idea, purpose, tone, and style of the passage. Remember the Golden Rule of "Order" from Chapter 1. Never spend so much time on one of these questions that you miss an opportunity to answer a quick, easy one.

TIP

If you see numbered sentences or paragraphs, expect a style question.

IMPORTANT STRATEGIES TO CONSIDER

Look for question stems in the right-hand column.

Most questions in the English section will simply pose four possible answer choices for an underlined word or phrase. Strategy and style questions contain specific prompts that precede answer choices. Scan ahead for these "question stems." They will alert you of an upcoming style question. Question stems that test your ability to think like a writer will look and sound similar to the following:

- To end this passage, the author wants to find a sentence that links the conclusions clearly to the introduction. Which of the following is the best choice?
- Which of the following sentences most effectively and clearly conveys the author's intended message?
- Given that all are true, which sentence best introduces the passage and clarifies the author's purpose?
- The author is considering deleting the preceding sentence from the paragraph. Should the author make this decision?

  F. Yes, because . . .
  G. Yes, because . . .
  H. No, because . . .
  J. No, because . . .

TIP

The question stem may give you a clue that you're dealing with a strategy and style question.

- In which order should the sentences in this paragraph appear?

  A. NO CHANGE
  B. 1, 3, 4, 2
  C. 2, 1, 4, 3
  D. 3, 2, 1, 4

- If the writer were to make this deletion, the essay would primarily lose:

  F. important information . . .
  G. logical flow . . .
  H. articulation of the main purpose . . .
  J. the appropriate tone . . .

LOOK FOR BRACKETED NUMBERS WITHIN OR BETWEEN PARAGRAPHS

Bracketed numbers within or between paragraphs indicate organization or strategy questions. If you see them, know that you will be asked to rearrange, add, or delete information. Passages with bracketed numbers will look like the one that follows:

> [1] Eighty degrees with brilliant sunshine provided the perfect backdrop for our trip. [2] The water cooled and refreshed us and was still high enough so that we rarely became stuck on sandbars. [3] A great blue heron stood on the bank of the river. [4] We watched it for awhile until this grand, yet shy bird flew away as we approached; it then landed behind us once we floated past its feeding area.

CONSIDER THE "BIG PICTURE"

Determine the main idea, purpose, tone, and style of the passage.

- **MAIN IDEA:** What is the topic? What is the author trying to say about the topic? Answering these two questions helps you with strategy and style questions.
- **PURPOSE:** Determining the author's purpose helps you decide whether or not information is relevant and logical. Does the author want to entertain, inform, explain, or persuade?
- **TONE:** You may be asked to consider whether or not the tone of a specific passage matches the author's purpose. To determine tone, seek to understand the author's attitude toward the topic. Is it distant? Sarcastic? Ironic?
- **STYLE:** While reading the passage, take note of the author's style. Is it conversational? Formal? Direct? Academic? Sensing the style of the passage will help you assess specific stylistic issues.

QUESTION CATEGORIES

Practice questions and explanations follow this brief discussion.

Relevance

- Relevance questions test your ability to determine which sentences or phrases are relevant to the essay and which ones can be omitted. Read the entire section or passage before answering a relevance question, as you may not completely understand the author's purpose until you have read the concluding sentence.
- Relevance questions also test your ability to determine whether a sentence adheres to or deviates from the focus of a paragraph. If a sentence seems off-topic, it's incorrect.

DEGREE OF DIFFICULTY CONCEPT: RELEVANCE AND SPECIFICITY

My sister was a dedicated snowboarder in her youth, and she still is. Every Sunday morning she would head up to the mountains, get in a few turns, and return in time to get her homework done.

If the word "Sunday" were deleted from the second sentence, the passage would primarily lose:

A. evidence that the narrator's sister was a snowboarder.

B. a detail that gives the sentence a different meaning.

C. further support for an earlier point.

D. a crucial link to the next paragraph.

EXPLANATION: (B) There are no shortcuts to "think like a writer" questions. Slow down and look for specific details. *Sunday* gives the sentence a particular meaning. It implies that the narrator's sister did other things during the week. Leaving out the word *Sunday* indicates that the narrator's sister may have snowboarded every day. Although C and D could be reasonable answers for some situations, B is the best answer based on the information given.

Meaning

- A question may ask you to identify the effect of changing, adding, or omitting a section on the purpose or tone or meaning of the writing.
- Meaning questions appear infrequently; you may only see one or two per test.

Clarity and Precision

- There may not be a question stem for a question that asks you to choose the most precise sentence or phrase to match the tone of a passage.
- In the case of a clarity or precision question, a section of the passage will be underlined and the options will offer alternative ways to say the same thing.

DEGREE OF DIFFICULTY CONCEPT: CLARITY AND PRECISION

I always stuck to skiing and still love it. Having tried, my sister never could make a snowboarder out of me. Now, when we go up together, she rides sideways, and I go straight down the hill.

Which of the following choices best emphasizes how much the narrator's sister wanted her brother to share her interest in snowboarding?

A. NO CHANGE

B. Because of my indifference about the sport,

C. Contrary to her thinking,

D. Despite her repeated attempts to change my mind,

EXPLANATION: (D) The key to these questions will usually be in the stem: "how much the narrator's sister *wanted* her brother to share her interest." Of the four possibilities, only one describes an action or thought that specifically points to the sister's desire for anything. Remember, ACT likes "showing" over "telling" and will often represent an idea with an action, especially in narrative writing.

Organization and Relationships

- If a passage has bracketed numbers prior to each paragraph, a question will appear that either asks you to place a sentence correctly within one of the paragraphs or to identify which order is best for paragraphs within an essay.
- ACT may bracket a specific sentence, or they may ask you to reorder a group of sentences. As a rule, ACT only chooses paragraphs that are organized in a traditional way, so just remember that paragraphs contain topic sentences, supporting details or examples, and concluding (sometimes transitional) sentences.

DEGREE OF DIFFICULTY CONCEPT: ORGANIZATION AND RELATIONSHIPS

PRACTICE QUESTION

(The following question refers to the entire passage.)

For the sake of logic and coherence, paragraph 2 should be placed:

A. where it is now.
B. after paragraph 5.
C. before paragraph 1.
D. after paragraph 3.

Of Note Here: Although we present this question without an actual passage to consider, you should still be able to conceptualize the main points:

1. You simply can't answer this question without understanding the content of the entire passage, so don't skip from underline to underline unless you want to give this point away.

2. When considering the arrangement of paragraphs, think about linear flow. (If it helps, imagine an outline of the passage.) In a coherent essay or narrative, at least on the ACT exam, "logic" and "coherence" mean "linear." Just order the events in a way that makes sense, and you'll have the correct answer.

A Word About Transitions

Organizational questions also test your knowledge of transitions, both between sentences and between paragraphs. Transitions should enhance clarity and support the logical sequence of ideas. Pay careful attention to the following transitional phrases:

- **TRANSITIONS THAT SIGNIFY CAUSE/EFFECT RELATIONSHIPS:** *therefore, as a result, because, consequently, so, thus*
- **TRANSITIONS THAT SIGNIFY CONTRAST:** *however, although, but, despite, on the other hand, though, while, yet*
- **TRANSITIONS THAT LEAD TO EXAMPLES OR CONVEY EMPHASIS, SIMILARITY, AND CONTINUATION:** *for example, for instance, in addition, in fact, likewise, moreover, similarly*

When the ACT asks you to identify the most appropriate transition, think about the relationships of the ideas involved. Does a contrast exist between clauses, sentences, or paragraphs? If not, the word *however* is inappropriate. As practice, try writing sentences that include each of the above transitional phrases. You will notice that the transitional word or phrase always dictates the rest of the sentence.

PRACTICE THINKING LIKE A WRITER

Answer the questions associated with the following sample passages and then assess your understanding of writing strategy and style questions with the explanations that follow.

Sample Passage 1

[1]

[1] This past summer my mother and I spent an afternoon tubing down the Niobrara River with my cousin Sarah and my Aunt Karla. [2] My mother called the tubing outfitter the week before to make arrangements. [3] We prepared for the trip by purchasing river-worthy snacks: licorice, soda, water, trail mix, and chips. [4] We then asked my brother to meet us at the end to pick us up and deliver us back to our car. [1] [5] When we reached the launch area, we placed our cooler of snacks and drinks in the tube that holds the cooler and then attached the tubes together.

[6] Each large tube has a smaller tube in the
          2
center and is covered with a canvas tarp that
          2
kept us from sitting in the water.
          2

[2]

[1] Eighty degrees with brilliant sunshine provided the perfect backdrop for our trip. [2] The water cooled and refreshed us and was still high enough so that we rarely became stuck on sandbars. [3] A great blue heron stood on the bank of the river. [4] We watched it awhile, until this grand yet shy bird flew away as we approached; it then landed behind us once we floated past its feeding area.

1. Adding ", which unbeknownst to us would be the most entertaining part of the trip" to the end of sentence 4 adds which of the following to the essay?
   A. whimsy
   B. sadness
   C. seriousness
   D. anticipation

2. The author is considering a different ending for this paragraph. Which of the following options matches the purpose of this paragraph?
   F. NO CHANGE
   G. OMIT the current sentence and leave sentence 5 as the final sentence of the paragraph.
   H. OMIT the sentence and replace it with the following sentence: "We jumped on the tubes, pushed off the edge of the river, and settled into a relaxing afternoon trip."
   J. Move sentence 6 so that it precedes sentence 5.

[5] My aunt's 60th birthday was the following
                                              3

weekend, and we chose to make this trip down
                                              3

the river our celebration with her.
                              3

[3]

[1] The trip was supposed to take four hours; however, it took five hours because we stopped at Smith Falls to enjoy the scenery and the spray from the waterfall. [2] The trip also took longer because we kept getting stuck in the slow-moving current, and we were too relaxed to get off our tubes to push the tubes into the stronger current. [3] Family acquaintances own an elk ranch near
                                              4

where we got off the river. As we relaxed in the sun,
                        4

we reminisced about previous tubing trips, family stories, and other travels we had experienced recently.

[4]

[1] As we reached the end of our trip, we heard a motor revving loudly, as if a vehicle was stuck in the mud. My mother and I hoped that it wasn't my brother; otherwise, we wouldn't have a ride home. My brother was waiting for quite a while because it took us longer to get down the river than anticipated. He was parked in the middle of the road taking a nap. A group of young campers tried to go around his vehicle and didn't see the large washout created by the river next to the road. Their small pickup truck dove headlights first into the washout and became stuck. When we reached the unloading area, my brother was trying, unsuccessfully,

3. The author feels that this sentence does not fit with this paragraph and would like to place it in the first paragraph. Which of the following options is most appropriate?
   A. after the first sentence of paragraph 1
   B. after the second sentence of paragraph 1
   C. after the third sentence of paragraph 1
   D. after the fourth sentence of paragraph 1

4. While revising this essay, the author senses that something is wrong with the placement or use of this sentence. Which of the following options is best?
   F. NO CHANGE
   G. Move this sentence so that it precedes the first sentence in this paragraph
   H. OMIT this sentence; it doesn't match the other details in the paragraph that describe the trip down the river.
   J. OMIT the sentence and replace it with the following sentence: "We ran out of bug spray trying to keep the biting flies off of us."

to help them out of the large ditch. [5] We were unable to help them out of their predicament, but we drove to the site of a nearby outfitter and sent someone back to help them get their

truck out of the ditch. [6]

5. The author would like to add a detail that best describes the humor of the situation without criticizing the driver's actions. Which of the following options most effectively meets this purpose?
   A. The sight of that small truck in the middle of that large ditch was quite humorous because of the massive size of the ditch and how ridiculous it was that the driver hadn't seen it.
   B. The truck was buried in the ditch.
   C. The image of that truck in the ditch was hysterical. I don't know how the driver hadn't seen the big hole in the ground.
   D. The truck sat precariously in the ditch as the driver climbed out of his window, looking like a shy turtle poking his head out of his shell.

6. The author is considering adding a sentence to this paragraph. Which of the following options wraps up the paragraph as well as the essay as a whole?
   F. NO CHANGE
   G. The memories of our tubing trip will probably blend in with the many other relaxing floats down the river and be forgotten, but the ending added a comedic twist that we will remember forever.
   H. The young campers eventually became unstuck and were able to continue with their relaxing weekend.
   J. We enjoyed our trip and hope to have another trip down the river next year.

Sample Passage 2

[1]

[7] [1] Fort Niobrara National Wildlife Refuge is nestled along the river and hosts longhorn cattle and prairie bison along with white-tail and mule deer. [2] Smith Falls, the tallest waterfall in Nebraska, is located on the Niobrara River, and Smith Falls State Park provides camping opportunities throughout the spring, summer, and fall. [3] Also, bird lovers may have the opportunity to view over 200 species of birds that live in the river valley. [4] A man-made boardwalk runs from the river valley to the base of the falls, providing

easy access for visitors. [8]

[2]

Local tubing and canoeing outfitters are
9

plentiful throughout the area. If you want to
9
be more active, you can rent a canoe, kayak, or raft. If you want a leisurely day without a paddle in sight, tubing is the activity for you. During the middle of the summer, sandbars appear in the river where you can stop and build a sand castle, swim in the water, or view the natural waterfalls. Many outfitters have camping areas along the river and help you get on and off the river or shuttle you to and from your vehicle. If you want to float down the river on the weekend, make plans early; outfitters may be completely booked as early as April for spring and summer weekends.

7. The author has been asked to write a section of a tourism brochure about the Niobrara River area near Valentine, Nebraska. Which of the following sentences creates the best introduction for the essay as a whole and the specific details included in this paragraph?
   A. NO CHANGE
   B. Valentine is the nearest town and provides many hotels and even some bed and breakfasts if you are seeking accommodations other than a tent.
   C. The Niobrara River valley near Valentine, Nebraska, offers a relaxing environment for water lovers and wildlife watchers.
   D. Besides floating down the river, the Niobrara River offers other opportunities for summer fun.

8. Which of the following sequences of sentences will make paragraph one most logical?
   F. NO CHANGE
   G. 1, 3, 2, 4
   H. 1, 4, 2, 3
   J. 1, 2, 4, 3

9. The author would like to revise this sentence so that it better reflects the content of the rest of the paragraph. Which of the following options best introduces the content of the paragraph?
   A. NO CHANGE
   B. Local tubing and canoeing outfitters can provide the proper equipment and accommodations for enjoying the river.
   C. Local tubing and canoeing outfitters can provide assistance getting on and off the river.
   D. Local tubing and canoeing outfitters can provide tubes and canoes for your river trip.

Bring lots of cash; the cost of going down the
10

river is pricey and you may want to have some
10

money left over to purchase souvenirs. Choosing
10

to visit the area during the middle of the week may make your trip planning easier, and the river is often less crowded at that time as well.

[3]

When you are not letting loose on the river,
11

local area activities provide even more family-friendly fun. Go on a horseback ride or drive out to Merrit Reservoir State Recreation Area for a fun afternoon at the lake. Merrit is located about thirty minutes from Valentine and offers camping, fishing, boating, and other water recreation activities. The Valentine National Wildlife Refuge, located forty minutes south of Valentine, protects thousands of acres of sand dunes, prairie, wet meadows, and natural lakes. The Niobrara River Valley and the area surrounding
12

Valentine are filled with western history and open spaces that take you back to a slower and more peaceful time.

10. The author is considering removing this sentence from the essay. Is this the best decision to make and why?

F. Yes, costs shouldn't be included when writing a travel brochure.

G. Yes, the tone of this sentence gives a negative impression of the outfitters and may deter tourists from visiting the area.

H. No, the sentence gives important information about the cost of the vacation.

J. No, the sentence adds a more relaxed tone to the essay, which is inviting to readers.

11. A. NO CHANGE
    B. When you are not relaxing on the river,
    C. When you are not chillin' on the river,
    D. While relaxing on the river,

12. Which of the following transitional phrases most effectively links the essay's introduction to the information in the last sentence?

F. NO CHANGE

G. Along with natural water and wildlife wonders, the Niobrara River Valley

H. Besides a variety of water sports, the Niobrara River Valley

J. Considering all of the wonderful activities and sights, the Niobrara River Valley

Answers Explained

1. **(D)** Category: Meaning

   By adding information that prepares the reader for the truck story at the end of the essay, the phrase adds more anticipation to the essay. Readers want to know why the end of the trip was the most interesting. Options A and B aren't reasonable choices; eliminate them immediately. If anything, the phrase adds more of a relaxed feel to the essay; therefore, option C, *seriousness*, doesn't make sense.

2. **(H)** Category: Relevance

   The last sentence of the first paragraph discusses the structure of the tubes. Because the purpose of this essay is to tell the story of the tubing trip, the information about the tubes is not important to the action; therefore, the sentence should be omitted. Option F (NO CHANGE) is incorrect. When considering option G, remember the purpose of the paragraph, which is to describe who was on the trip, how they prepared for the trip, and how they eventually ended up on the water. Sentence 5 doesn't show the individuals getting on the river, so it isn't an effective concluding sentence. Option H provides a conclusion for the introductory paragraph and moves the action of the narration forward. Narrative texts usually include information in chronological order. Without this sentence, it appears that the tubers remained on the bank of the river. Option J fails for the same reason option F fails. Regardless of where you put sentence 6, it doesn't provide information that fits the paragraph.

3. **(A)** Category: Relevance

   Option A is the best response. The sentence in question establishes the purpose of the trip and should be placed in the introductory paragraph. Because Aunt Karla is mentioned in the first sentence, referring to her 60th birthday party in the next sentence makes the most sense. Inserting the sentence anywhere else disrupts the flow of the paragraph.

4. **(H)** Category: Relevance

   The sentence in question has no relevance to the essay. The purpose of the second paragraph is to describe the sights of the trip. The fact that the narrator has an acquaintance with an elk ranch nearby is not an event that happened on the trip; therefore, it should be omitted, making options F and G incorrect. Only options H and J suggest omitting the sentence. Option J replaces the sentence with a sentence about bug spray. The rest of the paragraph contains descriptions of the beauty of the river, and a negative detail about the bug spray ruins the relaxed mood established throughout the rest of the paragraph. Option H is a stronger option than J.

5. **(D)** Categories: Relevance, Tone

   Option A describes the driver's actions as ridiculous and, therefore, criticizes the driver. The factual nature of option B does not reveal the humor of the situation. Option C is also too critical of the driver. The image of the driver climbing out the window like a turtle poking his head out of his shell gives the sentence a humorous tone without being too critical of the driver.

6. **(G)** Category: Organization

As it is written, the essay lacks a conclusion, ending instead with a detail that has little to do with the trip down the river. Option F does not work. Option G makes the truck story relevant to the rest of the essay, and reveals the emotional impact of the event on the narrator: The tubing trip is correctly described as relaxing, and the truck in the ditch makes it memorable as well. Option H shifts the focus too much on the truck stuck in the ditch, when the story is also about the trip down the river. Option J helps to wrap up the story, but it doesn't connect the truck incident to the rest of the essay.

7. **(C)** Category: Organization

The first sentence jumps immediately into detailed information about the wildlife refuge, leaving the reader confused about the purpose of the essay. Option A will not work. Option B expresses a specific detail about Valentine without offering a general introduction to the Niobrara River Valley. Option C is the correct response because the sentence introduces the area the essay discusses and suggests who might enjoy the Niobrara River Valley: water lovers and wildlife enthusiasts. Option D is incorrect because of the transitional phrase "besides floating down the river." The word *besides* indicates a contrast between two ideas, which necessitates a preceding sentence.

8. **(G)** Category: Organization

Sentence 3 feels out of place and needs to be linked to the other sentence that refers to the wildlife in the area (sentence 1). Another indicator that sentence 3 is linked to the other sentence about wildlife is the word *also*. Sentences 2 and 4 are connected because sentence 4 continues to give more detailed information about the waterfall and the boardwalk that leads to it. Sentence 3 disrupts the flow between these two sentences. The correct order is 1, 3, 2, 4 (option G).

9. **(B)** Category: Organization

Option A does not work because the original sentence only states that the outfitters are plentiful, which does not address the main content of the paragraph—the services provided by the outfitters. Option B is the best response because it shows that the outfitters provide accommodations and equipment. Option C is too general, and option D is too specific.

10. **(G)** Category: Relevance

Tourist brochures highlight the positive aspects of a community and never reveal the negative. Costs *are* relevant to a vaction, making Option F incorrect. The sentence in question does not put the outfitters in a positive light. Although tourist brochures do reveal the costs involved in planning a trip, they never label them as "pricey," as this sentence does. Option G is the correct response.

11. **(B)** Categories: Clarity and Precision

Even though a tourism brochure is a casual piece of writing, *letting loose* is too casual, which makes option A incorrect. Option B replaces *letting loose* with *relaxing*. The word *relaxing* appeals to a larger audience, which is important when developing a tourism brochure. Option C offers the word *chillin'* which is just as problematic as *letting loose*. The phrase "while relaxing on the river" (option D) changes the meaning of the paragraph. The intent of the paragraph is to give alternative activities for families when they are <u>not</u> on the river.

12. **(G)** Category: Organization

The last sentence feels out of place because it brings in new details about the area: western history and open spaces. It needs to be more connected to the rest of the essay, so F is not an option. Option G reviews the main contents of the essay by referring to the "variety of water and wildlife wonders." Because the essay discusses more than just the water sports in the area, option H doesn't include enough information. Option J employs the transitional word *considering*, which indicates a cause and effect relationship. The rest of the sentence does not reveal a cause and effect relationship, so option J is incorrect.

SIX CRITICAL CONCEPTS TO HELP YOU THINK LIKE A WRITER

1. Watch for question stems. They often ask you to consider revisions.

2. If paragraphs or sentences are numbered, an organization question is coming. Maintain a holistic sense of the passage as you answer detail questions, and refer to the numbers once you get to the organization question.

3. Answer all other questions first before tackling questions that ask you to consider entire paragraphs or an entire passage.

4. While you read, be cognizant of topic, main idea, purpose, tone, and style. When you attempt a strategy/style question, keep these concepts in mind.

5. Strategy and style questions test your understanding of the relevance and meaning of sentences, phrases, passages, and transitions. Consider the clarity and precision of language and the relationships between ideas.

6. Remember, there are no short cuts that help with style and strategy questions. Sometimes you'll have to slow down and work at them, but they will separate higher scores from lower ones!

ANSWER SHEET
English Practice Test

Sample Passage 1

1. Ⓐ Ⓑ Ⓒ Ⓓ
2. Ⓕ Ⓖ Ⓗ Ⓙ
3. Ⓐ Ⓑ Ⓒ Ⓓ
4. Ⓕ Ⓖ Ⓗ Ⓙ
5. Ⓐ Ⓑ Ⓒ Ⓓ

6. Ⓕ Ⓖ Ⓗ Ⓙ
7. Ⓐ Ⓑ Ⓒ Ⓓ
8. Ⓕ Ⓖ Ⓗ Ⓙ
9. Ⓐ Ⓑ Ⓒ Ⓓ
10. Ⓕ Ⓖ Ⓗ Ⓙ

11. Ⓐ Ⓑ Ⓒ Ⓓ
12. Ⓕ Ⓖ Ⓗ Ⓙ
13. Ⓐ Ⓑ Ⓒ Ⓓ
14. Ⓕ Ⓖ Ⓗ Ⓙ
15. Ⓐ Ⓑ Ⓒ Ⓓ

Sample Passage 2

1. Ⓐ Ⓑ Ⓒ Ⓓ
2. Ⓕ Ⓖ Ⓗ Ⓙ
3. Ⓐ Ⓑ Ⓒ Ⓓ
4. Ⓕ Ⓖ Ⓗ Ⓙ
5. Ⓐ Ⓑ Ⓒ Ⓓ

6. Ⓕ Ⓖ Ⓗ Ⓙ
7. Ⓐ Ⓑ Ⓒ Ⓓ
8. Ⓕ Ⓖ Ⓗ Ⓙ
9. Ⓐ Ⓑ Ⓒ Ⓓ
10. Ⓕ Ⓖ Ⓗ Ⓙ

11. Ⓐ Ⓑ Ⓒ Ⓓ
12. Ⓕ Ⓖ Ⓗ Ⓙ
13. Ⓐ Ⓑ Ⓒ Ⓓ
14. Ⓕ Ⓖ Ⓗ Ⓙ
15. Ⓐ Ⓑ Ⓒ Ⓓ

Sample Passage 3

1. Ⓐ Ⓑ Ⓒ Ⓓ
2. Ⓕ Ⓖ Ⓗ Ⓙ
3. Ⓐ Ⓑ Ⓒ Ⓓ
4. Ⓕ Ⓖ Ⓗ Ⓙ
5. Ⓐ Ⓑ Ⓒ Ⓓ

6. Ⓕ Ⓖ Ⓗ Ⓙ
7. Ⓐ Ⓑ Ⓒ Ⓓ
8. Ⓕ Ⓖ Ⓗ Ⓙ
9. Ⓐ Ⓑ Ⓒ Ⓓ
10. Ⓕ Ⓖ Ⓗ Ⓙ

11. Ⓐ Ⓑ Ⓒ Ⓓ
12. Ⓕ Ⓖ Ⓗ Ⓙ
13. Ⓐ Ⓑ Ⓒ Ⓓ
14. Ⓕ Ⓖ Ⓗ Ⓙ
15. Ⓐ Ⓑ Ⓒ Ⓓ

English Practice Test

6

SAMPLE PASSAGE 1

DIRECTIONS: The following passage has underlined words that may or may not contain errors or inappropriate expressions or that ask general questions about the passage. Compare each with the four alternatives in the right-hand column. If you think the original version is best, select A or F: NO CHANGE. If you think another alternative is best, circle the corresponding answer choice. Compare how you did with the answer explanations that follow.

Home Cooking

[1] Down the street from my mom's old house in Albuquerque, Padilla's Restaurant sits quietly

1.
    A. NO CHANGE
    B. Albuquerque Padilla's
    C. Albuquerque: Padilla's
    D. Albuquerque, Padillas

in a strip mall. [2] A gas station and a grocery

store occupying spots on either side of it, with all

2.
    F. NO CHANGE
    G. occupied
    H. occupy
    J. occupies

three structures built just out of sight of a main intersection. [3] As a kid I played tennis just a block

away, and as I got older, if she asked, I would stop

3.
    A. NO CHANGE
    B. if my mother asked,
    C. if my mother, asked
    D. —if she asked—

at the grocery store on the way home to pick something up for her. [4] Getting out, I'd feel proud of myself for being old enough to drive there. [5] One time, backing out in a hurry, I impaled my mother's tail light on the store's mailbox, right across the street from Padilla's. [6] Many don't notice the restaurant because of its location on

4.
    F. NO CHANGE
    G. restaurant, because of
    H. restaurant in spite of
    J. restaurant due to the fact that

Girard Street in an area that boasts little through traffic. [5]

If you stand just outside the front door of Padilla's, the sights, <u>noises, and stenches</u>
₆
practically pull you inside. The pungent spiciness of red and green chile and the warm sweetness of heated corn tortillas pull your nose inside.

<u>Once your through the door,</u> the sounds of dishes
₇
banging in the back and waitresses placing orders rise above the sounds of satisfied diners.

<u>If you scan the place,</u> and you'll see two rooms:
₈
one tiny and another larger. The second room seems like an add-on, as though the restaurant owners bought an adjacent business and knocked a wall down in order to seat more red chile fanatics.

Fast service and the <u>city's</u> best New Mexican
₉
food characterize a Padilla's dinner. Water, chips, and homemade salsa usually beat you to

the table. Hard-working waitresses, <u>people</u>
₁₀
<u>who know</u> turning tables earns them money,
₁₀
greet you as you push your chair in and ask if you'd "like a few more minutes."

5. For the sake of logic and coherence, sentence 6 should be placed:
   A. where it is now.
   B. before sentence 1.
   C. after sentence 1.
   D. after sentence 3.

6. In keeping with the tone of the essay, the author would be wise to change this phrase to which of the following?
   F. NO CHANGE
   G. thuds, and whiffs
   H. resonances, and odors
   J. sounds, and aromas

7. A. NO CHANGE
   B. Once you make it through the entrance;
   C. Once you walk through the door's entrance,
   D. Through the door,

8. F. NO CHANGE
   G. If you were to try to scan the place,
   H. Scan the place
   J. You scanned and inspected the place,

9. A. NO CHANGE
   B. cities
   C. citys'
   D. citys

10. F. NO CHANGE
    G. people who know
    H. ; people who knew
    J. ; who know

When I was a kid, we often wasted no time. Why not order right away if you already know which item on the memorized menu you want?

For my mother and stepfather, it was always the same order: chicken enchiladas, half red, half green (or "Christmas," as some call it) with extra onions and lettuce. I liked red chile enchiladas, sometimes with an over-easy egg. My sister was a little less

predictable, sometimes going with the tamales and

sometimes selecting a burrito with green salsa.

I still remember the cozy feeling in my stomach after a Padilla's meal. After wiping our plates clean with warm tortillas, we'd exit past clusters of families clinking forks and cooling their palates from red plastic cups. We'd then climb in our car and head home, arriving in about three minutes.

[1] I live in Denver now, and I wish the restaurant could pick itself up for one night and move into my new neighborhood. [2] The chile here's just not the same. [3] We craved it, just couldn't get our "fix" often enough. [4] Of course, a week later we'd come back to Padilla's all over again. [5] In fact, I'd say that the *only* thing that disappoints me about Padilla's is that it's not portable. [15]

11. The author is considering deleting the underlined sentence. If the writer did this, the paragraph would primarily lose:
   A. information comparing the author's experience at Padilla's with the experiences of the rest of his family.
   B. details describing Padilla's food.
   C. information informing the reader that the author frequents Padilla's.
   D. details about the fast service at the restaurant.

12. F. NO CHANGE
    G. ordering
    H. deciding
    J. coming to the decision of

13. A. NO CHANGE
    B. she would select
    C. selected
    D. she selects

14. F. NO CHANGE
    G. at which we arrived in about three minutes.
    H. where we arrived at in about three minutes.
    J. and arrive in about three minutes.

15. Which configuration represents the most effective sequence of sentences in this paragraph?
    A. NO CHANGE
    B. 4, 5, 3, 1, 2
    C. 2, 4, 5, 3, 1
    D. 4, 3, 5, 1, 2

DIRECTIONS: The following passage has underlined words that may or may not contain errors or inappropriate expressions or that ask general questions about the passage. Compare each with the four alternatives in the right-hand column. If you think the original version is best, select A or F: NO CHANGE. If you think another alternative is best, circle the corresponding answer choice. Compare how you did with the answer explanations that follow.

Unfathomable

[1]

On an August morning in 2008, a Serbian-American swimmer named Milorad Cavic glides toward the wall. The entire world believes he'll
1

win the biggest race of his life. Suddenly, a tsunami of chlorinated water rushes forward in the next lane. Two hands the size of Frisbees propel another swimmer's body toward the finish. In a moment impossible to see with the naked eye, the swimmer next to Cavic surges forward and arrives just before him.
2

This desperate attack, which seconds earlier
3

seemed in vain, has proven to be the difference. The swimmer in the lane next to Cavic has won.

[2]

The swimmer in the next lane is, of course,
4

Michael Phelps. His margin of victory is one one-hundredth of a second.

1. A. NO CHANGE
   B. believed he'd
   C. believed he was going to
   D. believe he'll

2. F. NO CHANGE
   G. his.
   H. his arrival.
   J. he does.

3. A. NO CHANGE
   B. lunge
   C. jump
   D. pounce

4. F. NO CHANGE
   G. in the next lane were,
   H. on the next lane is,
   J. in the next lane is

[3]

[1] The story of Michael Phelps at the Beijing Olympics includes countless mind-boggling specifics; eight gold medals, seven world records, two miraculous finishes, and a never-ending stream of priceless images: however, none of these details captures the essence of Phelps the athlete best than his astonishing win against Cavic in the 100-meter butterfly.

[2] This moment, seen only by underwater cameras, embodied Phelps's performance at the 2008 games. [3] Why? [4] Because it drove home the idea that no matter where he was in the pool—or in the eyes of the world for the other 200 weeks between Olympic meets—he inevitably came from nowhere, defeats his opponents and dominating our collective consciousness.

[4]

[1] Phelps is a rare athlete who *always* believes he can win, regardless of the odds or how many people doubt him. [2] Like Tiger

5. A. NO CHANGE
   B. specifics—eight gold medals
   C. specifics, eight gold medals
   D. specifics: eight gold medals

6. F. NO CHANGE
   G. images; moreover, none
   H. images; therefore, none
   J. images. None

7. A. NO CHANGE
   B. as good
   C. as well
   D. better

8. F. NO CHANGE
   G. only seen to underwater cameras,
   H. and seen by underwater cameras only,
   J. seen only by underwater cameras

9. A. NO CHANGE
   B. defeated his opponents
   C. defeating his opponents
   D. defeating his opponents—

10. The author is considering omitting the underlined phrase and rewriting the sentence. If she did so, the sentence would primarily lose:
    F. An important detail explaining why Phelps is the only truly rare athlete. The author should not remove the phrase.
    G. An important transition between paragraphs 3 and 4 that also explains why Phelps is a rare athlete. The author should not remove the phrase.
    H. Only a minor point about how Phelps responds to doubt. The author should remove the phrase.
    J. Nothing. The author should remove the phrase.

Woods, the only similarly dominant athlete in
11
recent memory, Phelps gets better as the stakes get
higher. [3] Normally an affable diplomat of his sport,
Phelps morphs instantly when necessary into a fierce,
relentless competitor.

[5]

[1] All week, Deborah Phelps's face had shown
television viewers the roots of Michael's success.
[2] Sure, his six-foot-seven-inch arm span
contributing too his achievements, but
12
family played at least as big a role. [3] When
Phelps finished his stunning run by helping his
team win the 400-meter medley relay, he took one
more swim, around an ocean of photographers
13

to hug his mother and sisters. ⎡14⎤ [4] When Phelps
kissed his mom on the cheek, it was clear that he
credited her with making his dreams possible. [5]
As spectators, we can only guess what they said to
each other. [6] What would you say to the person
who taught you that no matter where you were in
the pool, and regardless of the odds, you had the
ability to out-touch your opponent? ⎡15⎤

11. **A.** NO CHANGE
    B. similar dominant
    C. similar, dominant,
    D. similarly different

12. **F.** NO CHANGE
    G. contributed to
    H. contributed too
    J. contributed

13. **A.** NO CHANGE
    B. across an ocean
    C. across a desert
    D. over a mountain

14. In paragraph 5, sentence 3 would work best if
    the author placed it:
    F. where it is now.
    G. before sentence 1.
    H. after sentence 4.
    J. after sentence 5.

15. In order to explain that Michael Phelps has
    a sense of his place in history, the author is
    considering adding the following sentence to
    the essay:

    After his final race, Phelps seemed humbled
    by the complimentary words of Mark Spitz,
    whose "unbreakable" records Phelps broke in
    Beijing.

    If added, this sentence would most logically be
    placed:
    A. after sentence 1 in paragraph 3.
    B. after sentence 3 in paragraph 4.
    C. before sentence 1 in paragraph 5.
    D. The author would be better off omitting
    the sentence altogether.

DIRECTIONS: The following passage has underlined words that may or may not contain errors or inappropriate expressions or that ask general questions about the passage. Compare each with the four alternatives in the right-hand column. If you think the original version is best, select A or F: NO CHANGE. If you think another alternative is best, circle the corresponding answer choice. Compare how you did with the answer explanations that follow.

Wii Love It!

[1]

A video game system is like a new family member that everyone must adjust to.
₁

1. **A.** NO CHANGE
   B. member: to which everyone has to adjust
   C. member, to which everyone must adjust.
   D. member: everyone has to adjust to it.

I know: I bought one a few weeks ago. It
₂
arrived with much fanfare, a little like a newborn

2. **F.** NO CHANGE
   G. I know I
   H. I know, I
   J. I know; I

child. My three boys had gawked lighthearted
₃

3. **A.** NO CHANGE
   B. have gawked lightheartedly
   C. had gawked, lightheartedly,
   D. had gawked lightheartedly

at their cousin's system, just like children who
₄
are expecting a new brother or sister might
₄
want or need to spend a little extra time
₄
around a friend's baby brother or sister.
₄

4. **F.** NO CHANGE
   G. children, expecting a new brother or sister, may likewise want to spend time around a friend's baby brother or sister.
   H. as children expecting a new brother or sister might show curiosity toward someone else's baby.
   J. much as around a new baby, children might want to spend a little extra time who are expecting one, or need to.

We had never owned their own game system,
₅
unless you count the hand-me-down Nintendo 64 we inherited when my oldest son was three.

5. **A.** NO CHANGE
   B. We had never owned our own
   C. Having never owned our own
   D. We have never owned her own

None of us predicted the effects our new game
system would have on the family. It was fun,
₆

but it also made everyone in the family, except
my wife, temporarily insane, after the initial,
₇

tedious setup, we began playing.

Sam, the oldest of my three sons,
₈

took an immediate liking and got lots of
₉

enjoyment out of the sports games right away.
₉

Henry enjoyed the system somewhat but mostly

got frustrated—its hard to ski jump in perfect
₁₀

balance when you're four. Willie, my two-year-old,
didn't really understand the games, but he

did learned quickly that unplugging the little
₁₁

box made Sam and Henry fume in anger.

6. **F.** NO CHANGE
   G. It was fun
   H. It was fun;
   J. It was fun—

7. **A.** NO CHANGE
   B. insane. After
   C. insane; after
   D. insane. After,

8. **F.** NO CHANGE
   G. , the older of my three sons,
   H. the oldest of my three sons
   J. , the oldest of my three sons;

9. **A.** NO CHANGE
   B. liked
   C. immediately liked
   D. got lots of enjoyment out of

10. **F.** NO CHANGE
    G. it's
    H. it was
    J. it isn't

11. **A.** NO CHANGE
    B. learned fast
    C. learn more quickly
    D. learn quickly

[3]

Despite an occasional conflict, everything
                                        12
went good until Lego Star Wars arrived. One night,
      12
after my kids went to bed, I decided I should "figure
out" the new game for them. I played for five hours.
When I finally came to bed—at 3:00 A.M.—my wife,
Christina, looked sleepily at the clock and said,
"*What* are you doing?" At that moment, I wished I
had an answer besides, "I'm a thirty-five-year-old

moron who likes to played video games until
                          13
dawn. *Yawn*." But that's all I could come up with.
My wife rolled over, certain she had married the
wrong man.

[4]

    The next several days saw great conflict between
Sam and Henry because Sam, understandably,
was able to figure out Star Wars more quickly
then his brother was. Countless times after
                      14
work I heard the same complaint:

[5]

    "Dad, I'm trying to get over this bridge, but
Henry is in the other corner bumping his head
against the wall so I can't move. Can you help me?"

12. Which choice is the most effective first
sentence of paragraph 3?
   F. NO CHANGE
   G. Despite an occasional conflict, everything
   went fairly well until Lego Star Wars
   arrived.
   H. Besides the occasional conflict, nothing
   went well until Lego Star Wars arrived
   J. Lego Star Wars arrived, before which
   everything went well besides the
   occasional conflict.

13. A. NO CHANGE
   B. that likes to play
   C. who likes to play
   D. whom likes to play

14. F. NO CHANGE
   G. then his brother was able.
   H. than his brother was.
   J. than his brother had the ability to do.

[6]

Things have settled down a little now that a few weeks have passed. Sam and Henry now have a system for playing Star Wars together, which includes Henry "dropping out" periodically so Sam can conquer a particularly challenging section.

[7]

Now, while I am making their dinner, I often hear Sam squawking, "Drop out, Henry! Drop out!" I cringe a little. Inside, I hope desperately that our acquisition of a video game system doesn't set Sam, Henry, or William on a path that culminates in their high school guidance counselor using the same phrase. 15

15. In which order should the last four paragraphs be arranged?
   A. NO CHANGE
   B. 5, 4, 6, 7
   C. 6, 5, 4, 7
   D. 4, 6, 5, 7

ANSWER KEY
English Practice Test

Sample Passage 1

1. **A**	6. **J**	11. **C**
2. **H**	7. **D**	12. **G**
3. **B**	8. **H**	13. **A**
4. **F**	9. **A**	14. **F**
5. **C**	10. **F**	15. **D**

Sample Passage 2

1. **A**	6. **J**	11. **A**
2. **J**	7. **D**	12. **G**
3. **B**	8. **F**	13. **B**
4. **F**	9. **C**	14. **G**
5. **D**	10. **G**	15. **D**

Sample Passage 3

1. **D**	6. **F**	11. **D**
2. **J**	7. **B**	12. **G**
3. **D**	8. **F**	13. **C**
4. **H**	9. **B**	14. **H**
5. **B**	10. **G**	15. **A**

Answers Explained

PASSAGE 1

1. **(A)** The introductory dependent clause in the sentence, "Down the street from my mom's old house in Albuquerque," calls for a comma (see comma rule 1). Option B is incorrect because it lacks punctuation between the introductory dependent clause and the clause that succeeds it. Option C is incorrect because colons only come after an independent clause and before an example, explanation, short phrase, or list (see colon rule 1). Option D is incorrect because the name "Padilla's" implies possession and therefore needs an apostrophe (see apostrophe rule 1).

2. **(H)** Option F is incorrect because *occupy* is the main verb in the sentence. *Occupying* cannot stand on its own; it requires a helping verb such as *is* (*is occupying*), or else the result is a fragment. Option G is incorrect because of inconsistent verb tense. Because the rest of the paragraph is in present tense, the verb *occupy* must remain in present tense as well. Option J is incorrect because the subject, "A gas station and a grocery store," is plural and necessitates the plural verb *occupy*, not the singular verb *occupies*.

3. **(B)** Option A is incorrect because no antecedent precedes the underlined phrase to identify the *she* in the underlined portion. Option C is incorrect because the comma between *mother* and *asked* is unnecessary—you should never place a comma between the subject of a clause and the verb within the same clause. Option D is incorrect for the same reason that Option A is incorrect: Without a reference provided by an antecedent, it's incorrect to use a pronoun.

4. **(F)** Option G is incorrect because the second part of the sentence, "because of its location on Girard Street in an area that boasts little through traffic," is a dependent clause. Unless both "sides" of the sentence are independent, they do not need a comma between them (see comma rule 3). Option H is incorrect because the phrase "in spite of" implies that the second half of the sentence should contrast with the first. In fact, the second half of the sentence flows logically from the first: It makes sense that people wouldn't notice a restaurant on a street with little through traffic. Option J is incorrect because it is wordy. It is more economical to say "because" than it is to say "due to the fact that."

5. **(C)** Sentence 6 offers primary detail about the location of Padilla's and therefore works best after the first sentence. Option A is incorrect because the information contained in sentence 6 does not logically follow the secondary information about the car accident. Option B is incorrect because the sentence does not provide a proper introduction to the passage and therefore should not be the first sentence of the passage. Option D is incorrect because sentences 3 and 4 connect logically; breaking their flow by placing a sentence in between them creates an awkward arrangement of ideas.

6. **(J)** This question tests your sense of how words convey tone. Your best strategy is to gain a sense of the tone of the passage as a whole and then determine whether the connotations of the underlined words fit the tone of the passage. Option F is incorrect because the word *stenches* has a negative connotation and therefore doesn't fit the positive tone of the review. Option G is incorrect because the word *whiffs* is too colloquial and rarely used as a noun. Option H is incorrect for two reasons: the word *resonances* is out of place

within the context of the passage, and the word *odor* carries a slightly negative connotation that is rarely associated positively with food.

7. **(D)** Option A is incorrect because the use of *your* is incorrect. *Your* in the underlined portion actually means "you are" and therefore needs to be spelled *you're*. Option B is incorrect because the underlined portion is an introductory dependent clause, making the semicolon incorrect (see comma rule 1). Option C is incorrect because the phrase "door's entrance" is redundant. The word *door* implies an entrance, so *entrance* in this context is unnecessary.

8. **(H)** The answer to this question hinges on the word *and*, which allows you to rule out Options G and J immediately. The word *if* at the beginning of these answers makes the introductory clause dependent, which means the second half of the sentence must be independent. *And*, a subordinating conjunction, can't follow an "if" statement. Option J is incorrect for three reasons. First, verb tense is inconsistent. Second, the phrase "scanned and inspected" is redundant. Third, the entire phrase, if placed next to the nonunderlined portion of the sentence, renders the whole thought ungrammatical.

9. **(A)** *City's* shows possession and needs an apostrophe (see apostrophe rule 1). Option B is incorrect because *cities* is the plural form of the word, not the possessive form. Option C is incorrect because *citys'* is an incorrect spelling of the plural-possessive form of the word. Option D is incorrect because it is an incorrect spelling of the plural form of the word.

10. **(F)** The phrase "people who know turning tables earns them money" is a "BTW" phrase that needs a comma hug (see comma rule 2). Option G is incorrect because it is missing the first comma needed to offset the BTW phrase. Option H is incorrect because verb tense is inconsistent. Option J is incorrect because a semicolon is not appropriate (see semicolon rule 1).

11. **(C)** Option A is incorrect because the underlined phrase does not compare the diner's experience with the experiences of the rest of his family. Option B is incorrect because the phrase does not describe details about the food. Option D is incorrect because the phrase describes the family's tendency to order quickly, not the fast service of the restaurant.

12. **(G)** Option F is incorrect because the phrase "going with" is too colloquial and not specific enough. Option H is incorrect because the word *deciding* is only grammatical if a preposition follows it, as in "deciding on." Option J is incorrect because it is redundant. "Ordering" is more economical and specific than "coming to the decision of."

13. **(A)** This question is slightly tricky, because your answer to 12 dictates your answer to 13. Because of the rules of parallel structure, the verb form you choose must match the preceding verb, *ordering*. Options B, C, and D all break the rule of parallel structure, so all are incorrect. (See Chapter 3 for more information.)

14. **(F)** Option G is incorrect because the phrase "at which" is awkward in general but even more awkward when placed right next to the word *home*, which it describes. Option H is incorrect because the phrase "where we arrived at" misuses the preposition *at*. Option J is incorrect because the resulting sentence, "Then we'd climb in our car and head home and arrive in about three minutes," is wordy and ungrammatical.

15. **(D)** This question depends on your understanding of how sentences are organized within a paragraph. Obtaining the correct answer hinges on knowing that sentence 4 makes the best transition between the second-to-last paragraph and the last one. In any other combination, sentence 3 feels out of place. Furthermore, sentences 3 and 4 are a continuation of the previous paragraph, while sentences 1, 2, and 4 move on to talk about the author's relocation to Denver and his longing for the restaurant. Option A is incorrect because sentences 2, 3, and 4 make the paragraph seem disjointed and illogical. Option B is incorrect because sentence 5 sounds illogical when placed before sentence 3. Option C is incorrect because sentence 2 sounds illogical when placed in front of sentence 4.

PASSAGE 2

1. **(A)** This question tests subject-verb agreement and verb tense consistency. Option B is incorrect because the past tense "believed he'd" is inconsistent with the rest of the paragraph. Option C is also incorrect because it's written in past tense, which is inconsistent with the rest of the paragraph. Option D is incorrect because the phrase "The entire world," as one collective group, requires the singular verb *believes*. (See Chapter 3.)

2. **(J)** This question tests your knowledge of pronoun use. Option F, although it represents a form commonly used in spoken English, is technically incorrect. The subjective case of this pronoun is necessary because the verb *arrives* is implied at the end of the sentence—it would be incorrect to say "him arrives." (See Chapter 4.) Option G is incorrect because the possessive *his* creates the nonsensical phrase "just before his." Option H is incorrect because it creates a redundancy by placing *arrives* and *arrival* in the same phrase.

3. **(B)** This question tests your sense of style, especially relating to the connotations and specific definitions of words. The correct answer is hinted at in the preceding sentence when the author uses the word *surges*—obtaining the correct answer means finding its closest synonym. Option A is incorrect because the word *attacks* doesn't describe the situation—a desperate move forward—accurately. Option C is incorrect because the action described is not a *jump* but a move forward in the water. Option D is incorrect because the word *pounce* implies a move to quickly cover something, as a cat does to a mouse.

4. **(F)** Option G is incorrect because the plural verb *were* does not agree with the two nouns it links: *swimmer* and *Michael Phelps*. Option H is incorrect because of a preposition error: Conventional English dictates that the phrase "in the next lane" makes sense while "on the next lane" does not. Option J is incorrect because it lacks the comma necessary to separate the "BTW" phrase "of course" (see comma rule 2).

5. **(D)** This question tests your knowledge of punctuation. Colon rule 1 dictates that you should use a colon when it follows an independent clause and introduces an example, explanation, short phrase, or list.

6. **(J)** This question tests both your ability to punctuate properly and your sense of style with regard to ideas within a sentence. Option F is incorrect because the word *however*, succeeded by an independent clause, necessitates a semicolon, not a colon (see semicolon rule 1). Option G is incorrect because the word *moreover* implies a continuation of the thinking from the first part of the sentence, when in fact the second part of the

sentence contrasts with the first part. Option H is incorrect for the same reason: *therefore* implies continuation when in fact the beginning of the sentence contrasts with the end.

7. **(D)** Option A is incorrect because the result is the incorrect phrase "best than." Option B is incorrect because it uses the adjective *good* to modify the verb *captures*. Option C is incorrect because its result is the awkward phrase "as well than." Conventional English dictates that we use the phrase "as well as" in this case.

8. **(F)** Option G is incorrect because of the improper preposition *to*. Option H is incorrect because it creates the incorrect phrasing "this moment, *and* seen by underwater cameras only, embodied..." Option J is incorrect because it lacks the necessary comma to set apart this BTW phrase (see comma rule 2).

9. **(C)** This question tests your sense of style as it relates to parallel structure. Option A is incorrect because the verb form *defeats* fails to match the form of *dominating*, another verb within the same phrase. Option B is incorrect for the same reason. Option D is incorrect because it misuses a dash (see dash rule 2).

10. **(G)** This question tests writing strategy. Option F is incorrect because it is too extreme. Although Michael Phelps is a rare athlete, he is not "the only truly rare athlete." In fact, the paragraph goes on to describe another rare athlete, Tiger Woods. Option H is incorrect because the point of the sentence is not minor at all; in fact, it defines the topic of the entire paragraph. Option J is incorrect because, without the first sentence, the paragraph feels incomplete; its subject is not stated overtly enough.

11. **(A)** This question tests your knowledge of both adverb use and punctuation. Option B is incorrect because it contains an adjective, *similar*, modifying another adjective, *dominant*. Option C is incorrect because no comma is necessary between the word *dominant* and the word *athlete*. Option D is incorrect because the phase "similarly different" is paradoxical and therefore illogical in this case.

12. **(G)** Option F is incorrect because the verb *contributing* makes the first clause of the sentence dependent, which renders the entire sentence ungrammatical. Option H is incorrect because it employs the incorrect form of *too* (see Chapter 4). Option J is incorrect because the phrase "contributed his achievements"—as someone with an ear for conventional English knows—lacks the necessary preposition *to*.

13. **(B)** This question tests both your ear for prepositions and your understanding of figurative language. Option A is incorrect because the *ocean* of photographers implies a mass of people that Phelps must go *through*, not *around*. Option C is incorrect because *desert* does not complete the metaphor. It would not make sense, especially in an essay about swimming, to depict Phelps "swimming across a desert." Option D is incorrect for similar reasons. A mass of people is not a figurative *mountain* Phelps must climb; it's a figurative *ocean* he must cross.

14. **(G)** This question tests your sense of paragraph organization. In reading through the paragraph, you may have sensed some disorganization, which should have told you that answer A probably isn't the right choice. In fact, it's incorrect because sentence 1 refers to *Deborah Phelps* without introducing her. Although some readers might infer that the author is talking about Phelps's mother, her relationship with him is more obvious when sentence 1 follows sentence 3. Option H is incorrect because the information

in sentence 3—from a chronological standpoint—comes before the information in sentence 4, not after it. Option J is incorrect for the same reason: In the passage, Phelps must make his final "swim" across the crowd before we can guess what he says to his mother.

15. **(D)** This time-consuming question tests your sense of the passage as a whole. Answering it correctly involves a process of elimination. Option A is incorrect because a sentence about the historical context of Phelps's achievements doesn't fit within a paragraph that describes a single Olympic moment in detail. Option B is incorrect because, although the sentence makes more sense in paragraph 4, it disrupts the paragraph in two ways. First, it adds another piece of information not asserted by the topic sentence. Second, it attaches a final sentence to the paragraph without evaluating the significance of the sentence. In order to make this sentence fit, the author would have to develop paragraph 4 further. Option C is incorrect because a sentence about historical context does not fit within a paragraph that describes Phelps's relationship with his family.

PASSAGE 3

1. **(D)** This question tests your knowledge of prepositions, your understanding of punctuation, and your ability to distinguish between *whom* and *which*. Option A is incorrect because, in formal English, sentences may not end with a preposition. Option B is incorrect because a colon may not precede a prepositional phrase—no punctuation mark other than a comma should be considered in this instance (See Chapter 2). Option C is incorrect because of the phrase "to which." Because the author personifies the game system, he must use the word *whom*, which refers to a noun that is human. Option C also features an unnecessary comma after "member."

2. **(J)** This question tests punctuation. Both "I know" and "I bought one a few weeks ago" are independent clauses, so a semicolon must separate them. Option F is incorrect because colons are used only when they follow an independent clause and introduce an example, explanation, short phrase, or list. Option G is incorrect because, without punctuation, the sentence becomes a run-on. Option H is incorrect because a comma in this situation produces a comma splice.

3. **(D)** This question tests your ability to use adjectives and adverbs as well as your ability to spot inconsistencies in verb tense. Option A is incorrect because the adjective *light-hearted* cannot modify the verb *gawked*. Option B is incorrect because the present-tense verb *have* is inconsistent with the rest of the narrative, which is set in the past. Although the author editorializes in the present, he tells the story in the past. This underlined portion is clearly a part of the narrative. Option C is incorrect because the adverb *lightheartedly*, rather than being a nonessential or "BTW" phrase, simply modifies the verb *gawked* and therefore doesn't require a "comma hug" (see comma rule 2).

4. **(H)** This question tests your ability to use language economically. Option F is incorrect because the phrase "want or need" is wordy and because the repeated phrase "brother or sister" loads the sentence with too much verbiage. Option G is incorrect because the phrase "brother or sister" is repeated in the sentence, making it feel overloaded and clunky. Option J is incorrect because phrases and clauses are mixed together in a way that destroys the flow of the sentence and renders it unclear.

5. **(B)** This question tests both your understanding of sentence structure and your ability to maintain consistent verb tense. Option A is incorrect because the pronoun *we* does not agree in person with the pronoun *their*. Option C is incorrect because it produces a fragment—the first clause must be independent, because the rest of the sentence is not. Option D is incorrect because the verb *have* does not agree in tense with the rest of the sentence.

6. **(F)** This question tests your knowledge of punctuation. Two independent clauses with a FANBOYS word between them necessitate a comma (see comma rule 3). Option G is incorrect because, without punctuation, the sentence is a run-on. Option H is incorrect because a semicolon is unnecessary here: The subordinating conjunction *but* serves the same purpose (see comma rule 3 and semicolon rule 1). Option J is incorrect because, as we mention in Chapter 2, dashes are reserved for major breaks in thought (see dash rule 2).

7. **(B)** This question tests your knowledge of sentence structure. Option A is incorrect because it creates a comma splice: two independent clauses attached with just a comma. Option C is incorrect because the clause "after the initial, tedious setup, we got to playing" is not related to the previous clause closely enough to warrant a semicolon. Option D is incorrect because no comma is necessary between *after* and *the*.

8. **(F)** This question tests your knowledge of comparatives and superlatives, as well as your knowledge of punctuation. Option G is incorrect because the comparative word *older* can only be used when comparing two things. Option H is incorrect because the nonessential or BTW phrase "the oldest of my three sons" requires a comma hug (see comma rule 2). Option J is incorrect because a semicolon is not necessary following a nonessential, or BTW, phrase (see comma rule 2).

9. **(B)** This question tests your sense of economy in language. Option A is incorrect because it's redundant; "took an immediate liking" and "got lots of enjoyment" state essentially the same idea. Option C is also redundant; *immediately* and *right away* (a phrase following the underlined portion) have exactly the same meaning. Option D is incorrect because it's more economical to say "liked" than it is to say "got lots of enjoyment out of."

10. **(G)** This question tests your sense of the ideas in the sentence, your knowledge of punctuation, and your ability to maintain verb-tense consistency. Option F is incorrect because it employs the possessive spelling of *its* when the contraction *it's* is necessary. Option H is incorrect because the editorial comment "it's hard to ski jump in perfect balance when you're four" needs to be in present tense. Option J is incorrect because it isn't logical. It is hard for most young children to maintain perfect balance, so the phrase "it isn't hard" makes little sense.

11. **(D)** This question tests your knowledge of adverbs and adjectives, comparatives, and verb-tense consistency. Option A is wrong because the word "learned" is incorrect when placed next to the word "did." The result is the incoherent phrase "did learned." Option B is incorrect for the same reason, and because—in formal English writing—the adjective "fast" cannot modify the verb "learned." Option C is incorrect because the word "more" necessitates a comparison; without anything to compare, it is unnecessary.

12. **(G)** This question tests your sense of style and your knowledge of adjectives and adverbs. Option F is incorrect because, although common in colloquial English, the adjective *good* cannot modify the verb *went*. Option H is incorrect because the phrase "besides the occasional conflict" makes little sense in the same sentence as "nothing went well." The word *besides* implies a contrast, when in reality the phrases "occasional conflict" and "nothing went well" are closely related. Option J is incorrect because it breaks up the transition between paragraphs 2 and 3, disrupting the flow of the essay and making the beginning of paragraph 3 sound disjointed.

13. **(C)** This question tests your ability to identify when to use the words *who, whom,* and *that*. Option A is incorrect because the word *likes* must be succeeded by the infinitive *to play*, making *to played* ungrammatical. Option B is incorrect because the word *that* must be replaced by *who* when the sentence refers to a human being. Option D is incorrect because *who* is the subject of the clause. *Whom* is only correct in cases when it is the object (see Chapter 4).

14. **(H)** This question tests your ability to distinguish between *then* and *than*, as well as your sense of economy in language. Option F is incorrect because *then* refers to time and cannot be used when comparing two things. Option G is also incorrect, both because it employs the wrong *then* and because it contains the unnecessary word "able." Option J is incorrect because the phrase "had the ability to do" is wordy and redundant in the context of the rest of the sentence.

15. **(A)** This question tests your understanding of the essay's organization. Option B is incorrect because paragraph 4 sets up the quotation in paragraph 5 and therefore must precede it. Option C is incorrect for the same reason, and also because paragraph 6 sets up the central idea in paragraph 7 and therefore must precede it. Option D is incorrect because paragraphs 4 and 5 must go together and cease to make sense when separated by paragraph 6.

ONLINE PRACTICE TEST

For even more ACT English practice, remember you can access the online practice test at *barronsbooks.com/tp/ACT36*.

Math

Math

Overview of the Math Section

7

→ WORD PROBLEMS/MODELING
→ MULTIPLE-CHOICE QUESTIONS
→ USING THIS BOOK TO PREPARE
→ ACHIEVING A PERFECT MATH SCORE
→ MATH STRATEGIES
→ ONLINE VERSION OF THE ACT

You can earn a perfect score on the mathematics section of the ACT. Between your skills and knowledge, the tips in this book, and the time you put into preparing, you have everything you need. The math portion of the ACT is an assessment of content knowledge through algebra 2 (or the equivalent). That means a typical junior is on track for completing the necessary coursework to ace the math. So why doesn't everyone earn a perfect score? Well, the challenge is completing 60 questions in 60 minutes. Be efficient and manage your time.

Questions are based on everything from elementary algebra to trigonometry. The different types of questions are mixed throughout the test. The elementary algebra questions appear more frequently in the beginning of the test and are sprinkled throughout the latter part of the test. The opposite is true of the intermediate algebra, coordinate and plane geometry, and trigonometry questions. This means you can expect to move through the test more quickly in the beginning and to slow your pace toward the end.

What makes the math section of the ACT challenging is not the content but rather the time limit. You have 60 minutes to correctly answer 60 questions (and most are word problems), so you will not have enough time to carefully solve each question. Employ strategies for finding the correct solution without fully working out each problem. By understanding the makeup of the test, you will be better able to plan your attack and get closer to reaching the perfect score. It can be done!

WORD PROBLEMS/MODELING

The test is composed mostly of word problems. You must solve word problems at every opportunity so they become natural for you. The more word problems you read and solve, the faster you will be at identifying what the problem is asking and determining the most efficient way of solving it. Whether your math teacher assigns word problems or not, solve them whenever you can.

The latest version of the ACT has at least 25% of the questions identified as modeling questions. The widely accepted description of what constitutes a modeling question is that the context is one for which people in the real world would genuinely use mathematics to solve the problem. The student is called upon to decontextualize the problem, identify the appropriate mathematical model to solve the problem, use the information in the problem with

 TIP

The ability to decipher and solve word problems is the key to acing the math section.

the appropriate model to solve it, and then recontextualize the solution in order to provide the answer in terms of the original problem. Many of the word problems you encounter will be authentic situations. If you practice word problems at every opportunity, you will be well prepared for the modeling subset of the assessment.

You will receive a score for the category of Modeling, and the questions that are reported in this category will also be reported in a math content category. You will notice that the math categories add up to 100% of the 60 questions. At least 25% of those questions will fall into the modeling category. This score will be helpful if you choose to take the assessment more than once since it will indicate how well you are doing with word problems on the test.

MULTIPLE-CHOICE QUESTIONS

Multiple-choice questions may sound like a slam dunk, but there is a catch. Among the answer choices are wrong answers that are the results of common mistakes. Test writers include decoys among choices (wrong answers that look right) by working problems incorrectly. It is important to answer the problems quickly, but remember to balance your pace with accuracy. Be sure to go as quickly as you can while avoiding careless mistakes. A quick re-read of the question will help you confirm the reasonableness of your solution.

Types of Problems

TIP

Almost half of the math consists of elementary algebra.

Now that you're aware of the makeup of the exam, let's look at the good news. First of all, you are allowed to use a graphing calculator on the exam. (There are restrictions on the type of graphing calculator, which we will discuss later.) About forty percent of the test requires the skills you learned in middle school. These skills include operations with rational numbers and proportional reasoning. In this book, we will refer to this content as elementary algebra. The ACT refers to this category as Integrating Essential Skills and will report these skills as their own category. The other categories for the ACT make up 57–60% of the test and are referred to as Preparing for Higher Mathematics. This means that about 25 questions will be concepts and skills that call upon from your pre-algebra coursework and should be quick and easy to solve. In addition to these two main categories, you will receive a score for the category of Modeling and more than 25% of the questions will include applying a mathematical model to a situation in order to solve the problem. The test will begin with mostly elementary algebra problems and then move into the types of problems that are likely to involve multiple steps. There will be some elementary algebra problems sprinkled throughout the remainder of the exam.

MAKEUP OF THE TEST QUESTIONS

40–43% Integrating Essential Skills
57–60% Preparing for Higher Mathematics
- 31–40% High School Algebra
  - 7–10% Number & Quantity
  - 12–15% Algebra
  - 12–15% Functions
- 12–15% Geometry (including Trigonometry)
- 8–12% Statistics & Probability

More than 25% of the questions will incorporate Modeling.

USING THIS BOOK TO PREPARE

The purpose of the mathematics section of this book is to familiarize you with the exam and prepare you to obtain a perfect score on the math section of the ACT. Six chapters make up the math portion of the book. The first chapter is an overview of the math section test. The next three chapters focus on various content areas of the test. The fifth chapter includes mini-lessons on conic sections, trigonometry, and graphing calculator use, and the sixth chapter is a practice test.

The graphing calculator can be a great time saver—but only if you know how to use it.

The content chapters will be where you spend most of your time and energy. In each of the content chapters you will find an explanation for the more common topics assessed in that content area. Each topic comes with example problems and solution explanations. Throughout these chapters, you'll see content/formula boxes as well as tip boxes. Use the boxes later as a quick review of what you learned. Each content chapter will end with 12 practice questions. For this mini-test, you will need to time your performance. For elementary algebra problems, you will want to average 30 seconds per question. For the more difficult material covered in the other two chapters, you will want to average 80 seconds per question. Be sure to use the strategies provided in this section to help you solve the questions accurately and quickly.

The last two chapters include mini-lessons and a practice test. Even if you are familiar with the topics, you will want to read through the mini-lessons because they focus on the specific ways the topics are addressed on the ACT. In trigonometry, for example, the focus is on right triangle and circular trigonometry. Knowing this will help you focus your studies and preparation. Your graphing calculator can be a great tool, but only to the extent that you are familiar with using it. The use of the graphing calculator is highlighted in the Intermediate Algebra chapter as well as the mini-lesson chapter. Following the mini-lessons is a 60-question practice test. The practice test is important because it mixes all of the topics covered in the math section of this book. When taking the practice test, be sure to simulate a testing environment as best as you can (time, clear space free of distractions and noise, no reference materials).

ACHIEVING A PERFECT MATH SCORE

As mentioned earlier, your skills and knowledge of mathematics will not be enough to ensure a perfect score on the ACT. You will need to take an active role, which means using the book in the most effective way as well as working outside of the book to train yourself for the exam.

Engage with the Material in This Book

When studying, focus most of your attention on your weak spots.

Feel free to write in the margins and highlight the text. (If you are borrowing the book, use removable highlighter tape and sticky notes). When taking notes in the text, use language that will help you remember what you learned. Your notes can act as a review when you come back to the book. Highlight and code items that you want to re-read later. Mark areas that require further study. You can also write questions in the text that you want to ask your math teacher.

Work Through the Content Chapters

The three content chapters are a review of the mathematics you already know. Read each chapter in the order it is presented, and work through each example before reading the solution explanation. Be sure to mark both your strong and weak areas. You will want to quickly review your strong areas and pay more attention to weak areas. Each content chapter includes practice problems specific to the material in the chapter. Treat these problems as a practice test and don't forget to give yourself time constraints. Simulate a test environment and solve the problems without reference materials.

Both Time and Accuracy Are Important

Whether you are doing the problems in one focus area or using the sample test at the end of this section, time yourself. A great strategy is to set a timer for slightly less than the allotted time (this will help you with your pacing). When the time has elapsed, change pencil or pen colors and continue to work through the problems. This will show you how much additional time you use. Once you have attempted every problem, use the answer key to check your answers. Over the course of your preparation, your goal should be to improve both your time and your accuracy. The key to a perfect score is simple: get all the questions correct within the allotted time.

Mini-Lessons Are Important, Too

The fifth chapter of this section includes mini-lessons for conic sections (circles, ellipses, hyperbolas), circular trigonometry, and graphing calculator. For some students, these lessons may not be necessary, and for others they will be beneficial. Depending on your coursework to date, read through the lessons to review the topics and make your own judgment. If you need additional instruction on these topics, talk with your math teacher about resources available at your school.

Focus on ACT Preparation in Your Math Class

Use your math class as practice before the big day. This book will be key in helping you understand what is on the test and identifying your strengths and weaknesses. You can do a lot to improve your ACT math score simply by changing what you do in your regular math class. Focus on these four areas to improve your performance: word problems, your personal weak spots, the ballpark approach, and the graphing calculator.

TIP

Don't use time constraints when learning new material.

WORD PROBLEMS make up a good portion of the ACT. Take the initiative to solve all available word problems in your math textbook as you learn a new unit of study. While these problems may not cover the same content as problems on the ACT, they will help you to hone your word problem-solving skills. When working with word problems, pay special attention to determining the important information in the problem, selecting the appropriate mathematical model, and identifying a strategy to solve the problem. Be sure to re-read the problem to ensure your solution is answering the question and is reasonable. Treat each problem as a practice ACT question.

WEAK AREAS can be strengthened with the help of your math teacher. Once you have worked through this book, take a list of your weak areas along with specific questions to your teacher. Request additional help AND additional practice problems in the areas that frustrate you. Your teacher has access to more resources than you do. Do not underestimate your teacher's dedication to your success.

THE BALLPARK APPROACH will help you throughout the ACT math test. When solving any problem in your math class, begin by guessing a range that the answer will fall in. Using this technique with the problems in your math class will give you lots of practice. Write your guess down, solve the problem, and then evaluate your guess. Reflect on ways that you can guess more accurately in the future. You'll be surprised how useful this technique can be when you are attempting to solve 60 questions in 60 minutes.

THE GRAPHING CALCULATOR's usefulness depends on how well you know how to use it. Increase your comfort with the graphing calculator by using it as often as possible. For starters, use it to help you determine a ballpark answer before solving problems by hand. Make sure to review your calculator's statistics, probability, and counting functions. Enlist the help of your classmates who seem the most savvy with their calculators.

MATH STRATEGIES

As you begin your quest for a perfect ACT score, let's look at seven key strategies for approaching math questions.

TIP

Set a timer for 80 seconds and sit in silence. It is longer than you think.

> ### SEVEN KEY MATH STRATEGIES
>
> - Buy Time
> - Solve It (Whenever You Can)
> - Draw/Label Pictures
> - Ballpark and Eliminate
> - Plug in the Answer Choices
> - Use Your Graphing Calculator
> - Make an Educated Guess*
>
> *Since this book is focused on helping you obtain a PERFECT score, guessing is included only as a last resort.

BUYING TIME is the first—and most important—strategy. One minute per problem will not be sufficient for solving the more difficult problems. You can buy time for those problems by solving the easiest problems in 30 seconds or less. These problems include topics from pre-algebra through parts of algebra 1. They will not be marked in any special way, so it will be up to you to identify them as being easy and solve them quickly. The next chapter will help you with both identifying these problems and solving them efficiently. Unfortunately, even 80 seconds will not be enough time to completely solve some of the more advanced problems, so you'll need to pair this strategy with some others.

Beyond the elementary algebra problems, there will be several problems you can solve quickly (and only you can identify these). Use this book to help you determine which types of problems, in addition to the elementary problems, you are able to solve quickly. Make a list of the types that are easy for you. Review this list prior to the test. When you see a problem that is typically easy for you—**SOLVE IT!** Don't over-think this strategy. If you find it easy to solve in the allotted time (30 seconds or 80 seconds), go for it.

When a picture is provided, use the information in the word problem to **LABEL THE PICTURE**. If there is no picture and you find yourself trying to visualize the situation in your mind's eye, **DRAW THE PICTURE** on paper. It is easier to work with an actual drawing that is labeled than it is to keep the information straight in your mind. This will reduce the chance of mistakes *and* the time it takes you to solve the problem (our two key areas for ensuring success).

Once you've determined that a problem won't be *easy* to solve, you will want to begin with a **BALLPARK-AND-ELIMINATE** strategy—ballpark the answers and eliminate the choices that aren't in the ballpark. Begin practicing this strategy with problems you are facing in math class today. Use your knowledge and experience to identify a general range of results, whether the answer is numerical or graphical, and then attempt to solve the problem. On the ACT, you may still end up testing out the solutions that your ballpark answer does not eliminate, but using this technique will reduce the number of solutions you need to test.

PLUG IN ANSWER CHOICES when the answers are numerical. This can be quicker than solving the problem because it simply requires substitution rather than actual algebra. When using this strategy, start with the middle choice because the answers are listed in numerical order. Once you have tried one number, determine if you should go to a higher or lower answer choice for your next attempt.

YOUR GRAPHING CALCULATOR can be a lifesaver. Say you recognize a problem as a combination or permutation but don't remember the formula. Your graphing calculator will solve it for you. What if you are given a list of data and asked for some measure of central tendency? Your graphing calculator can calculate that for you, too. If you are given a graph and asked to find the equation, you can enter each answer choice into your calculator and examine the resulting graph. Be attentive to the "window" of the answer choices. Work on becoming even more proficient with your graphing calculator and plan on using it on the ACT. Practice with it as you work through this book and you'll know when to turn to it during the exam. Remember, your calculator is only a time-saver if you're quick with it.

The last resort is to make an **EDUCATED GUESS**. This will not guarantee you a perfect score, but it is certainly better than leaving any problem blank. First, complete all the problems that you can answer correctly and quickly, skipping the ones you find difficult. When you have a few minutes left in the testing time, go back to the problems you skipped. Remember, the key to guessing is to make an *educated* guess. Use your ballpark answer or your graphing calculator to eliminate incorrect choices. Narrow your choices as much as you can before guessing.

ONLINE VERSION OF THE ACT

The ACT may be available online in your area. If both the online and the paper and pencil versions are available to you, consider which assessment delivery will provide you with the best opportunity to complete 60 questions in 60 minutes. Practice with the questions in this book and the full-length online practice test to monitor your performance in each version.

The drawing and labeling of pictures is an important aspect of solving many math problems. If the assessment is administered online, you may need to sketch key features of the problem on your scratch paper as you solve it. This may or may not cause you to take more time. It may be that the act of sketching key components aids you in solving the problem quickly.

There is an advantage to practicing with Test Nav if you will be taking the ACT online. Test Nav is the platform that the ACT will be delivered on. Familiarity with this platform will save you some time during the test. In particular, there are two tools you should practice using. The bookmarking tool allows you to mark questions you would like to come back to later. You should bookmark questions that you choose to skip or questions you have answered that you would like to review if you have time. The eliminator tool can be used to mark incorrect answer choices with an X in order to avoid re-reading choices that you already know to be incorrect. On the paper and pencil practice tests, you practice marking wrong answer choices with an X once you determine the choice to be incorrect.

What is key when preparing for the ACT is that you simulate the environment you will experience during the actual test. If you will be taking the assessment online, do not write on the actual problems in this book during the practice test. Instead, imagine the question is on a screen and use scratch paper to work through the problem. Remember to time yourself in this situation and work on improving your speed as you improve your accuracy.

So, there you have it! You now have an idea of what will be in the math section of the ACT, tips for using this book, and strategies for taking the test. Perhaps you have already written notes in these margins and highlighted the key points. Refer back to this chapter when working through the next five and again after you have worked through the entire math section of this book.

ONLINE PRACTICE TEST

Remember, you can access the full-length online practice test at *barronsbooks.com/tp/ACT36* or by scanning the QR Code below.*

*Be sure to have your copy of *ACT 36*, 4th edition on hand to complete the registration process.

Elementary Algebra

8

→ **INTRODUCTORY PROBABILITY AND STATISTICS**
→ **PRE-ALGEBRA TOPICS**
→ **EXPRESSIONS AND EQUATIONS**
→ **EXPONENTS/POLYNOMIALS**
→ **FACTORING POLYNOMIALS**
→ **PRACTICE SET: ELEMENTARY ALGEBRA**

Elementary algebra is just that—elementary! It calls upon the skills you learned in middle school through part of first-year algebra, including probability, percents, proportion, expressions, equations, and polynomials. Graphing problems are in another section. When you come across an elementary algebra problem, don't over-think it! The key here is to trust that the problem is, in fact, easy and straightforward.

Your pre-algebra and basic algebra skills should be strong enough that you can work out these problems in 30 seconds or less. Spending time looking for patterns or clues to select an answer without solving the problem may be a waste of time. The most difficult problems in this category are factoring problems, which we'll get to at the end of this chapter.

This section of the test is your chance to buy time. Elementary algebra will make up about 25 of the 60 questions in the math section of the ACT. Know your basics and you have a great opportunity to earn yourself more time to think on the remaining 35 questions. Review each of the topics in this chapter and time yourself on the practice problems. Remember, limit yourself to 30 seconds or less on each problem. If an area is taking more time, find some practice problems on that topic and work to pick up your speed.

INTRODUCTORY PROBABILITY AND STATISTICS

The good news is that the probability and statistics material tested on the ACT is what you learned in middle school. You will use fractions and percents along with your knowledge of probability to solve simple problems.

Simple Probability

You won't have to memorize any formulas for these questions. Instead, you will use your understanding of the general concept to solve straightforward problems. To review, you will recall that the probability of something happening is represented as the fraction of the number of favorable outcomes divided by the number of possible outcomes. For instance, when you roll a six-sided die, the probability of rolling a 2 is 1/6 because there is one 2 (favorable outcome) out of six possibilities.

Try the following problem and then read the solution/explanation to review the concept.

PRACTICE QUESTION

A bag contains 4 red balls, 5 green balls, and 3 blue balls. If a ball is selected at random from the bag, what is the probability that the ball selected will be green?

A. $\dfrac{1}{5}$

B. $\dfrac{1}{12}$

C. $\dfrac{5}{60}$

D. $\dfrac{5}{12}$

E. $\dfrac{5}{7}$

EXPLANATION: (D) The answer is simply $\dfrac{5}{12}$ because there are 5 green balls and a total of 12 balls (or possible outcomes). Probability is always the number of choices considered successes divided by the number of choices that exist.

Simple Statistics

When you first started learning about statistics, you examined data sets and found the measures of central tendency and the range of the data. Those are the only parts of statistics that you will be called upon to know for the ACT. In other words, you will use *mean, median, mode,* and *range*.

- **MODE** is the number that occurs most often in a data set (there may be more than one mode).
- **RANGE** is the difference between the smallest data value and the largest.

Most likely, the statistics problems you encounter will involve mean or median. Examples and explanations of these two concepts follow.

MEAN

The mean is determined by adding all of the data in a data set and dividing by the number of data. The problems on the ACT will not always be as straightforward as that, but they will be simple. The following example demonstrates how the mean might be used to solve a problem. Give it a try and check the solution/explanation to see if you solved it the same way.

REMEMBER

Mean **is the total value of a data set divided by the number of data in the set (the average).**

PRACTICE QUESTION

Julia went to Cancun during summer vacation. She recorded the number of pesos she spent on the first five days of her trip in the table below. How many pesos did she spend on the sixth day to make the mean expenditure per day (for six days) 220?

July	1	2	3	4	5	6
Pesos spent	250	100	150	100	400	?

F. 120
G. 200
H. 220
J. 320
K. 1000

EXPLANATION: (J) The answer to this problem is 320. In order for the mean of six pieces of data to be 220, the sum of the data must be equal to 6(220) or 1320. If you subtract the sum of the pesos spent over the first five days (1000) from 1320, you have 320 left, which must have been spent on day 6.

MEDIAN

The median of a set of data is the value of the piece of data that is in the middle when all data are listed in increasing or decreasing order. This is considered one of the measures of central tendency, along with mode and mean. In order to find it, you must first list the numbers (data) in numerical order and then locate the middle value by counting the total number of data (how many there are). When there is an odd number of data in your set, you will simply select the value in the middle of the list (once rewritten in numerical order). When there is an even number, you will find the two values in the middle and then find the average of those two numbers. Here are two examples that demonstrate both cases.

REMEMBER

Median **is the middle number (or average of two middle numbers) when data are written in numerical order.**

PRACTICE QUESTIONS

1. What is the median of the following 9 numbers?

   61, 14, 72, 25, 36, 48, 57, 17, 81
   A. 14
   B. 81
   C. 48
   D. 5
   E. 42

2. Find the median of the following set of data.

42, 13, 76, 61, 5, 21, 13, 37

F. 33
G. 21
H. 33.5
J. 29
K. 13

EXPLANATIONS

1. **(C)** The first step in solving this problem is to list the numbers in numerical order from least to greatest. The set would then be listed as 14, 17, 25, 36, 48, 57, 61, 72, 81. There are nine total numbers, and if you move in evenly from either side, you will end up at the fifth term, which is 48. The median of this data set is 48.

2. **(J)** Again, you will first reorder the data in numerical order from least to greatest. The set will then be written as 5, 13, 13, 21, 37, 42, 61, 76. If you move in evenly from each side, you will end up with two values, 37 and 21, in the middle. Neither of these is the median. The median is 29, which is the average of 37 and 21.

PRE-ALGEBRA TOPICS

The quickest, easiest way to solve problems in this section is to use the context rather than trying to remember formulas or procedures. You may not have practiced these skills out of context in a few years, but you still know how to do the math. You use percents when you are shopping at the mall. You use formulas and solve for variables in formulas all the time in your science classes. Finding patterns and using tables is second nature to you. So, again, do not over-think this. These problems should be as easy as they appear, and each of them should take you under 30 seconds to solve. Read about each topic, try the examples, and review the solution/explanations.

Percents

If a percent problem is completely straightforward, use your calculator and move on. However, it is likely that percent problems will not be completely straightforward and will require a working knowledge of the meaning of percents. Remember that *percent* means "per one hundred" and you can always convert the number to a fraction or decimal. For instance, 47% is the same as $\dfrac{47}{100}$ or 0.47 (47 hundredths). When you are finding a percent of a number, you multiply. If you are not comfortable with percents, use the context and your common sense to help you. For example, if you know what 10% of a number is, you can find 1% or 5% by using a tenth or half of 10%. Take a look at the following example along with the solution/explanation.

You may be given information involving percent in a table and asked to solve problems based on the values given. This is a simple case of reading a table and applying your knowledge of percent. A common example of this type of problem would be a loan chart in which varying payment schedules are listed depending on the amount borrowed and the percent of interest charged.

At a given lunch period, 75% of the students buying lunch selected pizza. 60% of the students who did not select pizza selected chicken nuggets. What percent of the students selected something other than pizza or chicken nuggets?

A. 0%

B. 10%

C. 15%

D. 25%

E. 40%

EXPLANATION: (B) For this problem it is easiest to suppose that there are 100 total students. If 75% chose pizza, then 75 students chose pizza and 25%, or 25 students, did not select pizza. If 60% of the students who did not select pizza (25) selected chicken nuggets, then 40% of the 25 did not select either. 40% of 25 is equivalent to $\frac{4}{10}$ of 25, which is 10 or 10%. In this case you are finding percents of percents. Whenever possible, make the problem more concrete for yourself.

TIP

When working with percents, you may want to draw a circle or a fraction bar.

Formulas

You will see two types of formula problems on the ACT. You will be evaluating formulas, and you will solve a formula for a given variable.

Evaluating formulas is simple—you don't even have to know the formula that you are asked to evaluate. In the past, you have probably worked with geometric formulas and distance formulas. For example, you may have been given the area and width of a rectangle and asked to find the length, using the geometric formula $A = lw$. Using the distance formula, $d = rt$, you might be given the time and distance and asked to find the rate at which a car is traveling. No matter the formula, you will be expected to use the problem to find the values of all but one variable, substitute those values in, and solve the equation for the remaining variable.

The second type of formula problem is one in which you are simply given a formula and asked to solve for a particular variable. If you have taken chemistry or physics, you have done this before. If you have not, don't let this kind of problem intimidate you. Solving a formula for a given variable is actually easier than evaluating a formula. Again, it is not necessary to be familiar with the formula you are asked to manipulate. Simply use the same algebraic properties that you would use when solving equations for a variable. Keep things balanced and you should be fine! Here are three examples for you to work through to become more comfortable with these types of problems.

1. The circumference of a circle is given by the formula $C = \pi d$ where d is the diameter of the circle. The formula for the area of a circle is $A = \pi r^2$. If the area of the circle is 9π, what is the circumference of the circle?

   A. 9π

   B. 9

   C. 6π

   D. 6

   E. 3π

2. The Pythagorean theorem is $a^2 + b^2 = c^2$. Solve for a.

   F. $a = c - b$

   G. $a = c^2 - b^2$

   H. $a = \dfrac{c^2 - b^2}{2}$

   J. $a = \sqrt{c - b}$

   K. $a = \sqrt{c^2 - b^2}$

3. The perimeter of an ellipse is found using the formula $p = \dfrac{\pi}{2}\sqrt{2(h^2 + w^2)}$. Solve this formula for w.

   A. $\sqrt{\dfrac{2p^2}{\pi^2} - h^2} = w$

   B. $\sqrt{\dfrac{2}{\pi^2}(p^2 - h^2)} = w$

   C. $w = \dfrac{\pi}{2}\sqrt{2(h^2 + p^2)}$

   D. $w = \dfrac{\pi}{2}\sqrt{2(p^2 - h^2)}$

   E. $\dfrac{2p^2}{\pi^2} - h^2 = w$

EXPLANATIONS

1. **(C)** This problem is simple even though it requires more than one step. First you use the area of 9π to recognize that r^2 is equal to 9. Therefore, r is the square root of 9, which is 3. The diameter is twice the radius of 3, so the diameter is 6 and the circumference is 6π.

2. **(K)** This is a straightforward and very common problem. The solution $a = \sqrt{c^2 - b^2}$ is found by first subtracting b^2 from both sides and then taking the square root of both sides.

3. **(A)** Yes, this formula and the solutions can appear intimidating. There are exponents and radicals, and you may not even know what an ellipse is. In order to solve this problem, you will need to use multiple steps and equation-solving skills. You will square both sides, multiply by a reciprocal, subtract a value, and take the square root of both sides. Really, the process is not difficult, but you must be careful about the exponents and parentheses. Follow the process on the next page.

First, square both sides of the equation to eliminate the radical.

$$(p)^2 = \left(\frac{\pi}{2}\sqrt{2(h^2+w^2)}\right)^2 \text{ which results in } p^2 = \frac{\pi^2}{4} \cdot 2(h^2 + w^2)$$

Simplifying this will give you $p^2 = \frac{\pi^2}{2} \cdot (h^2 + w^2)$. In order to isolate the parentheses you

will need to multiply both sides by $\frac{2}{\pi^2}$.

$$\left(\frac{2}{\pi^2}\right)p^2 = \left(\frac{2}{\pi^2}\right)\left(\frac{\pi^2}{2}(h^2+w^2)\right), \text{ which results in } \frac{2p^2}{\pi^2} = (h^2 + w^2).$$

The next step is to subtract h^2 from both sides.

$$\frac{2p^2}{\pi^2} - h^2 = (h^2 + w^2) - h^2, \text{ which results in } \frac{2p^2}{\pi^2} - h^2 = w^2.$$

Now, taking the square root of each side will isolate w and therefore solve for w.

$$\sqrt{\frac{2p^2}{\pi^2} - h^2} = \sqrt{w^2}, \text{ resulting in } \sqrt{\frac{2p^2}{\pi^2} - h^2} = w$$

Factors and Multiples

On the ACT you will be asked to solve problems involving factors and multiples without those terms being used specifically. You should be able to move from a number to its factors or its multiples with ease. Check your skill with the following example.

PRACTICE QUESTION

One light flashes green every 15 seconds and a second light flashes red every 6 seconds. If they flash together and you begin counting seconds, after how many seconds will they next flash together?

F. 75
G. 60
H. 30
J. 18
K. 15

EXPLANATION: (H) The solution is 30 seconds. This problem involves your knowledge of multiples, yet it does not specifically ask you to find multiples. In this case, selecting the larger number and finding its multiples while checking to see if the smaller number is a factor of each multiple is the quickest way to solve the problem. 6 is not a factor of 15, but it is a factor of 30.

TIP

When solving equations, keep things balanced. In other words, anything that you do to one side, you must do to the other side.

REMEMBER

Factors and *multiples* are opposite terms. For example, 9 is a factor of 72, and 72 is a multiple of 9.

EXPRESSIONS AND EQUATIONS

Absolute Value

The absolute value of a number is the distance the number is from zero on the number line. You may know this simply as the positive of the number. Similarly, the absolute value of an expression is the distance of the value of that expression from zero. When you are asked to work with the absolute value of an expression, treat the contents of the absolute value as a group, find the value of the contents, and then take the absolute value of that value. For instance, $|3 - 7| = |-4|$. -4 is four units from zero on the number line, which means that $|-4| = 4$. You may be given a problem like $|x - 7| = 5$ and asked to find x. In this case, you need to work backwards and understand that the contents of the absolute value symbol may be positive or negative 5 because both are 5 units away from zero. Therefore, you would need to solve for either value and report all possible solutions to the equation. In this case, you would find that $x - 7 = 5$ results in $x = 12$ and $x - 7 = -5$ results in $x = 2$. So, there are two solutions to this problem $x = 12$ or 2.

PRACTICE QUESTION

Solve $|x - 13| = 5$ for x.

A. 18
B. 8 or 18
C. −18
D. −2
E. 8

EXPLANATION: (B) If $|x - 13| = 5$, then $x - 13 = 5$ or $x - 13 = -5$. If $x - 13 = 5$, then $x = 18$. If $x - 13 = -5$, then $x = 8$. So the solution is $x = \{8, 18\}$.

Absolute Value Inequalities

Absolute values indicate a distance from zero. If an absolute value is less than or greater than a number, it indicates that the distance of the contents of the absolute value from zero is less than or greater than that number. If the distance is greater than a number, then the solutions are one *or* the other, because you cannot be in both regions at the same time. If the solution is less than a number, the solutions must both be in play at the same time so you would use **and** to describe the two solutions.

Solve $|x - 13| > 5$ for x.

F. 18
G. 8 or 18
H. $x < 8$ or $x > 18$
J. $8 < x < 18$
K. 8

EXPLANATION: (H) If $|x - 13| > 5$, then $x - 13 > 5$ **or** $x - 13 < -5$. If $x - 13 > 5$, then $x > 18$. If $x - 13 < -5$, then $x < 8$. So the solution is $x < 8$ **or** $x > 18$ (it cannot be both so you must use **or**).

Proportion

Proportions are simply a special kind of equation. They can help you solve problems when you have a relationship that is established and you are missing one piece of information out of four. For instance, if you know that in order to mix a fruit drink you need to use 1 cup powder for 3 cups of water, and you have 5 cups of powder available, you can determine that you need 15 cups of water. 1 is to 3 as 5 is to . . . ? You can use a proportion to set up the equation $\frac{1}{3} = \frac{5}{x}$. You can solve this problem by multiplying both sides by $3x$ to eliminate the fractions. You would then have $x = 15$. Proportion problems will not always be this simple and may involve expressions, but the premise is the same. There will be an established relationship, you will set up a proportion, you will multiply by the denominators to eliminate fractions, and then you will solve the equation.

Gordon recently learned that his shadow is proportional to his height. He also learned that the shadows of other objects are proportional to their height. At three o'clock, his shadow measured 4 feet and the shadow of the tree in his front yard measured 18 feet. If Gordon is 6 feet tall, how tall is the tree?

A. 108 feet
B. 72 feet
C. 27 feet
D. 24 feet
E. 9 feet

EXPLANATION: (C) This proportion can be set up two ways. One way is $\frac{4}{18} = \frac{6}{x}$ and the other is $\frac{4}{6} = \frac{18}{x}$ or $\frac{2}{3} = \frac{18}{x}$. Either way, you may notice that the ratio of 4 to 6 is equivalent to 2 to 3. Then, using the same ratio for 18 to x, 9 goes into 18 twice and 9 times 3 is 27. You could also multiply by the denominators to find that $4x = 108$ and that $108/4 = 27$. Using the second proportion would result in the same equation.

Solving Multi-Step Linear Equations

Because you've probably had a lot of practice solving equations, it will be best to solve linear equations rather than checking the answer options. Checking the answers requires that you perform the operations multiple times (as many as it takes for you to find the correct answer). This will take more time than solving the equation once for the variable in question.

Linear equation problems will call on you to distribute, combine like terms, and use multiplication, division, addition, and subtraction to isolate the variable. When faced with a multi-step linear equation, hit autopilot and get to work without wasting time considering whether to solve or not. Solving will be the most efficient method!

PRACTICE QUESTION

Solve $2(4x + 7) - 3(2x - 4) = 20$ for x.

F. $\dfrac{9}{7}$

G. -3

H. 9

J. 13

K. 23

EXPLANATION: (G) Distribute 2 and −3 through their respective parentheses to result in $8x + 14 - 6x + 12 = 20$. Then, combine like terms to result in $2x + 26 = 20$. Subtract 26 from both sides of the equation so that $2x = -6$ and divide by 2 on both sides to find that $x = -3$.

TIP

If an equation has fractions in it, multiply through by the least common denominator to eliminate all fractions.

Writing Linear Equations

The ACT will ask you to demonstrate your skill at writing linear equations. The most typical scenario is one in which you are given a situation and asked to depict the situation with variables in an equation. Try your hand at the following example. You may find that the context makes it easier for you to move to an equation.

PRACTICE QUESTION

Josie would like to have wireless Internet in her apartment. Her phone company charges a $60 installation fee and $39.99 per month. Write an equation that will help Josie determine her cost (c) to have wireless for any given number of months (m).

A. $60 + 39.99\ m = c$

B. $39.99 + 60\ m = c$

C. $60 = 39.99\ m$

D. $c = 60 - 39.99\ m$

E. $c = 60\ m - 39.99$

EXPLANATION: (A) The initial cost is $60, and that will be charged no matter how many months Josie has wireless Internet in her apartment. The monthly cost of $39.99 needs to be multiplied by the number of months that Josie has service. So, the total cost equals 39.99 $m + 60$.

Linear Equations: Special Cases

There will be problems that ask you to represent one value in terms of another in order to reduce the equation to two variables. For instance, there are times when you will be asked to work with consecutive integers, consecutive odd integers, or consecutive even integers. In these cases, you name the first integer x and write the second integer in terms of the first: $x+1$ in the case of consecutive integers and $x + 2$ in the case of consecutive even or odd integers.

Another special case of linear equations is a problem in which you are given a table of values and asked to write a rule for the given pattern. If there is a common difference, then you may simply use your knowledge of slope intercept to determine the value of the pattern for the zero term, and use the common difference as the slope. If there is no common difference, the equation is not linear and you may want to plug values into each of the possible solutions. Be careful here because it is possible that more than one choice will work for some of the values in the table, but only one will work for all the values.

TIP

Use *x* as your variable and define all other variables in terms of *x*.

EXPONENTS/POLYNOMIALS
Multiplying Monomials

In order to multiply monomials, you must use the product property of exponents. Remember that when you multiply monomials you can combine common bases by adding their exponents. This works because $x^3 \cdot x^5 = (xxx) \cdot (xxxxx) = xxxxxxxx = x^8$. This same problem could be solved simply by adding the exponents $x^3 \cdot x^5 = x^{3+5} = x^8$. Of course, the monomials you are asked to multiply will be more complicated than these, but the premise remains the same. Give it a try here and see just how simple multiplying monomials is.

TIP

If you come across a pattern that does not have a common difference, guess and check with the solutions to determine the correct answer.

PRACTICE QUESTION

The product of $(3m^5n^7)(-4mn^3)$ is equivalent to:

F. $-12m^5n^{10}$

G. $-12m^4n^4$

H. $-12m^{12}n^4$

J. $-12m^5n^{21}$

K. $-12m^6n^{10}$

EXPLANATION: (K) 3×-4 is -12, $m^5m = m^6$, and $n^7n^3 = n^{10}$. So, the product of $(3m^5n^7)$ $(-4mn^3)$ is equivalent to $-12m^6n^{10}$.

TIP

When multiplying common bases, remember the product property: $x^a \times x^b = x^{a+b}$. For example, $x^3 \times x^5 = x^{3+5} = x^8$.

Adding Polynomials

Adding polynomials is as easy as combining like terms. Be careful that the terms are in fact alike and that you keep track of the signs of the coefficients. Feel free to write in the ACT problem book and cross off the terms that you have added so that you do not forget any. Also, writing the solutions in decreasing order will help you keep track of your work and make it easier to match your solution to the solution choices given. You may not have to work through the entire problem if you keep track of your answer's similarity to the choices given. Note: if you take the assessment online you may need to write the problem on scratch paper in order to solve it.

What polynomial must be added to $7x^2 + 14x - 8$ to result in a sum of $5x^2 + 18x + 1$?

A. $-2x^2 - 4x + 7$

B. $2x^2 - 4x + 9$

C. $-2x^2 + 4x + 9$

D. $-2x^2 + 4x + 7$

E. $2x^2 + 4x + 9$

EXPLANATION: (C) In order to get from $7x^2$ to $5x^2$, you would need to add $-2x^2$, to get from $14x$ to $18x$, you would need to add $4x$, and to get from -8 to 1 you would need to add 9. Therefore, the polynomial you would need to add to $7x^2 + 14x - 8$ to result in a sum of $5x^2 + 18x + 1$ would be $-2x^2 + 4x + 9$.

Distributing

Distributing is a skill that you use all the time. It is simply multiplying a monomial across a polynomial. In the case of multiplying two binomials, you take one monomial at a time and multiply it across the second binomial. This is the distributive property and is often called FOIL (first, outer, inner, last). Also, multiplying two polynomials together requires taking each monomial from the first polynomial and multiplying it across the second polynomial. Be careful to watch the signs when distributing and to combine all like terms once you have performed the multiplication. Again, because this skill is probably such a natural process for you, it is most efficient to perform the distribution rather than look for a shortcut to the solution.

Which is the equivalent form of $(x - 3)(x^2 + 4x - 8)$?

F. $x^3 + x^2 - 20x + 24$

G. $x^3 + 7x^2 + 4x - 24$

H. $x^3 + 7x^2 + 20x - 24$

J. $x^3 + x^2 - 12x + 24$

K. $x^3 + x^2 + 4x + 24$

EXPLANATION: (F) First multiply x through $(x^2 + 4x - 8)$ so that you are simply looking at $x(x^2 + 4x - 8) = x^3 + 4x^2 - 8x$. Then multiply -3 through $(x^2 + 4x - 8)$ so that you are simply looking at $-3(x^2 + 4x - 8) = -3x^2 - 12x + 24$ and then add your like terms. You have $x^3 + 4x^2 - 8x - 3x^2 - 12x + 24 = x^3 + x^2 - 20x + 24$.

FACTORING POLYNOMIALS

Although you learned factoring in your first algebra class, you were most likely in your second algebra class before you were fluent at the procedure. The elementary algebra problems on the ACT will ask you to factor quadratics that are relatively simple. That is to say, the leading coefficient is either 1 or a prime number. You may need to factor out a common term to notice the leading coefficient to be 1 or a prime number. For problems that have composite leading coefficients, you will find other strategies for factoring in the next chapter. Here, we will concentrate on simple factoring. Two types of problems that require factoring are those involving rational expressions and those involving quadratic equations.

To achieve a perfect score on the ACT, you must be able to factor quickly and correctly. You will need to call on this skill to aid you in solving more complex problems. In this chapter, however, the factoring will not be complex or difficult.

Simple Factoring

Let's review simple factoring! First, factor out a common term if possible. You ought to be left with a leading coefficient of either 1 or a prime number. Next, write two parentheses and place a binomial in each.

Given the expression $ax^2 + bx + c$ where a is equal to one, start filling in your factors with $(x\_\_\_\_)(x\_\_\_\_)$. Then consider two numbers whose product is c and whose sum is b (keeping the signs in mind). If c is negative, the two factors will have opposite signs; when you add the numbers together you will be adding a positive number and a negative number. If c is positive, the two factors will have the same sign (it may be positive or negative). When you add them together, you will find the sum of the numbers and keep the sign (watch the sign of b to determine the sign of the factors).

Here is an example to illustrate the concept. Give it a try.

PRACTICE QUESTION

Which of the following is the factored form of $x^2 - 7x + 10$?
- **A.** $(x - 7)(x - 3)$
- **B.** $(x + 4)(x + 3)$
- **C.** $(x - 4)(x - 3)$
- **D.** $(x - 5)(x - 2)$
- **E.** $(x + 5)(x + 2)$

EXPLANATION: (D) In this case, the leading coefficient is 1. You simply need to identify two factors of positive 10 whose sum is -7. The factors are -5 and -2. The factored form is $(x - 5)(x - 2)$.

TIP

When multiplying a term from the first polynomial, be sure to take the sign of the coefficient as part of the term.

REMEMBER

Factoring helps you find the expressions that can be multiplied together to equal the polynomial.

Factoring with Prime Numbers

Now, let's review what this process will be like if a is a prime number. The factors will start out with $(ax\_\_\_\_\_)(x\_\_\_\_\_)$. This time, you will multiply a by c and determine which factors you are looking for. Find two factors of ac that add up to b. Then, work on the placement of factors of c (one will be multiplied by a and one will be multiplied by 1, and the resulting products will be added to equal b) so that the correct factors of ac add up to b. Try the following example. You will absolutely need to be able to factor expressions when simplifying rational expressions in the next chapter.

PRACTICE QUESTION

Which of the following is the factored form of the expression $3x^2 + 5x - 12$?

F. $(3x - 4)(x + 3)$
G. $(3x + 4)(x - 3)$
H. $(3x - 6)(x + 2)$
J. $(3x + 6)(x - 2)$
K. $(x - 4)(3x + 3)$

EXPLANATION: (F) The leading coefficient is not equal to 1 and it is prime, so the first step is to establish that the factors will begin with $(3x\_\_\_\_\_)(x\_\_\_\_\_)$. Now, two factors of -36 whose sum is 5 are 9 and -4. You know that the two numbers placed in the parentheses must have a product of -12 and that you need your middle terms to be $9x$ and $-4x$ to give you a sum of $5x$. Using 3 and -4 as the factors of -12 and placing the 3 in the position that will be multiplied by the 3 in the first spot will give you 9. Placing these factors into the product of the binomials results in $(3x - 4)(x + 3)$. If you were to distribute this to check it, you would get $3x^2 + 9x - 4x - 12 = 3x^2 + 5x - 12$. Notice that the middle terms are $9x$ and $-4x$, which match the factors of $-36x$ and whose sum is $5x$.

Solving Quadratics

Once you have a quadratic equation set equal to zero and factored, the solution is simple. Problems that are categorized as elementary algebra will be in factored form already. For problems that are not yet factored, we will review strategies for solving non-linear equations in the next chapter. For now, let's review how to solve a factored equation that equals zero. Simply use the zero property of multiplication, which states that if the product of two or more terms equals zero then one or more of those terms must equal zero. If $x \times y \times z = 0$ then either x and/or y and/or z equal zero. So, when you have $(x - 7)(x + 4) = 0$ you know that either $x - 7 = 0$ (in which case $x = 7$) and/or $x + 4 = 0$ (in which case $x = -4$). The solution to the equation $(x - 7)(x + 4) = 0$ is $x = \{-4, 7\}$.

Which of the following is not a solution of $3(x-8)(x-3)(x+4)(x+7)=0$?

F. -4

G. 0

H. 3

J. 8

K. -7

EXPLANATION: (G) Since the equation is in factored form, you simply set each factor equal to zero and find the value of x that would make it true. $3=0$ cannot be true for any x. $x-8=0$ is true when $x=8$, $x-3=0$ is true when $x=3$, $x+4=0$ is true when $x=-4$, and $x+7=0$ is true when $x=-7$. So, the solutions are $x=\{8, 3, -4, -7\}$. 0 is not a solution of this equation.

PRACTICE SET: ELEMENTARY ALGEBRA

The following problems are all typical of the 25 elementary algebra problems on the ACT. These types of problems will occur most frequently at the beginning of the test, and some will be mixed in throughout the test. While practicing, challenge yourself to complete each problem in 30 seconds or less. Time yourself on the following 12 questions, and attempt to complete them in 6 minutes or less.

In the directions on the exam, you will be told to choose the correct answer and fill in the corresponding oval on the answer sheet. You will be reminded not to linger on problems that you are struggling to solve. In order to recognize when you are lingering, practice in a timed setting. You will be reminded that you are allowed to use a calculator on any problems but that it may not be the best choice every time. The directions will include a few final clarifying points, and then you will start the test.

You are not required to do the problems in any particular order. Moving through the test in numerical order will present you with a higher concentration of elementary algebra problems at the beginning, allowing you to move through the first part quickly and then take more time per problem as you continue through the test.

TIP

Don't linger over any one problem. Move on, then come back to it if you have time.

1. To increase the mean of 8 numbers by 5, by how much would the sum of the 8 numbers need to increase?
   A. 5
   B. 10
   C. 20
   D. 40
   E. 80

2. When $\frac{1}{7}n + 3 = \frac{-1}{5}(n-20)$, what is the value of n?

   F. $\frac{1}{12}$

   G. $\frac{35}{12}$

   H. $\frac{12}{35}$

   J. 12

   K. 35

3. Cathy has a coupon for 10% off at her favorite CD store. When she arrives at the store she finds that the CDs are already on sale for 25% off. She would like to put an expression into her calculator to determine the cost of a CD after the 25% and additional 10% discounts. Using p for the original marked price, which of the following expressions will give her the discounted price?
   A. $p - .35p$
   B. $p - .35$
   C. $p - .325p$
   D. $p - .325$
   E. $p - .10p$

4. For all x, $(2x+5)^2(-3x+7) = ?$
   F. $-12x^2 + 70$
   G. $-6x^2 - x + 35$
   H. $4x^2 + 20x + 25$
   J. $4x^2 + 17x + 32$
   K. $-12x^3 - 32x^2 + 65x + 175$

5. The Key Club at the local high school is sponsoring an Easter egg hunt at the park. 250 children register for the hunt. The Key Club members decide that it is more fair if they separate the children into age groups. The children are divided into four age categories, as shown in the following table.

Age category	Under 2	2–5	6–10	Over 10
Number of children	25	53	125	47

70 eggs that have special prizes in them will be distributed proportionally to each age category. How many prizes will the club members award to the children in the 6–10 age range?

A. 18
B. 27
C. 32
D. 35
E. 53

6. The number 0.07 is 1000 times as large as which of the following numbers?

F. 0.7
G. 0.07
H. 0.007
J. 0.0007
K. 0.00007

7. Which of the following is equal to $\dfrac{\frac{3}{4}-\frac{1}{3}}{\frac{3}{4}+\frac{1}{3}}$?

A. $\dfrac{5}{12}$

B. $\dfrac{-5}{12}$

C. $\dfrac{-5}{13}$

D. $\dfrac{5}{13}$

E. $\dfrac{13}{5}$

8. Find the simplified form of $\dfrac{-10x^2-35x+20}{3x^2+12x}$.

F. $\dfrac{-5(2x-1)}{3x}$

G. $\dfrac{-5}{3}$

H. $\dfrac{-5(2x^2+7x+4)}{3x^2+12x}$

J. $-7x^2-23x+20$

K. $\dfrac{-10}{3}-\dfrac{35}{12}+20$

9. If $8-5x=-47$, then $2x=$?

A. 7.8
B. 15.6
C. 11
D. −11
E. 22

10. The formula $d=rt$ is called the distance formula. In this formula, d represents the distance traveled, r represents the rate of speed, and t represents the time traveled. If a person travels 90 miles in $2\frac{1}{2}$ hours, what is the value of r?

F. 36 mph
G. 45 mph
H. 72 mph
J. 180 mph
K. 225 mph

11. The product of $(-4x^6y^7)(-2xy^3)$ is:

A. $8x^7y^{10}$
B. $8x^6y^{10}$
C. $8x^6y^{21}$
D. $8x^7y^{21}$
E. $-8x^6y^{10}$

12. A bag contains 4 red gumballs, 7 green gumballs, 2 white gumballs, and 5 blue gumballs. How many additional white gumballs must be added to the 18 gumballs in the bag so that the probability of drawing a gumball that is not white is $\frac{2}{3}$?

F. 3
G. 4
H. 5
J. 6
K. 7

Answers Explained

1. **(D)** The sum of the 8 numbers would need to increase by 5 for each number, so multiply 5 by 8 to get 40.

2. **(G)** Multiplying $\frac{1}{7}n+3=\frac{-1}{5}(n-20)$ by 35 simplifies to $5n + 105 = -7(n - 20)$, which simplifies to $5n + 105 = -7n + 140$, which simplifies to $12n = 35$, which means that n must equal $\frac{35}{12}$.

3. **(C)** A discount of 25% would leave 75% of the cost. Taking an additional 10% off the 75% remaining is equivalent to an additional 7.5% off the original price (10% of 75 is 7.5). $25\% + 7.5\% = 32.5\%$ total discount. The original price minus 32.5% of the original price is the discounted price. 32.5% is equivalent to $\frac{32.5}{100}=0.325$.

4. **(K)** On the actual test, if you recognize that the answer should include a cubic, select the answer without solving. If you did not already solve it, solve it now and review the given solution.

$$(2x+5)^2(-3x+7)$$
$$=(4x^2+20x+25)(-3x+7)$$
$$=-12x^3-60x^2-75x+28x^2+140x+175$$
$$=-12x^3-32x^2+65x+175$$

5. **(D)** 125 children in the 6–10 age group is $\frac{1}{2}$ of the 250 total runners. 35 prizes is half of the total of 70 prizes. Setting this up as a proportion would give you $\frac{125}{250}=\frac{x}{70}$ or $\frac{1}{2}=\frac{x}{70}$, which means that $x=35$.

6. **(K)** $0.07/1000=0.00007$

7. **(D)**

$$\frac{\frac{3}{4}-\frac{1}{3}}{\frac{3}{4}+\frac{1}{3}}=\frac{\frac{5}{12}}{\frac{13}{12}}=\frac{5}{12}\times\frac{12}{13}=\frac{5}{13}$$

Alternately, this can be solved by multiplying both the numerator and denominator by 12 as a first step.

$$\frac{12\left(\frac{3}{4}-\frac{1}{3}\right)}{12\left(\frac{3}{4}+\frac{1}{3}\right)}=\frac{9-4}{9+4}=\frac{5}{13}$$

8. **(F)**

$$\frac{-10x^2-35x+20}{3x^2+12x}=\frac{-5(2x^2+7x-4)}{3x(x+4)}$$
$$=\frac{-5(2x-1)(x+4)}{3x(x+4)}$$
$$=\frac{-5(2x-1)}{3x}$$

9. **(E)**

$$8 - 5x = -47$$
$$-5x = -55$$
$$x = 11 \text{ so, } 2x = 22$$

10. **(F)**

$$d = rt$$
$$90 = r(2.5)$$
$$\frac{90}{2.5} = r$$
$$36 \text{ mph} = r$$

11. **(A)** $(-4x^6y^7)(-2xy^3) = -4(-2)x^{6+1}y^{7+3} = 8x^7y^{10}$

12. **(J)** There are 16 gumballs that are not white out of 18 total gumballs. 16 out of 24 would give you $\frac{2}{3}$ probability of selecting a gumball that is not white. $18 + 6 = 24$, so you would need to increase the number of white gumballs by 6.

Intermediate Algebra/ Coordinate Geometry

9

The questions in this category come from your algebra 1 and algebra 2 coursework (coordinate geometry is another way to say "graphing"). These questions will be sprinkled in with the elementary algebra in the beginning of the test and show up with greater regularity as you move through the test.

If you have done well with the elementary algebra portion and averaged 30 seconds per question, you will have earned yourself the flexibility to average 80 seconds for each question in this section. Some of the questions will be very easy and simply require that you find the slope or translate points. Others will be more difficult, requiring more thought and problem-solving skill. This is where you will have to decide whether a problem is best solved by graphing calculator, by hand, or if you should use another strategy for determining the solution more quickly. The key is to solve the easy problems and to use other strategies to determine solutions for the more difficult ones.

INSIDE THE ACT 36 MIND

The graphing calculator will come in handy for both coordinate geometry and intermediate algebra problems.

WHAT TO EXPECT

Coordinate geometry is simply another way of saying "graphing." Some of the problems in this section will be solved quickly and easily. These kinds of questions may simply ask you to translate points on the coordinate plane or to identify an even or odd function. In either of those cases, you will be able to select the answer from the choices quickly. Other problems will be more complicated, and it will take less time for you to solve them another way. In the case of more difficult problems, your deep understanding of the topic is what will make it possible for you to obtain a perfect score on the ACT mathematics section.

Intermediate algebra is generally all of the solving you have learned to do. The equations will include composite functions and rational expressions and converting from logarithmic to exponential, among other topics. All of these are topics you know well and you will excel at if you keep the time limit in mind.

Conic sections is a topic that you learned in algebra 2 and is considered coordinate geometry, but you may not have spent much time on it in your class. If you are not comfortable with this topic, please see the fourth chapter of this section for an overview of conic sections. Once you have the basics down, you will be able to use your extensive knowledge of solving and graphing functions to solve problems involving conics.

This category will be mixed throughout the exam with a heavier concentration in the latter part of the exam. Keep in mind that these problems should be solved in an average of 80 seconds each. When working through this chapter, try the examples on your own before reading the solution/explanation.

Let's start with the topics that may be a little less familiar, then go into the areas that you know better, and finish up with conic sections. Remember: There will only be nine questions from intermediate algebra on the ACT, so you will not necessarily see questions on each of the following topics. If you want a perfect score, however, you will need to be prepared for anything.

SEQUENCE AND SERIES

A sequence is simply an ordered list of numbers. A series is the sum of a given number of terms in a sequence.

Arithmetic Sequence and Series

TIP

A sequence can be arithmetic or geometric. An arithmetic sequence has a common difference between terms and is linear. A geometric sequence has a common ratio between terms and is exponential.

An arithmetic sequence has a common difference and is linear. It can be represented with your typical linear equation where y is the value of each term, m is the common difference (constant rate of change), x is the number of terms minus 1, and b is the value of the first term. For instance, if the sequence is 5, 9, 13, 17, 21, etc., then you can represent any term by the equation $y = 4x + 5$ where x is the number of terms minus 1. This is written in terms of sequence by using the explicit formula $a_n = a_1 + (n - 1)d$, where d is the common difference, n is the number of terms, and a_1 is the first term in the sequence. With this formula you can find the value of any variable in the formula given the values of the other variables. You may be asked to find the first term given the nth term, the common difference, and the value of n. Similarly, you may be given all but the common difference and asked to find that. Memorize this formula and you will be able to answer any arithmetic sequence problem quickly.

> ### ARITHMETIC SEQUENCE FORMULA
> $a_n = a_1 + (n - 1)d$, where d is the common difference, n is the number of terms, and a_1 is the first term in the sequence.

A series is the expression for the sum of a finite sequence (a set number of terms). For instance, given the finite sequence 5, 8, 11, 14, 17, 20 the corresponding series would be $5 + 8 + 11 + 14 + 17 + 20$ with a value of 75. The sum of a finite sequence can be found using the formula $S_n = \frac{n}{2}(a_1 + a_n)$ where a_1 is the first term, a_n is the nth term, and n is the number of terms in the sequence. To use this formula you simply need to be given or to determine the values of the first and last terms in the sequence. You may need to use the formula given above for an arithmetic sequence in order to find the information necessary to determine the arithmetic series.

> **ARITHMETIC SERIES FORMULA**
>
> $S_n = \frac{n}{2}(a_1 + a_n)$, where a_1 is the first term, a_n is the nth term, and n is the number of terms in the sequence.

To solve the following problem, you will need to use the series formula to determine n and then use the sequence formula to determine d.

PRACTICE QUESTION

If the first term in an arithmetic series is 3 and the last term is 136, and the sum is 1390, what are the first four terms?

A. 3, 9, 27, 81
B. 3, 10, 17, 24
C. 3, 12, 36, 94
D. 3, 14, 28, 108
E. 3, 15, 30, 121

EXPLANATION: (B)

$1390 = \frac{n}{2}(3 + 136)$, so $\frac{n}{2} = \frac{1390}{139} = 10$, which means that $n = 20$. Given that $n = 20$, and the first and last terms are 3 and 136, you can use the sequence formula to determine d. $136 = 3 + 19d$ or $133 = 19d$ or $7 = d$. This means that the first four terms are 3, 10, 17, and 24.

As long as you know your formulas, problems like this one should not be too difficult for you.

TIP

Memorize the formulas listed throughout the mathematics section of this book!

Geometric Sequence and Series

A geometric sequence is exponential and can be recognized by the fact that it is non-linear. Upon more careful inspection, you will also notice a common ratio between terms in the sequence. Keep in mind: the *ratio* must be common. If a pattern does not have a common difference or a common ratio, it is simply a pattern and is not an arithmetic or a geometric sequence.

Examples of a geometric sequence: 4, 12, 36, 108 . . . or 100, 20, 4, 0.8 . . . . Notice that it does not have to be increasing.

Similar to an arithmetic sequence or series, there are formulas for determining a given term in a geometric sequence and for determining a value of a geometric series. It is less likely that you will encounter a geometric series question on the ACT, but you should memorize the formula just in case you do. In the formulas for geometric sequence and series, r stands for the common ratio. In the two examples above, $r = 3$ for the first sequence and $r = 1/5$ for the second sequence.

> ### GEOMETRIC SEQUENCE FORMULA
>
> $a_n = a_1 \times r^{n-1}$, where r is the common ratio, n is the number term, a_n is the nth term in the sequence, and a_1 is the first term in the sequence.

You will want to be familiar with the sequence formula and the series formula.

> ### GEOMETRIC SERIES FORMULA
>
> $S_n = \dfrac{a_1(1 - r^n)}{1 - r}$, where r is the common ratio, n is the number term,
>
> and a_1 is the first term in the sequence.

COMBINATIONS AND PERMUTATIONS

TIP

Once you know whether the problem places significance on the order of the results or not, your calculator can do the rest. Use MATH, then PRB to find the formula.

Combinations and permutations are methods for determining the number of ways that different items can be grouped together. The main difference between the two is whether order matters or not. A great way to remember the difference between combinations and permutations is to think of the difference between ice cream scoops served in a bowl and ice cream served on a cone. If you have 10 flavors to choose from and you select 3 scoops to be served in a bowl, you could find the number of different combinations of the choices. If you were going to serve the scoops on a cone then the order would matter and you would find the number of different permutations of choices. Simply put, there are more permutations than combinations.

Combinations (Order Does Not Matter)

In the case of combinations, you have a number of something and you want to know the number of ways that you can select some of that whole set. You will use the formula $_nC_r = \dfrac{n!}{r!(n-r)!}$ for $0 \leq r \leq n$. In this formula, n is the total number of choices and r is the number you are selecting from that total. You will not be told whether a problem is a combination problem or a permutation problem so you will have to recognize it as such.

Here's an example of a combination problem: There are 15 children in a class and 5 will be selected to perform classroom jobs this week. How many different ways can the children be chosen?

$$_{15}C_5 = \frac{15!}{5!(15-5)!} = \frac{15 \cdot 14 \cdot 13 \cdot 12 \cdot 11}{5 \cdot 4 \cdot 3 \cdot 2 \cdot 1} = 3003$$

This calculation can be done simply on your graphing calculator. Type 15, then press MATH, select PRB, 3: $_nC_r$, then type 5 and ENTER to receive the same result of 3003.

> ### COMBINATION FORMULA
>
> $_nC_r = \dfrac{n!}{r!(n-r)!}$ for $0 \leq r \leq n$.

Permutations (Order Does Matter)

In the case of permutations, order does matter and the calculation is a little different. It still involves factorials ($n!$) and division, and it can still be done quite simply on the calculator. For permutations the formula is $_nP_r = \dfrac{n!}{(n-r)!}$ for $0 \le r \le n$. Again, n is the total number of choices and r is the number that you are selecting from that total. For an example of where order matters, let's use a horse race. There are 10 horses running and you need to determine the number of ways that 1st, 2nd, and 3rd place can be arranged. Whenever order matters, the calculation is a permutation and not a combination.

$$_{10}P_3 = \frac{10!}{(10-3)!} = \frac{10 \cdot 9 \cdot 8 \cdot 7 \cdot 6 \cdot 5 \cdot 4 \cdot 3 \cdot 2 \cdot 1}{7 \cdot 6 \cdot 5 \cdot 4 \cdot 3 \cdot 2 \cdot 1} = 10 \cdot 9 \cdot 8 = 720$$

You will find the same result by using your graphing calculator. Type 10, then MATH, select PRB, select 4: $_nP_r$, then type 3 and ENTER.

PERMUTATION FORMULA

$$_nP_r = \frac{n!}{(n-r)!} \text{ for } 0 \le r \le n.$$

MATRICES

A matrix is an array of numbers. A matrix is described by its dimensions, by stating the number of rows by the number of columns. Addition, subtraction, and scalar multiplication can be performed on matrices. Matrices can also be cross multiplied. On the ACT, matrices can be used to solve a system of equations. They can also be used to determine coordinates of a geometric figure following a transformation.

If you are very comfortable with matrices and like to use them for geometric transformations and/or solving equations, go for it. If you are not comfortable with them and cannot use your calculator to solve them quickly don't try it. Use other, more familiar strategies for performing geometric transformations and/or solving systems.

You should review basic operations involving matrices in case you run into a problem on the ACT. It pays to be prepared.

Adding and subtracting matrices can be done with like-dimensioned matrices. You simply add or subtract corresponding elements (elements in the same position as each other).

For example:

$$\begin{bmatrix} 5 & 7 & -3 \\ 2 & -1 & 4 \\ 1 & 3 & -2 \end{bmatrix} + \begin{bmatrix} 6 & -2 & -1 \\ -2 & 3 & 5 \\ -6 & 2 & 2 \end{bmatrix} = \begin{bmatrix} 11 & 5 & -4 \\ 0 & 2 & 9 \\ -5 & 5 & 0 \end{bmatrix}$$

or

$$\begin{bmatrix} 5 & 7 & -3 \\ 2 & -1 & 4 \\ 1 & 3 & -2 \end{bmatrix} - \begin{bmatrix} 6 & -2 & -1 \\ -2 & 3 & 5 \\ -6 & 2 & 2 \end{bmatrix} = \begin{bmatrix} -1 & 9 & -2 \\ 4 & -4 & -1 \\ 7 & 1 & -4 \end{bmatrix}$$

TIP

Unless you are very comfortable with matrices and your graphing calculator, don't use them to perform geometric transformations or to solve systems of equations.

Scalar multiplication is when a constant is multiplied by a matrix. In this case, the constant is multiplied by each element and the resulting matrix has the same dimensions as the original matrix.

For example:

$$3\begin{bmatrix} -2 & 5 \\ -3 & -1 \end{bmatrix} = \begin{bmatrix} -6 & 15 \\ -9 & -3 \end{bmatrix} \quad \text{or} \quad -2\begin{bmatrix} 3 \\ -1 \\ 2 \end{bmatrix} = \begin{bmatrix} -6 \\ 2 \\ -4 \end{bmatrix}$$

TIP

Operations on matrices are most efficiently done in your head.

These operations are most quickly done by hand even though they can also be done using a graphing calculator. Entering the matrices into a calculator takes time and may result in an error with data entry. If you have a problem with addition, subtraction, or scalar multiplication of matrices, examine the problem and perform the operation in your head as you look for the answer among the answer choices.

RATIONAL EXPRESSIONS AND FUNCTIONS

A rational expression is simply a fraction involving variables. In order to simplify it, you will need to remember your rules of exponents. You will also need to factor quadratics and simply factor common terms out.

> **RULES OF EXPONENTS**
>
> Product Rule $\quad x^m \cdot x^n = x^{m+n}$
>
> Quotient Rule $\quad \dfrac{x^m}{x^n} = x^{m-n}$
>
> Power Rule $\quad (x^m)^n = x^{mn}$

For example, $\dfrac{2x^4 y^3}{3x^9} \cdot \dfrac{-9x^2}{5y} = \dfrac{-6y^2}{5x^3}$

TIP

Watch for a negative sign to be the difference between having a common term to cancel or not.

Most often with rational expressions, the problem will involve polynomials, which must be factored in order to be simplified.

For example, $\dfrac{x^4}{x^2+2x+1} \div \dfrac{5x^2}{x^2-1} = \dfrac{x^4}{(x+1)(x+1)} \cdot \dfrac{(x+1)(x-1)}{5x^2} = \dfrac{x^2(x-1)}{5(x+1)}$

A function is rational when the simplified form contains a variable in the denominator. What makes these functions unique is the fact that there are values of x for which the function is undefined. Any value of x that would make the denominator of the simplified form equal to zero is undefined and will show up on the graph as an asymptote. Knowing where that will occur is an excellent way to narrow your solution choices. In order to determine this you must simplify the rational function using factoring. A much faster way is to graph the function on your calculator and play with your window until you can match the given function to the solution choice. If the value of x would make both the denominator and the numerator zero, it will show up as a hole in the graph rather than an asymptote.

LOGARITHMIC AND EXPONENTIAL FUNCTIONS

Logarithmic and exponential functions are inverses of each other. Be sure that you commit the properties of both to memory. Many problems involving these functions can be solved by converting to the opposite function and using the properties of both.

Converting Between Logarithmic and Exponential Functions

On the ACT, the most likely use of either exponential equations or logarithmic equations will be in solving an equation involving the opposite function. For instance, if you are solving an exponential equation in which the variable is in the exponent, you will use logs to bring it down. If you are solving a logarithmic equation in which x cannot be isolated, you will use an exponential function to solve.

> If $y = b^x$, then $\log_b y = x$ and vice versa.

Logarithmic Functions

Three things to have in your toolbox when working with logarithms are the conversion from logarithmic to exponential, the properties of logarithms, and the change of base formula.

Regardless of the base you are working in, you can use the properties of logarithms to simplify an equation or expression.

TIP

If you can convert the logarithmic equation to base 10 (common logarithm) or base e (natural logarithm), you can use your calculator to determine values.

> **PROPERTIES OF LOGARITHMS**
>
> Product Property $\quad \log_b MN = \log_b M + \log_b N$
>
> Quotient Property $\quad \log_b \dfrac{M}{N} = \log_b M - \log_b N$
>
> Power Property $\quad \log_b M^x = x\log_b M$

When you are dealing with a logarithmic equation that is neither common nor natural, you will simplify it and then either convert it to an exponential equation to solve for x or use the change of base formula to convert it to a common logarithm, which can be solved on your calculator.

TIP

When using the change of base formula, be sure to change the base to something you can use to solve the problem. Base 10 can be solved using a calculator.

> **CHANGE OF BASE FORMULA**
>
> $$\log_b M = \frac{\log_c M}{\log_c b}$$
>
> (This formula will convert from any base to any base.)

Exponential Functions

An exponential function has the variable in the exponent. The graph of the function increases or decreases exponentially and cannot cross the x axis since there is no value of x that will make the function equal 0. You can solve an exponential equation by expressing both sides of the equation in the same base so that the exponents can be set equal and you can solve for the variable.

When you cannot express each side of the equation in terms of an equivalent base, use logarithms to solve the equation. Exponential and logarithmic functions are inverses of each other. One can be used to undo the other and vice versa. Also the graphs are inverses of each other. If you can convert from exponential to logarithmic, you can use logs to solve exponential equations.

TIP

If you can express both sides of the equation using the same base, the exponents can be set equal to each other. $b^x = b^y$ means that $x = y$.

> If $y = b^x$, then $\log_b y = x$ and vice versa.

You can use your graphing calculator to graph both exponential and logarithmic functions. Be sure to mind your window. Remember that finding an x for a given value of the function simply means determining the x value that corresponds to the given y. You can do this using the TRACE key and tracing the graph of the function to the given y. This may be quicker than solving the equation, assuming the equation is already written in $y =$ or $f(x) =$ form.

GRAPHING LINEAR FUNCTIONS AND INEQUALITIES

You can graph a line or an inequality using your graphing calculator. However, this may not always be the fastest way to solve the problem. If the equation/inequality is written in standard form ($ax + by = c$) then determine the x and y intercepts and find the corresponding graph from the answer choices. If the equation/inequality is written in slope-intercept form ($y = mx + b$) then plug it into your calculator, double-check the window settings, and graph.

SYSTEMS OF EQUATIONS AND INEQUALITIES

A system can be solved using substitution, elimination, or graphing. If you are given one equation and a value for either x or y, the fastest way to solve it is by using substitution. Simply substitute the value you are given into the equation to find the value of the other variable and find the point of intersection in the answer choices. If the equation is written in standard form, you will have to decide whether it is fastest to solve for y and use your calculator, or to use elimination to find the value of one variable and then use substitution for the second variable. If the equation is written in $y =$ or $f(x) =$ form, then the graphing calculator is absolutely the fastest way to solve it. Simply plug the equations into $y =$, graph them, and calculate the intersection.

QUADRATIC FUNCTIONS

Graphing, factoring, and solving quadratic functions should be almost second nature for you. To save time on the ACT, consider the fastest way to solve a quadratic. You will have your graphing calculator for the entire test. Does it take more time to factor and solve or to graph and calculate x intercepts? In most cases, graphing is faster. In cases where the roots are irrational or imaginary, solving using the quadratic formula is fastest.

> ### QUADRATIC FORMULA
>
> If $ax^2 + bx + c = 0$, then $x = \dfrac{-b \pm \sqrt{b^2 - 4ac}}{2a}$ where $a \neq 0$

As you know, a quadratic function may have one real solution, two real solutions, or nonreal solutions. This classification can be determined quickly by using only the discriminant of the quadratic formula. If $b^2 - 4ac$ is equal to zero, there is one real solution; if it is less than zero, there are imaginary or complex solutions; and if it is positive, there are two real solutions.

FUNCTION NOTATION

$F(x) =$ is synonymous with $y =$. With function notation you may be asked to substitute for x by finding f(a given number). You may also be asked to perform operations on functions (addition, subtraction, multiplication, and division), which is as simple as having each function in parentheses and simplifying.

Composition of functions is different than operations on functions. With composition of functions, you are being asked to find f of g of x, which can be written as $f(g(x))$ or $(f \circ g)(x)$.

$$\text{Given that } f(x) = 2x^2 + 9 \text{ and } g(x) = -3x,$$
$$(f \circ g)(x) = 2(-3x)^2 + 9 = 2(9x^2) + 9 = 18x^2 + 9$$

Note that $(g \circ f)(x) = -3(2x^2 + 9) = -6x^2 - 27$, which is not the same as $(f \circ g)(x)$.

Operations on those functions are different; $f(x) + g(x)$ is simply $2x^2 - 3x + 9$.

In most cases you will be asked to find the value of the resulting function for a given x. You should perform the operation or composition using the variables, then substitute the value of x into the resulting function.

CONIC SECTIONS

Conic sections result when a plane intersects a double cone. If you slice a double cone (where the points meet in the center), you get one of four shapes: a parabola, a circle, an ellipse, or a hyperbola. You have probably worked extensively with parabolas because they are the graph of a quadratic function. If you consider the vertex form of the equation of a quadratic and all that you know about that form, you can easily transfer your knowledge to circles, ellipses, and hyperbolas (plural of *hyperbola*).

> ### PARABOLA
>
> $y = a(x - h)^2 + k$ or $f(x) = a(x - h)^2 + k$
>
> where (h, k) is the vertex and a determines the orientation and width of the resulting graph.

Use your understanding of the vertex form of a parabola to understand the vertex form of the equations for circles, ellipses, and hyperbolas. In all four cases, (h, k) is an important point. In a parabola, (h, k) is the vertex. In a circle, (h, k) is the center point. In an ellipse, (h, k) is the

TIP

You do not have
time to complete
the square in
both variables on
this test.

point that is equidistant from the extremes in x and the extremes in y. In a hyperbola, (h, k) is the point that is between the two vertices of the graph.

With a quadratic equation, you can complete the square in order to write the equation in vertex form. Similarly, completing the square in both x and y will give you the standard form of the equations of a circle, an ellipse, or a hyperbola. With 60 questions in 60 minutes, you do not have time to do extensive work with each problem. In the case of conic sections, recognize which conic you are dealing with and be ready to go from an equation in standard form to a graph or vice versa. More explanation and examples of graphs are included in the final chapter of the mathematics section of this text. For now, review the standard form of each equation.

CIRCLE

$$(x - h)^2 + (y - k)^2 = r^2$$

where (h, k) is the center and r is the radius of the circle.

ELLIPSE

$$\frac{(x - h)^2}{a^2} + \frac{(y - k)^2}{b^2} = 1$$

where (h, k) is the center, a is the distance from the center in x, and b is the distance from the center in y.

HYPERBOLA

$$\frac{(x - h)^2}{a^2} - \frac{(y - k)^2}{b^2} = 1$$

where (h, k) is the center, a is the distance from the center to the vertex of each branch on the x-axis, and b is the vertical distance from the vertex of each branch to an asymptote.

The topics in this chapter are familiar to you, and your first instinct may be to go on autopilot and solve every problem. But don't forget about your timing—80 seconds can fly by. Use your graphing calculator whenever it is quickest. The last chapter of the mathematics section will include a graphing calculator review and conic section explanation. Review these items carefully and memorize the formulas. Create a formula sheet for yourself by copying each formula or standard form. The act of copying the formulas with their name will aid in the memorization. To obtain the perfect score, timing will be everything!

PRACTICE SET: INTERMEDIATE ALGEBRA/COORDINATE GEOMETRY

REMEMBER

For more extra-challenging practice, you can go online for the Challenge Round with 50 difficult questions.

The following problems are all typical of the intermediate algebra/coordinate geometry problems on the ACT. These types of problems will be sprinkled among the beginning test questions and then make up about half of the questions toward the end of the test. While practicing, challenge yourself to complete each problem in 80 seconds or less. In order to accomplish this, you will need to make a split-second decision about your strategy and then move full-speed ahead. Time yourself on these 12 questions and attempt to complete them in 16 minutes or less.

In order to improve your time, set a timer and work through the problems in the allotted time without guessing. When the time has ended, finish the questions in an alternate color and track the amount of time you take to finish. Check your answers. Note the strategy you use and challenge yourself to try other strategies and compare efficiencies. The key is to establish efficiency—to choose the correct answers as quickly as possible. Guessing will not earn you a perfect score.

1. What is the real value of x in the equation,
   $\log_2 80 - \log_2 5 = \log_3 x$?
   A. 8
   B. 48
   C. 75
   D. 64
   E. 81

2. In the standard (x, y) coordinate plane, the midpoint of $\overline{AB}$ is $(8, -5)$ and B is located at $(12, -1)$. If (x, y) are the coordinates of A, what is the value of $x + y$?
   F. -8
   G. -7
   H. -5
   J. 7
   K. 8

3. A function F is defined as follows:
   for $x > 0$, $F(x) = x^6 - x^3 - 17x - 17$
   for $x < 0$, $F(x) = -x^6 - x^3 + 17x - 17$
   What is the value of $F(-1)$?
   A. -34
   B. -2
   C. 0
   D. 2
   E. 34

4. For $i^2 = -1$, $(1 - 3i)^3 = ?$
   F. -26
   G. -8
   H. $-10 + 30i$
   J. $-26 + 18i$
   K. $10 + 18i$

5. Tickets to the annual Follies Show at Littleton High School are $4 for adults and $2.50 for students. There is a cost of $750 to produce the show. If the x-axis represents the number of adult tickets sold and the y-axis represents the number of student tickets sold, which graph represents all the possible combinations of ticket sales that allow the junior class to at least cover the cost of the show?

A.

B.

C.

D.

E.

6. What are the real solutions of $2|x|^2 + 4|x| - 6 = 0$?

F. $\{1\}$

G. $\{-1,1\}$

H. $\{1,-3\}$

J. $\{1,3\}$

K. $\{-3,3\}$

7. The sum of the real numbers x and y is 17. Their difference is 3. What is the value of xy?

A. -140

B. -60

C. 11

D. 70

E. 140

8. For all $x > 5$, $\dfrac{5x^2 - x^3}{x^2 - x - 20} = ?$

F. $\dfrac{-x^2}{x+4}$

G. $\dfrac{x^2}{x+4}$

H. $\dfrac{-5+x}{20}$

J. $\dfrac{5x-x^2}{x-19}$

K. $\dfrac{-5x+x^2}{x-19}$

9. A circle in the standard (x, y) coordinate plane has center $(5, -3)$ and radius 4 units. Which of the following equations represents this circle?

A. $(x+5)^2 + (y-3)^2 = 4$

B. $(x-5)^2 + (y+3)^2 = 4$

C. $(x+5)^2 + (y-3)^2 = 8$

D. $(x-5)^2 + (y+3)^2 = 16$

E. $(x+5)^2 + (y-3)^2 = 16$

10. Consider the functions $f(x) = \sqrt{x}$ and $g(x) = x^2 - b$. In the standard (x, y) coordinate plane, $y = f(g(x))$ passes through the point $(3, 5)$. What is the value of b?

F. 16

G. 4

H. −2

J. −4

K. −16

11. For what value of k does $4x^2 + kx + 25 = 0$ have exactly one real solution for x?

A. 5

B. 10

C. 15

D. 20

E. 25

12. What is the slope of the line through $(-3, 7)$ and $(2, 5)$ in the standard (x, y) coordinate plane?

F. $-\dfrac{5}{2}$

G. $-\dfrac{2}{5}$

H. undefined

J. $\dfrac{2}{5}$

K. $\dfrac{5}{2}$

Answers Explained

1. **(E)** Given the problem $\log_2 80 - \log_2 5 = \log_3 x$, you must simplify before converting logarithmic to exponential to solve. To simplify, recall that subtraction of logs is equivalent to the log of the quotient (and vice versa). So, $\log_2 80 - \log_2 5 = \log_3 x$ is equivalent to $\log_2 \frac{80}{5} = \log_3 x$, which is equivalent to $\log_2 16 = \log_3 x$, which can be converted to exponential by writing $2^{\log_3 x} = 16$. Since $16 = 2^4$, you have $2^{\log_3 x} = 2^4$, which means that $\log_3 x = 4$ or $3^4 = x$, so $x = 81$.

2. **(H)** A midpoint has coordinates that are the average of the coordinates of the endpoints. For this problem, that means that $\frac{12+x}{2} = 8$ and $\frac{-1+y}{2} = -5$, which simplify to the point $(4, -9)$. You were not asked to find the endpoint but rather the sum of the coordinates of the endpoint, which would be $4 - 9 = -5$.

3. **(A)** Since the value of x is -1, you must substitute this value into the equation for x values < 0. When you substitute -1 in for x in the function $F(x) = -x^6 - x^3 + 17x - 17$, you have $-(-1)^6 - (-1)^3 + 17(-1) - 17$ or $-1 + 1 - 17 - 17 = -34$.

4. **(J)** In order to solve $(1 - 3i)^3 = ?$, you will need to FOIL, simplify, and then FOIL and simplify again. $(1 - 3i)(1 - 3i)(1 - 3i)$ simplifies to $(1 - 6i + 9i^2)(1 - 3i)$. Remembering that $i^2 = -1$, you know that $(1 - 6i + 9i^2)(1 - 3i) = (1 - 6i - 9)(1 - 3i) = (-8 - 6i)(1 - 3i)$, which simplifies to $-8 + 18i + 18i^2 = -8 + 18i - 18 = -26 + 18i$.

5. **(C)** In order to solve this problem, you must first develop the inequality $4x + 2.5y \geq 750$, then solve for y to find that $y \geq \frac{-8}{5}x + 300$, and then use your graphing calculator to graph the equation. Or you could simply find the x and y intercepts to be $(0, 300)$ and $(187.5, 0)$ and select the graph with those intercepts and the shading indicating greater than or equal to.

6. **(G)** In order to solve this equation, you will first treat it as if the absolute value symbols are not included. For the simple quadratic $2x^2 + 4x - 6 = 0$ you will factor out 2 and factor to get $2(x - 1)(x + 3) = 0$. Solving this quadratic gives you the solutions 1 and -3. This is where the absolute value comes back into play. You have $|x| = 1$ or $|x| = -3$. Since the absolute value cannot equal a negative number, you eliminate the choice -3. Now you have $|x| = 1$, which means that $x = 1$ or $x = -1$ leaving you with the solution $\{-1, 1\}$.

7. **(D)** This problem poses a system of the equations $x + y = 17$ and $x - y = 3$. Solving this by elimination, you find that $2x = 20$ and $x = 10$. You substitute 10 in for x in either equation to find that $y = 7$. You were asked to find the product xy, so $10 \times 7 = 70$.

8. **(F)** Factor both the numerator and the denominator in order to simplify.

$$\frac{5x^2 - x^3}{x^2 - x - 20} = \frac{x^2(5 - x)}{(x - 5)(x + 4)} = \frac{-x^2(x - 5)}{(x - 5)(x + 4)}$$

For the last step, factoring out a negative sign helps you to see that you have $(x - 5)$ in both the numerator and the denominator. This can be simplified to $\frac{-x^2}{x + 4}$.

9. **(D)** For a circle with center point (5, –3) and radius 4, you simply plug the corresponding values into the standard form of a circle equation $(x - h)^2 + (y - k)^2 = r^2$ where the center is (h, k) and the radius is r. Therefore, $(x - 5)^2 + (y + 3)^2 = 16$.

10. **(K)** $f(g(x)) = \sqrt{x^2 - b}$, and when the point (3,5) is substituted into this equation, you have $5 = \sqrt{3^2 - b}$ or $5 = \sqrt{9 - b}$. In order to eliminate the radical, you square both sides, resulting in $25 = 9 - b$, which simplifies to $16 = -b$ or $-16 = b$.

11. **(D)** To determine the possible values for k such that the quadratic has exactly one root, you use the discriminant $b^2 - 4ac = 0$. If $\sqrt{b^2 - 4ac}$ equals zero, the solution of the quadratic will simply be $\frac{-b}{2a}$. In this case you have $k^2 - 4(4)(25) = 0$ or $k^2 - 400 = 0$, meaning that $k^2 = 400$ and k can equal either –20 or 20. Since only 20 is a choice, it is the value choice for which there is exactly one solution to the quadratic.

12. **(G)** $m = \dfrac{y_2 - y_1}{x_2 - x_1} = \dfrac{7 - 5}{-3 - 2} = \dfrac{2}{-5} = -\dfrac{2}{5}$

Plane Geometry/
Trigonometry

10

→ **ANGLES AND RELATIONS AMONG PARALLEL AND PERPENDICULAR LINES**

→ **PROPERTIES OF CIRCLES**

→ **SOLVING FOR ANGLES IN TWO-DIMENSIONAL SHAPES**

→ **TRANSFORMATIONS**

→ **REASONING AND PROOF**

→ **VOLUME**

→ **SPECIAL RIGHT TRIANGLES**

→ **RIGHT TRIANGLE TRIGONOMETRY**

→ **VALUES OF TRIGONOMETRIC FUNCTIONS**

→ **PRACTICE SET: PLANE GEOMETRY/TRIGONOMETRY**

The questions in this category come from your geometry coursework as well as some algebra 2 or trigonometry. These questions will be sprinkled in with the elementary algebra in the beginning of the test and show up with greater regularity as you move through the test.

Most of this portion of the test is based on your geometry coursework. You will be required to solve problems that involve the properties of polygons, triangles, circles and angles, transformations of shapes, area, surface area and volume, and reasoning and proof. Grouping your review of these concepts into big ideas will help you recall the many things you know well. Many of the problems in this category will involve more complex problem-solving and some thought beyond surface knowledge of properties. Review the topics and problems discussed in this chapter very carefully. Use your reasoning skills to pull your knowledge together and solve the problems as efficiently as possible.

A very small part of the overall exam (about 4 out of 60) will be based on trigonometry. This could include using trigonometry to solve right triangles, unit circles, graphs of trigonometric functions, and using trigonometric identities to solve equations involving trigonometric identities. If you have not had a full course on trigonometry, you can still work toward a perfect score on the ACT. Simply review the mini-lesson in the next chapter and try your hand at the sample problems here. You may also ask your current mathematics teacher for an overview of these topics. The key will be to know enough about the topics to use your graphing calculator and solve the problems quickly and correctly.

ANGLES AND RELATIONS AMONG PARALLEL AND PERPENDICULAR LINES

Perpendicular lines meet at a right angle, which measures 90 degrees. This fact will come up in many problems involving angles. A problem may state that the sides are perpendicular rather than indicating the angle size. Perpendicular lines tend to appear in problems involving triangles, where you will need to use either the Pythagorean theorem or right triangle trigonometry. You will be expected to know that the height of a triangle meets the base at a right angle, the diagonals of a kite are perpendicular, and a tangent to a circle meets the radius at a right angle. These angles will be used to form right triangles that you will be asked to solve.

> **PYTHAGOREAN THEOREM**
> $a^2 + b^2 = c^2$

The Pythagorean theorem may be used to solve for a side length of a right triangle or to determine whether a triangle is a right triangle or not.

For example, you may be asked whether or not a triangle with side lengths 5, 8, and 11 is a right triangle.

Use the Pythagorean theorem with 5 and 8 as the lengths of the legs and 11 as the length of the hypotenuse. Since $25 + 64 \neq 121$, this is not a right triangle.

Parallel lines will come up in problems involving quadrilaterals and problems involving parallel lines cut by a transversal. Everything you know about parallels cut by a transversal can be applied to quadrilaterals involving parallel sides (or parallelograms which include rectangles, rhombi, squares, and trapezoids).

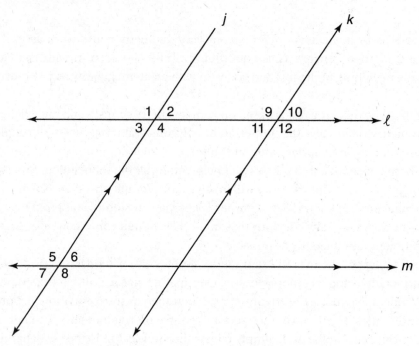

TIP

Corresponding and vertical angles are congruent and linear pairs are supplementary.

Lines l and m are parallel and lines j and k are parallel. The m∠2 = 73°, find the measure of the other 11 angles.

- Angles 2 and 6 and 2 and 10 are corresponding and therefore congruent.
- Angles 2 and 3, 6 and 7, and 10 and 11 are vertical and therefore congruent.
- Angles 2 and 1, 2 and 4, 6 and 5, 6 and 8, 10 and 9, and 10 and 12 are linear pairs and therefore supplementary.

The ACT may replace angle names with variable expressions, requiring you to find the value of the variable as an additional step.

PROPERTIES OF CIRCLES

Everything your teacher taught you about circles is fair game: chords, arcs, semicircles, inscribed and central angles, tangents and the angles they form with a radius.

Key things to remember:

- Central angle occurs at the center and cuts the circle at an arc whose measure is equivalent to the measure of the angle.
- An inscribed angle occurs on the circle land its measure is half the measure of the corresponding central and arc measure.
- A line tangent to the circle will meet the radius of the circle at a 90° angle.
- The diameter is the longest chord, and it divides the circle into two semicircles.
- The area of a sector of the circle can be found by multiplying the area of the entire circle by the fraction of the circle the sector includes.
- The area of a segment of a circle can be found by determining the area of the sector and subtracting the area of the triangle.

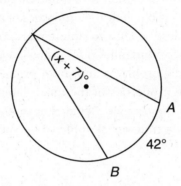

Find x.

Solution: Since the inscribed angle is half of the arc measure, $(x+7)° = 21°$ and $x = 14°$.

SOLVING FOR ANGLES IN TWO-DIMENSIONAL SHAPES

Problems requiring you to find angle measures are assessing your knowledge of properties and theorems. You will need to call on your knowledge of linear pairs, vertical angles, exterior angles, sums of angles, and many other concepts.

For example, find the exterior angle x for a regular hexagon.

TIP

A regular hexagon is made up of six equilateral triangles.

The sum of the angles in a hexagon can be found by using the formula $(n-2)180°$ where $n = 6$. $4(180°) = 720°$. Since this hexagon is regular, each interior angle is congruent and measures 120°. Angle x is a linear pair with an interior angle and therefore measures 60°.

Properties of Triangles

Triangle properties will come up when you are working with almost any shape, reasoning and proof, angles, circles, area, and volume. You will need to know triangle congruence in order to use the information from one triangle to find angles and side lengths in another. You will use properties of isosceles triangles to find area and perimeter of regular polygons.

The height of an isosceles or equilateral triangle can be found by using the Pythagorean theorem if you know the length of the base and the side. Triangle properties can also be used to solve problems involving a kite (the diagonals of a kite meet at a right angle). Triangle sum and the reflexive property are also key properties to keep in mind when solving problems involving triangles.

Properties of Quadrilaterals

A rectangle, square, and rhombus are special parallelograms. Recalling the properties of parallelograms and then the properties that make these quadrilaterals special will be an easy way to keep all of the information straight in your mind. Be sure to review both general trapezoids and isosceles trapezoids. Also review the properties of a kite.

When reviewing all properties, be sure to note congruence of angles, supplementary angles, properties of diagonals, and parallel sides. Knowledge of the properties of quadrilaterals will help you solve angle problems and proof problems. Triangles may be placed within a quadrilateral, and the properties of the quadrilateral will give you clues to side lengths and angle measures of the triangle. Remember that angle relationships of a set of parallel sides being crossed by a transversal apply when you have a problem involving a parallelogram.

PROPERTIES OF QUADRILATERALS

Parallelogram: opposite sides parallel and congruent

Rectangle: a parallelogram with four 90° angles

Rhombus: a parallelogram with four congruent sides

Square: a parallelogram with four 90° angles and four congruent sides

Trapezoid: exactly one set of parallel sides

Isosceles trapezoid: one set of parallel bases and two congruent sides

Kite: two sets of consecutive congruent sides

TRANSFORMATIONS

Transformation is the general term for translations, reflections, and rotations. All of these transformations can occur on the coordinate plane but are not restricted to it. A rotation of a two-dimensional figure may produce a three-dimensional figure.

A translation moves the figure on the coordinate plane. You will find the resulting figure by changing each coordinate by the prescribed amount. For instance, if the figure is to move right 5 and down 3, you will add 5 to the x coordinate of each vertex and subtract 3 from the y coordinate of each vertex. By plotting the new vertices and connecting them, you will have the translated figure.

A rotation moves a figure about a fixed point by a given angle. A rotation of 360 degrees will result in the original figure. A rotation of 180 degrees results in the reflection of the figure. A rotation of 20 degrees simply turns the figure about the point of rotation by 20 degrees.

A reflection results in the mirror image of the figure about a given line. To find the resulting figure you need only to imagine that the line of reflection is a mirror and either imagine or plot what the reflection would be on the opposite side of the line.

REASONING AND PROOF

When you solve problems that involve multiple steps and require you to recall properties of geometric shapes, you are using your reasoning skills. You use your reasoning skills in a more formal way when you are required to perform a proof. On the ACT, the questions are all multiple choice. That means that the proof questions will be restricted to things that can be done within the constraints of the multiple-choice format.

Some ways that you may encounter proofs on multiple-choice questions are:

- Select which statement is true based on the given information.
- Which statement is not true based on the given information?
- Which reason is accurate for the given statement?
- Which statement is accurate for the given reason?

These are only examples of what you may run into on the ACT. In any case, you will be required to recall properties of geometric figures along with the reflexive property, triangle congruence, and of course CPCTC (corresponding parts of congruent triangles are congruent).

> **TRIANGLE CONGRUENCE**
> SAS, SSS, and ASA are each sufficient for proving that two triangles are congruent.

VOLUME

Volume is simply the area of the base times the height of the object. Properties of triangles and the Pythagorean theorem or right triangle trigonometry may be required to determine the information you will need to use in the formula.

Volume of an oblique three-dimensional shape is equivalent to the volume the shape would have if it were not oblique. You must be sure to use the actual height of the object and not the length from the base to the top on the outside of the object.

TIP

The volume of a pyramid is $\frac{1}{3}$ times the area of the base times the height. The volume of a cone is $\frac{1}{3}$ times the area of a circular base times height.

Height always
hits the base or
an extension of
the base at a
90° angle.

SPECIAL RIGHT TRIANGLES

There are two special right triangles. One is the 30–60–90 triangle and the other is the 45–45–90 triangle. The 30–60–90 triangle is half of an equilateral triangle, and the 45–45–90 triangle is half of a square. Knowing the relationship between the side lengths of these two triangles may save you time on the test. You can discover these relationships by using variables for the side lengths (with the 30–60–90, the shorter leg is half the length of the hypotenuse, and with the 45–45–90, the two legs are congruent) and using the Pythagorean theorem to solve for each variable.

30–60–90 TRIANGLE

If you use h for the hypotenuse, the short leg = $\frac{1}{2}h$ and the long leg = $\frac{h}{2}\sqrt{3}$.

45–45–90 TRIANGLE

Using h for the hypotenuse, each leg = $\frac{\sqrt{2}}{2}h$.

TIP

Use SOH–CAH–TOA
to remind you
that

$\sin\theta = \frac{opp}{hyp}$

$\cos\theta = \frac{adj}{hyp}$

$\tan\theta = \frac{opp}{adj}$

RIGHT TRIANGLE TRIGONOMETRY

Right triangle trigonometry is basically summed up by the acronym SOH–CAH–TOA. When working with right triangles, the sine of an angle is equivalent to the length of the opposite side (to the angle) divided by the length of the hypotenuse (SOH). The cosine of an angle is equivalent to the length of the adjacent side (to the angle) divided by the hypotenuse (CAH). The tangent of an angle is equivalent to the length of the opposite side (to the angle) divided by the adjacent side (TOA). These formulas allow you to solve for all side lengths and all angles given that you have either two sides or a side and an angle value.

A right triangle is typically labeled with capital letters naming the angles and corresponding lowercase letters naming the sides. Note the general right triangle here.

For example, find the values of all side lengths and angles in triangle *ABC*.

To find side b, use tangent and the opposite and adjacent sides. To find side c, use cosine and the adjacent and hypotenuse sides. To find angle A, use the complementary nature of the two non-right angles in a right triangle.

TIP

It is important to use given information whenever possible. Doing so reduces rounding errors.

$$\tan 55 = \frac{b}{24}, b = 24 \tan 55, b = 34.2756 \text{ or } 34$$

$$\cos 55 = \frac{24}{c}, c = \frac{24}{\cos 55}, c = 41.8427 \text{ or } 42$$

$$\text{Angle } A = 90° - 55° = 35°$$

VALUES OF TRIGONOMETRIC FUNCTIONS

The value of a trigonometric function can be found quickly and easily using your graphing calculator. It happens to correspond to the x and y coordinates of points along the unit circle as a ray is extended from the origin at the given angle. The relationship to the unit circle helps you understand the trigonometric function, but that understanding is not required for a perfect score on the exam. You need to be able to use your graphing calculator and be familiar with the range of values and behavior of the graph of the function. This will allow you to check the answer obtained on the calculator.

Graphing Trigonometric Functions

A graphing calculator will graph a trigonometric function quickly. The key is to set the window appropriately and to set the mode correctly to radians or degrees, depending on the form the angle is written in.

When a graphical representation of a trigonometric function is the problem, knowing the parent functions and transformations on the trigonometric graphs will allow you to quickly select the correct answer choice.

Know your parent functions:

$$f(x) = \sin(x)$$

$$f(x) = \cos(x)$$

$$f(x) = \tan(x)$$

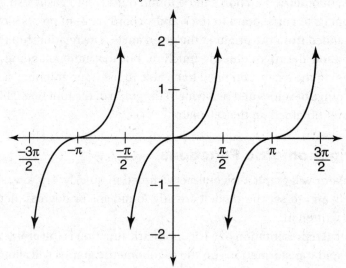

In the general form $f(x) = a \sin b (x - h) + k$, $|a|$ is the amplitude, $\dfrac{2\pi}{b}$ is the period (assuming x is in radians and b is greater than zero), h is the horizontal shift, and k is the vertical shift.

Use of Trigonometric Identities

Trigonometric identities are ways of representing trig functions in terms of one another. These allow you to substitute one function (in an expression) for another. This is helpful when you have an equation involving more than one trig function and you do not have the value of the angle. Review the list of common trig identities in the next chapter. You may run into a problem involving trig identities on the ACT but they do not appear on every test. The most common or basic identities are $\sin \theta = \sqrt{1 - \cos^2 \theta}$ or $\cos \theta = \sqrt{1 - \sin^2 \theta}$. These identities can be used to replace either $\sin \theta$ or $\cos \theta$ with an expression involving the other.

For example, simplify the expression $(1 + \sin \theta)(1 - \sin \theta)$.

To simplify this, you will first multiply it out to get $1 - \sin^2 \theta$, which is equivalent to $\cos^2 \theta$.

Solving Trigonometric Equations

Solving trigonometric equations is very similar to solving any other equation. You will want to isolate the variable and solve. When you are solving for an angle, you will have to isolate the entire trigonometric function and then use the inverse function to find the angle measure. When the inverse function is taken, it is taken of both sides of the equation. You may be required to use a trigonometric identity to simplify the equation of one function in order to isolate and solve.

With a complicated equation that requires multiple steps to isolate the variable, it may be quicker to use your calculator to check the solutions. Find the value of each side of the equation with a given solution choice and check to see the two sides are equal.

PRACTICE SET: PLANE GEOMETRY/TRIGONOMETRY

The following problems are typical of the plane geometry/trigonometry problems on the ACT. These types of problems are sprinkled among the beginning test questions and are more likely found toward the end of the test. While practicing, challenge yourself to complete each problem in 80 seconds or less. In order to accomplish this, you will need to make a split-second decision around strategy and then move full-speed ahead. Time yourself on these 12 questions and attempt to complete them in 16 minutes or less. Remember that if you will be taking the online version of the ACT, you will want to practice using scratch paper to solve problems.

In order to improve your time, set a timer and work through the problems in the allotted time without guessing. When the time has ended, finish the questions in an alternate color and track the amount of time you take to finish. Check your answers. The key is to establish efficiency—to select the correct answers as quickly as possible. Guessing will not earn you a perfect score.

In the directions on the exam you will be told to choose the correct answer and fill in the corresponding oval on the answer sheet. You will be reminded not to linger on problems that you are struggling to solve. (In order to know when you are lingering, you will want to practice in a timed setting.) You will be reminded that you are allowed to use a calculator on any problem but that it may not be the best choice every time. (You'll know from your practice when the use of a calculator is most appropriate.) The directions will include a few final clarifying points, and then you will begin.

1. Which of the following is not a property of a parallelogram?
    A. Opposite sides are congruent.
    B. Consecutive angles are supplementary.
    C. Diagonals are congruent.
    D. Opposite sides are parallel.
    E. The sum of the angles is 360°.

2. Find the x value for which l is parallel to m.

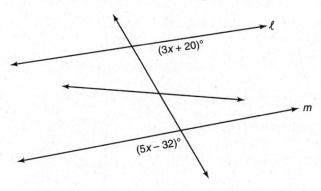

    F. 6
    G. 16
    H. 20
    J. 24
    K. 26

3. Which is the equation of the trigonometric function graphed here?

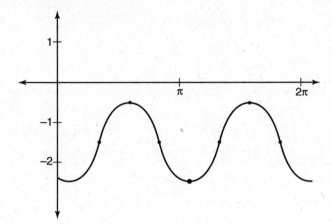

A. $y = \sin 2x - \dfrac{\pi}{3}$

B. $y = \sin 2\left(x + \dfrac{\pi}{3}\right)$

C. $y = \sin 2\left(x - \dfrac{\pi}{3}\right)$

D. $y = \sin 2\left(x - \dfrac{\pi}{3}\right) - \dfrac{3}{2}$

E. $y = \sin 2\left(x + \dfrac{\pi}{3}\right) - \dfrac{3}{2}$

4. Which of the following are the dimensions of a right triangle?
- **F.** 0.6, 0.8, 0.12
- **G.** 2, 3, 4
- **H.** 9, 12, 15
- **J.** 9, 13, 21
- **K.** 18, 23, 25

5. Find the volume of a cone with a slant height of 15 inches and a base with a 16-inch diameter.
- **A.** 271π
- **B.** 320π
- **C.** 960π
- **D.** 1280π
- **E.** 3248π

6. Find the coordinates of point $A(-7, 3)$ when it is reflected about the line $y = x$.
- **F.** $(-7, -3)$
- **G.** $(-3, 7)$
- **H.** $(3, -7)$
- **J.** $(3, 7)$
- **K.** $(7, 3)$

7. Find x.

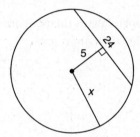

- **A.** 7
- **B.** 11
- **C.** 12
- **D.** 13
- **E.** 15

8. Solve for x, given that the area is 120.

- **F.** 7
- **G.** 11
- **H.** 12
- **J.** 14
- **K.** 15

9. When constructing wheelchair ramps, the ramp must not rise more than 1 inch for every foot of ramp. What is the maximum angle the ramp can make with the ground for a 3-foot ramp?

A. 4.8°
B. 14.34°
C. 14.47°
D. 19.47°
E. 90°

10. By which postulate or theorem are triangle ABC and triangle DBC congruent?

F. SAS
G. SSS
H. AAS
J. ASA
K. Cannot be determined from the given information.

11. Find x.

A. 2.16
B. 3
C. 4.33
D. 5
E. 10

12. Find the arc measure of the arc cut by one side of a circumscribed regular hexagon.

F. 30°
G. 60°
H. 120°
J. 180°
K. 240°

Answers Explained

1. **(C)** While diagonals are congruent when the parallelogram is a rectangle, this is not necessarily true for all parallelograms.

2. **(J)** When l is parallel to m, the two angles are supplementary because each is congruent to the linear pair of the other. Since they are supplementary, $5x - 32 + 3x + 20 = 180$, $8x - 12 = 180$, $8x = 192$, and $x = 24$.

3. **(D)** The graph has a period of 2, and it is translated $\frac{\pi}{3}$ to the right and $\frac{3}{2}$ down. The period of 2 means that the curve completes a cycle between 0 and π. Translating right and down translates each point right and down.

4. **(H)** To determine whether or not a triangle is a right triangle, substitute the values into the Pythagorean theorem and check to be sure the sentence is true. $9^2 + 12^2 = 15^2$, $81 + 144 = 225$.

5. **(A)** The slant height and the diameter can be used with the Pythagorean theorem to find the height of the cone. $15^2 - 8^2 = 161$, and the square root of 161 is approximately 12.6885. This height along with the radius can be used in the formula for the volume of a cone $\left(\frac{1}{3}\pi r^2 h\right)$ to find that the volume is approximately 270.69π or 271π.

6. **(H)** When reflecting about $y = x$, use the y coordinate of the original point to determine the x coordinate and the x coordinate of the original point to determine the new y coordinate. This is the same as graphing the point and the line $y = x$, then folding the graph along the line $y = x$ and drawing a point where the original point lands.

7. **(D)** The segment from the center perpendicular to a chord bisects the chord. If the radius is drawn to meet the endpoint of the chord, a right triangle will be formed with legs measuring 5 and 12 and hypotenuse of x. Use the Pythagorean theorem to find that the hypotenuse measures the square root of the sum of 12^2 and 5^2, which is 13.

8. **(J)** Use the Pythagorean theorem to find that the height of the trapezoid is 8. Then use the formula for the area of a trapezoid, $A = \frac{1}{2}(b_1 + b_2)h$, to get $120 = \frac{1}{2}(19 + x - 3)8$, which means that $120 = 4(16 + x)$, $30 = 16 + x$, and $x = 14$.

9. **(A)** The ratio of height to hypotenuse (ramp length) is constant at 1 inch to 12 inches. You may choose to use 3 inches to 36 inches for this problem. Either way, use the sine function to determine the angle, $\sin\theta = \frac{1}{12}$. Then, taking the inverse sine of both sides will give you the answer of $4.8°$.

10. **(K)** $BC \cong BC$ by the reflexive property and $\angle A \cong \angle D$ and $AC \cong CD$ are given. Even though you are given three pieces of information, they are not in the correct order to provide sufficient evidence to determine congruence. When there are two sides and an angle congruent, the angle must fall between the two sides to be sufficient evidence that the triangles are congruent.

11. **(E)** Triangles *ABC* and *AED* are similar because all angles are congruent. Since the triangles are similar, $x + 4$ is to 7 as $3x + 4$ is to 17. Setting up the proportion and cross multiplying results in $17x + 68 = 21x + 28$. Solving for x gives you $40 = 4x$ and $10 = x$.

12. **(G)** One angle of a regular hexagon is 120°, and it cuts the corresponding arc to result in a measure of 240°. That leaves 120° to be divided by two chords that are equivalent in length, making each arc measure 60°.

Mini-Lessons As Review

11

- → **MINI-LESSON: CONIC SECTIONS**
- → **MINI-LESSON: STATISTICS AND PROBABILITY**
- → **MINI-LESSON: TRIGONOMETRY**
- → **MINI-LESSON: GRAPHING CALCULATOR**
- → **KEYS TO ACHIEVING MATH PERFECTION**

The math section of the ACT includes content that is familiar to most juniors in the United States. What is challenging about obtaining a perfect score is the time constraint. By familiarizing yourself with the content, vocabulary, and formulas that will appear on the test, and being armed with your graphing calculator, you will increase your pace while taking the exam.

Depending on the coursework you have completed, you may need a deeper explanation of conic sections and trigonometry. A mini-lesson on each of these topics is included in this chapter. These mini-lessons are intended to give greater context to the information you studied already in previous chapters. Also in this chapter, we will review how to use a graphing calculator on the ACT.

Remember that reading through this book once is not sufficient studying for a perfect score on the exam. You should have marked the book along the way with highlights and notes. Be sure to go back through the math section and study those topics that were unfamiliar or difficult for you the first time through. Review the formulas to the point of memorization. Give yourself some time away from the text and then come back with fresh eyes and read through it again, practicing the problems again as well. Good luck!

MINI-LESSON: CONIC SECTIONS

Conic sections are slices of a cone and can be a parabola, circle, ellipse, or hyperbola. This is a complex topic, but our goal is simply to give you enough information to solve problems on the ACT. The general form of the equation can be determined by completing the square on each variable. The general form of the equation will tell you which transformation to make on the graph of the parent function.

Circles and Ellipses

Circles have the general equation of $(x - h)^2 + (y - k)^2 = r^2$ where (h, k) is the center and r is the radius.

For example, $x^2 + y^2 = 9$ is a circle centered at $(0, 0)$ with a radius of 3.

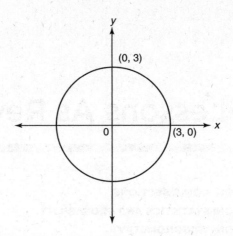

Ellipses are very similar to circles. The difference is that they extend a different amount in x and in y. So, instead of being shaped like a circle, they are shaped like an oval. In the equation this shows up as denominators under the x and y expression, and the equation equals 1 instead of a radius squared. The general equation for an ellipse is $\dfrac{(x-h)^2}{a^2} + \dfrac{(y-k)^2}{b^2} = 1$, where (h, k) is the center, a is the amount that the ellipse extends horizontally from the center, and b is the amount that the ellipse extends vertically.

For example, $\dfrac{x^2}{25} + \dfrac{y^2}{49} = 1$ is an ellipse centered at $(0, 0)$, which extends to -5 and 5 on the x-axis, and to 7 and -7 on the y-axis.

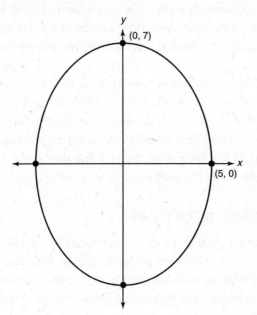

Hyperbolas

Hyperbolas are a bit trickier than circles and ellipses, but the nice thing is that they are easy to spot in a graph or an equation. The equation of a hyperbola is very similar to that of an ellipse. The difference is that, instead of a sum, it is a difference. There are two possibilities, one where the y term is subtracted from the x term, and the reverse. There will be a reference point at (h, k), a will tell you about the horizontal distance from the reference point, and b will tell you about the vertical distance from the reference point. A difference is that these references describe a box that lies between the points that make up the solution of the equation and the graph. In this case, a picture is worth a thousand words. Examine the graphical representations of the following:

$$\frac{(x-h)^2}{a^2} - \frac{(y-k)^2}{b^2} = 1$$

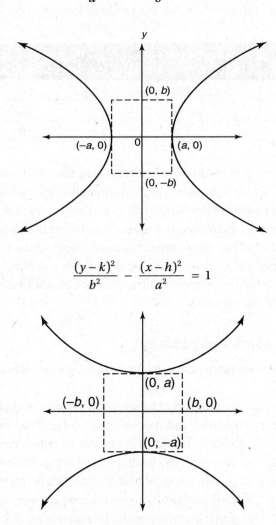

$$\frac{(y-k)^2}{b^2} - \frac{(x-h)^2}{a^2} = 1$$

The key points to remember about a hyperbola are the subtraction sign in the equation, and the general characteristics of the graph based on (h, k), a, and b.

MINI-LESSON: STATISTICS AND PROBABILITY

When you learned that 8–12% of the ACT questions are in the subcategory of Statistics and Probability, you may have worried that you chose to take trigonometry and pre-calculus instead of a course in statistics and probability. You do not need to be concerned. The content in this subcategory is not the formal content in the high school level course. The ACT includes content that should be familiar to any high school graduate from their studies in typical math courses and the general studies in other content areas.

Topics covered in most of the score ranges for this subcategory include the content that is addressed in Chapter 8 of this book (Elementary Algebra). Even the highest scoring students in this subcategory are using skills and knowledge that you are likely to have. Just to be sure, let's review a few key areas that are understood by students who score between 33 and 36.

Two-way Frequency Tables

Two-way frequency tables allow you to review the frequency of one variable in terms of a second variable. To illustrate this point, review the two-way frequency table below.

High School Students	Participate in Extracurricular Activities	Do Not Participate in Extracurricular Activities	Total
Lower Classmen	327	422	749
Upper Classmen	217	467	684
Total	544	889	1433

Consider the questions that could be asked regarding this particular two-way frequency table. Note that you will need to consider the proportionality reflected in relationships rather than simply comparing raw numbers. While 120 more lower classmen than upper classmen participate in extracurricular activities, it is important to communicate those numbers in terms of the total number of lower or upper classmen. Because the total for each category is different sizes, the numbers by themselves would provide a skewed analysis. In this case, 44% of lower classmen participate in extracurricular activities, and 32% of upper classmen participate in extracurricular activities.

Conditional and Joint Probability

Using the two-way frequency table above, we will examine joint, marginal, and conditional probability.

The probability of two independent events happening is joint probability. We can create a table reflecting the joint probabilities and the marginal probabilities by dividing each number by the total number of students. The joint probabilities (when two events are true) are reflected inside the table. For instance, the probability of a lower classman participating in extracurricular activities is 0.23. The marginal probabilities are in the margins and disregard one of the two variables. The probability of a student being a lower classman is 0.52, or the probability of a student NOT participating in extracurricular activities is 0.62.

High School Students	Participate in Extracurricular Activities	Do Not Participate in Extracurricular Activities	Total
Lower Classmen	0.23	0.29	0.52
Upper Classmen	0.15	0.33	0.48
Total	0.38	0.62	1.0

Conditional probability is found when you are asked about the probability of one event under the condition that another event is true. For example, find the probability of a student being a lower classman given that the student participates in extracurricular activities. In this case, only use the Participate in Extracurricular Activities column to find the probability of being a lower classman in that column. Divide 0.23 by 0.38 and the probability is 0.61. Conversely, the probability of being an upper classman given that the student participates in extracurricular activities is 0.15 divided by 0.38 or 0.39. Notice that the two probabilities will add up to 1 (the probability of being either lower or upper classman given that the student participates in extracurricular activities).

The Role of Randomization

Without randomization, there may be bias in the data, and it would be inappropriate to make generalizations to the larger group. Randomization is accomplished by applying a systematic process to selecting the sample.

Statistical Modeling

Simply put, statistical modeling is similar to modeling in general. It is a way of taking a situation and applying a mathematical model to it in order to predict values. In the case of a statistical model, it is important to consider the difference between the actual or observed values and the values generated by the model. This is easiest to understand in terms of a scatter plot and a line of best fit. The closer the line of best fit is to each actual value (scatter plot point), the more accurate the equation of the line is in predicting a value that will occur. Additionally, a line is not the only statistical model, and other functions should be considered when selecting a mathematical model for actual data.

MINI-LESSON: TRIGONOMETRY

The topic of trigonometry makes up a very small portion of the test and really works to separate the advanced students from the rest. Students who are not working toward a perfect score may be inclined to skip the four problems that involve trigonometry. For those (like you!) who seek a perfect score, no topic in this category is beyond comprehension. These can be four easy problems for you. The problems can come from any of the following topics, but it is unlikely that all four topics will be included. At the very least, you should expect to come across a right triangle trigonometry question.

Right Triangle Trigonometry

Right triangle trigonometry is used to find side lengths and angle values in right triangles. Specifically, angles and side lengths of right triangles can be found using sine, cosine, and tangent functions. As you know, right triangles have sides called legs and a hypotenuse (the longest side, which is opposite the right angle). Use SOH–CAH–TOA to remind you that $\sin \theta = \dfrac{opp}{hyp}$, $\cos \theta = \dfrac{adj}{hyp}$, and $\tan \theta = \dfrac{opp}{adj}$.

Solving these equations for an angle will require you to take the inverse function of each side in order to eliminate the function. This is done easily on your calculator. Try it now by taking $\sin^{-1}(\sin 30)$. Notice that the angle is in degrees, so you will want to be sure your calculator is set to degrees. The inverse sine of the sine of 30 equals 30.

Graphs of Trigonometric Functions

The graphs of sine, cosine, and tangent functions can be found using your graphing calculator. Use the TRACE key on your calculator to examine characteristics of the graphs of each of these functions. You will notice that there is no value for the tangent of $\frac{\pi}{2}$, $\frac{3\pi}{2}$, and all the multiples of those angles. This is because the value of the adjacent side (x-value) at those locations along the unit circle is zero. As you know, the result of dividing by zero is undefined. Looking more specifically at sine and cosine, you will notice key characteristics at x-values of 0, $\frac{\pi}{6}$, $\frac{\pi}{4}$, $\frac{\pi}{3}$, and multiples of these angles. Take some time to examine characteristics of these graphs using your calculator.

Trigonometric Transformations

In the chapter on plane geometry and trigonometry, you examined the parent functions of sine, cosine, and tangent. The period for a parent function of sine or cosine is 2π, and the range is from -1 to 1. As with the other functions, (h, k) shifts the parent function by $-h$ horizontally and k vertically. So, examining the general equation of a sine function, $f(x) = a \sin b\,(x - h) + k$, $|a|$ is the amplitude (affects the range), $\frac{2\pi}{b}$ is the period (notice that when b is 1 the period is 2π), h is the horizontal shift, and k is the vertical shift. Set the graphing window on your calculator and explore how changes to the equation affect the graph of the function. Before you examine the graph, try predicting what you think will occur on the basis of the change you make to the equation.

Trigonometric Identities

For the purposes of the ACT, you will focus on three trigonometric identities in one. Consider a right triangle where the hypotenuse is 1 (think "unit circle"). You have the length of one leg (along the x-axis) valued at $\cos\theta$ and the length of the other leg (along the y axis) valued at $\sin\theta$. Using the Pythagorean theorem, you find that $\sin^2\theta + \cos^2\theta = 1^2$ or $\mathbf{\sin^2\theta + \cos^2\theta = 1}$. This is the basic trigonometric identity. Using this identity, you can solve for either $\sin^2\theta$ or $\cos^2\theta$ by simply subtracting. This gives you two more identities to use: $\mathbf{\sin^2\theta = 1 - \cos^2\theta}$ and $\mathbf{\cos^2\theta = 1 - \sin^2\theta}$. Each of these identities can be solved further by taking the square root of both sides. These identities are especially helpful when you are trying to solve an equation involving both sine and cosine. You can use either equation to substitute in for either $\sin(x)$ or $\cos(x)$, which will allow you to work with one trig function.

MINI-LESSON: GRAPHING CALCULATOR

Your graphing calculator will help you tremendously if you know how to use it for the different types of problems on the ACT. Briefly review the following topics concerning your graphing calculator.

Computation

- Fractions. Remember that you may need to tell your calculator to give you the answer in the form of a fraction so that it matches the answer choices.
- Exponents. The x^2 key is handy, but you may also need to use the $\wedge$ symbol when working with a different power.

- Roots. Square roots are easy, but be sure to locate the key for finding a cube root as well.
- Logarithms. Base 10 and base e (ln) are readily available. Be sure you know the change of base formula and practice changing bases to base 10 and solving with your calculator.
- Trigonometry (radians or degrees). Know whether the problem involves radians or degrees and practice changing from one to the other. You may encounter problems that are set up using radians and degrees throughout the exam.

Statistics

- Lists. A list will only be useful if you are very fast and accurate at filling it in and you are using it for something that you can't do faster without a list. Be sure your lists are all empty before you start the test.
- Basic statistics. If you decide to enter data into a list, you can use your calculator to find the mean, median, and standard deviation of your data.

Graphing

- Window settings. Your window settings will depend on the graph in question. You will need to estimate the window required and set your calculator accordingly.
- TRACE and CALCULATE. TRACE can be used to find points along the graph, and CALCULATE is especially helpful when locating intercepts and maximums or minimums.

Know when to use your graphing calculator. It may be that the most efficient way to solve a problem is *without* the calculator *at all*. For areas that you are weak in, speed is less important than accuracy—use the calculator. Sometimes you will use the calculator to check the answer choices rather than to solve the problem itself.

Practice making these decisions and working within time limits on the practice math test that follows. You may even want to code your practice test by writing a "c" next to the problems you use your calculator for and then reviewing that code once you have completed the practice test.

Now that you've reviewed all the math concepts tested on the ACT, it's time to take a full-length practice test to see how well you do. Good luck!

KEYS TO ACHIEVING MATH PERFECTION

You selected this particular preparation book because you believe in yourself. You have read through the chapters and have a good idea of the content you will encounter on the ACT. Use this book as your reference tool and your classroom as your practice gym. Remember what you have learned here:

Seek Out Word Problems

Whether your teacher assigns them or not, solve word problems at every opportunity. Whenever possible, draw and label a diagram that depicts the situation in the math problem. This is an efficient way to gather key information from the word problem so that you can pull that information quickly into your formula or an equation.

Double-check for Reasonableness

When you are solving a problem that has taken a bit more time, it is important to do a quick double-check. Re-reading the problem will help you ensure that you didn't get off track and answer a different question than was asked. The solutions to other questions are available only as decoy choices. At the same time, check for reasonableness. This should be done in about 5 seconds, and this will help you avoid losing points unnecessarily.

Practice Using Your Graphing Calculator

Practice using your graphing calculator often and in a variety of ways. Use it to solve problems when appropriate to the topic in class. Also use it to determine a ballpark estimate in order to practice this crucial strategy.

Get Accustomed to the Time Crunch

When working on homework that is review (material you have previously learned), set a timer for the number of problems times 80 seconds per problem. Solve the problems as efficiently as you can and switch pen colors when the timer goes off. This is a stiff time limit when you are not able to practice the strategies related to multiple choice. It is still great practice and will help you get used to the pressure of the timed testing environment.

Seek Additional Help

Seek additional help from your teacher on content that seems least familiar to you. If you do not have much experience with conic sections, for example, ask your teacher to loan you a book that has good explanations, and practice problems in it. You know what areas you need extra help in, and it is up to you to get it.

With your intelligence and education along with the strategies in this book, the perfect score in math is within your reach!

Work Toward Efficiency

Note the strategy you use and the time it takes to solve different types of problems. Challenge yourself to explore different strategies.

Memorize Formulas and Properties

Create a master list of key formulas and properties. Create and use flash cards of these formulas to help you memorize them.

ANSWER SHEET
Math Practice Test

1. Ⓐ Ⓑ Ⓒ Ⓓ Ⓔ
2. Ⓕ Ⓖ Ⓗ Ⓙ Ⓚ
3. Ⓐ Ⓑ Ⓒ Ⓓ Ⓔ
4. Ⓕ Ⓖ Ⓗ Ⓙ Ⓚ
5. Ⓐ Ⓑ Ⓒ Ⓓ Ⓔ
6. Ⓕ Ⓖ Ⓗ Ⓙ Ⓚ
7. Ⓐ Ⓑ Ⓒ Ⓓ Ⓔ
8. Ⓕ Ⓖ Ⓗ Ⓙ Ⓚ
9. Ⓐ Ⓑ Ⓒ Ⓓ Ⓔ
10. Ⓕ Ⓖ Ⓗ Ⓙ Ⓚ
11. Ⓐ Ⓑ Ⓒ Ⓓ Ⓔ
12. Ⓕ Ⓖ Ⓗ Ⓙ Ⓚ
13. Ⓐ Ⓑ Ⓒ Ⓓ Ⓔ
14. Ⓕ Ⓖ Ⓗ Ⓙ Ⓚ
15. Ⓐ Ⓑ Ⓒ Ⓓ Ⓔ
16. Ⓕ Ⓖ Ⓗ Ⓙ Ⓚ
17. Ⓐ Ⓑ Ⓒ Ⓓ Ⓔ
18. Ⓕ Ⓖ Ⓗ Ⓙ Ⓚ
19. Ⓐ Ⓑ Ⓒ Ⓓ Ⓔ
20. Ⓕ Ⓖ Ⓗ Ⓙ Ⓚ

21. Ⓐ Ⓑ Ⓒ Ⓓ Ⓔ
22. Ⓕ Ⓖ Ⓗ Ⓙ Ⓚ
23. Ⓐ Ⓑ Ⓒ Ⓓ Ⓔ
24. Ⓕ Ⓖ Ⓗ Ⓙ Ⓚ
25. Ⓐ Ⓑ Ⓒ Ⓓ Ⓔ
26. Ⓕ Ⓖ Ⓗ Ⓙ Ⓚ
27. Ⓐ Ⓑ Ⓒ Ⓓ Ⓔ
28. Ⓕ Ⓖ Ⓗ Ⓙ Ⓚ
29. Ⓐ Ⓑ Ⓒ Ⓓ Ⓔ
30. Ⓕ Ⓖ Ⓗ Ⓙ Ⓚ
31. Ⓐ Ⓑ Ⓒ Ⓓ Ⓔ
32. Ⓕ Ⓖ Ⓗ Ⓙ Ⓚ
33. Ⓐ Ⓑ Ⓒ Ⓓ Ⓔ
34. Ⓕ Ⓖ Ⓗ Ⓙ Ⓚ
35. Ⓐ Ⓑ Ⓒ Ⓓ Ⓔ
36. Ⓕ Ⓖ Ⓗ Ⓙ Ⓚ
37. Ⓐ Ⓑ Ⓒ Ⓓ Ⓔ
38. Ⓕ Ⓖ Ⓗ Ⓙ Ⓚ
39. Ⓐ Ⓑ Ⓒ Ⓓ Ⓔ
40. Ⓕ Ⓖ Ⓗ Ⓙ Ⓚ

41. Ⓐ Ⓑ Ⓒ Ⓓ Ⓔ
42. Ⓕ Ⓖ Ⓗ Ⓙ Ⓚ
43. Ⓐ Ⓑ Ⓒ Ⓓ Ⓔ
44. Ⓕ Ⓖ Ⓗ Ⓙ Ⓚ
45. Ⓐ Ⓑ Ⓒ Ⓓ Ⓔ
46. Ⓕ Ⓖ Ⓗ Ⓙ Ⓚ
47. Ⓐ Ⓑ Ⓒ Ⓓ Ⓔ
48. Ⓕ Ⓖ Ⓗ Ⓙ Ⓚ
49. Ⓐ Ⓑ Ⓒ Ⓓ Ⓔ
50. Ⓕ Ⓖ Ⓗ Ⓙ Ⓚ
51. Ⓐ Ⓑ Ⓒ Ⓓ Ⓔ
52. Ⓕ Ⓖ Ⓗ Ⓙ Ⓚ
53. Ⓐ Ⓑ Ⓒ Ⓓ Ⓔ
54. Ⓕ Ⓖ Ⓗ Ⓙ Ⓚ
55. Ⓐ Ⓑ Ⓒ Ⓓ Ⓔ
56. Ⓕ Ⓖ Ⓗ Ⓙ Ⓚ
57. Ⓐ Ⓑ Ⓒ Ⓓ Ⓔ
58. Ⓕ Ⓖ Ⓗ Ⓙ Ⓚ
59. Ⓐ Ⓑ Ⓒ Ⓓ Ⓔ
60. Ⓕ Ⓖ Ⓗ Ⓙ Ⓚ

Math Practice Test

12

DIRECTIONS: You have 60 minutes to complete 60 questions. Time yourself—that's important! Read and solve each problem.

If a problem is difficult, move to the next problem and come back to the skipped problem after you have gone through the entire math section of the exam. Your calculator can be used on any problem you choose.

Keep your pacing and strategies in mind. You should be able to work more quickly at the beginning of the test because it includes a greater concentration of elementary algebra questions. This also means that the strategy for most of the beginning questions will be to solve the problem. As you move through the test, you will want to use different strategies, and the problems will take more time.

Do not linger over problems that take too much time. Solve as many problems as you can, then return to the others in the time you have left.

Remember that figures are not drawn to scale. You must rely on the explanation in the problem for relative conditions on the illustration (congruence, similarity, etc.).

1. What is the equation of a circle that includes a point at $(1, -2)$ and is centered at $(4, 2)$?

   A. $(x-4)^2 + (y-2)^2 = 5$
   B. $(x-4)^2 + (y-5)^2 = 2$
   C. $(x+4)^2 + (y+2)^2 = 5$
   D. $(x-4)^2 + (y-5)^2 = 25$
   E. $(x-4)^2 + (y-2)^2 = 25$

DO YOUR FIGURING HERE

2. Simplify $(4x^2 + 2x^2 - 3(x - 7)) - (-2x^4 - 2x^2 + 3x - 5)$.

   F. $10x^2 - 6x + 26$
   G. $6x^4 + 4x^2 + 26$
   H. $6x^4 + 4x^2 - 6x + 26$
   J. $2x^4 + 8x^2 - 6x + 26$
   K. $2x^4 - 6x + 26$

3. Find $2x(x - 3y) + 2y^2$ when $x = -6$ and $y = 3$.
   A. -9
   B. 54
   C. 81
   D. 126
   E. 198

4. Bennett is twice as old as his daughter Alissa, who is three years younger than her brother Neal. If the sum of their ages is 63, how old is Neal?
   F. 15
   G. 18
   H. 20
   J. 23
   K. 30

5. When Corina performs in a cheerleading competition she makes 2 mistakes in every 3 minutes of performance. If she performs for a total of 18 minutes in the competition tonight, how many mistakes will she make?
   A. 12
   B. 15
   C. 16
   D. 27
   E. 30

6. Each student in the choir must earn $2500 to attend a performance in Ireland this summer. To earn the funds they are selling candy bars and t-shirts. For each candy bar sold, the singer earns $1 credit, and for each t-shirt the singer earns $5.75. Which equation represents the number of candy bars (x) and t-shirts (y) that must be sold by each singer to ensure that he/she can attend the performance?
   F. $(x + 1) + (y + 5.75) \geq 2500$
   G. $5.75x + y \geq 2500$
   H. $x + 5.75y \geq 2500$
   J. $6.75xy \geq 2500$
   K. $6.75(x + y) \geq 2500$

7. Quadrilateral *ABCD* is a kite. Which of the following cannot be determined?

A. $m\angle 3 = 21°$
B. $m\angle 1 = 90°$
C. $m\angle 2 = 69°$
D. $AD \cong CD$
E. $AB \cong CB$

8. Which of the following is the factored form of $2x^2 - 3x - 9$?

F. $(2x - 3)(x - 9)$
G. $(2x - 9)(x + 3)$
H. $(3x + 2)(x - 3)$
J. $(2x + 3)(x - 3)$
K. $(x + 3)(2x - 3)$

9. Madison surveyed the student body and found that 3 out of 7 students go by a nickname. In a class of 35 students, how many students can Madison predict will go by a nickname?

A. 8
B. 10
C. 15
D. 21
E. 28

10. What is one value of *x*, if $|x - 7| = 5$?

F. -35
G. -12
H. -2
J. 12
K. 35

11. Which of the following is equivalent to $(3x-7)(x+4)$?

A. $12x^2-10x-7$
B. $3x^2+5x-28$
C. $3x^2-3x-28$
D. $3x^2-28$
E. $4x-3$

12. Which three-dimensional figure is formed by rotating a right triangle about a leg?

F. prism
G. sphere
H. cone
J. cylinder
K. pyramid

13. Find $33+(4-3^2)-24\div8$.

A. $\dfrac{7}{4}$

B. $\dfrac{5}{2}$

C. 7
D. 25
E. 31

14. Which of the following is a solution of $-7\sqrt[2]{3x-8}+3=-4x+7$ for x.

F. -8
G. -0.18
H. 0.18
J. 8
K. No real solution

15. Determine the expression that represents $m\angle R$ in triangle PQR given that side $PQ=7$, side $QR=9$, and $m\angle P=110$.

(Note: The law of sines states that the ratio of the side lengths to the sines of the opposite angle are equal for any triangle.)

A. $\sin^{-1}\left(\dfrac{7\sin110°}{9}\right)$

B. $\sin^{-1}63\sin110°$

C. $\sin^{-1}\left(\dfrac{\sin110°}{63}\right)$

D. $\dfrac{7\sin110°}{9}$

E. $\dfrac{\sin110°}{63}$

16. On Crazy Hair Day, 17% of the girls dyed their hair pink, but not one boy dyed his hair pink. If 39% of the total student body are girls, what percent of the total student body wore pink hair on Crazy Hair Day?

- **F.** 2.3%
- **G.** 6.6%
- **H.** 10.4%
- **J.** 17%
- **K.** 22%

17. Simplify $\dfrac{3x^5y^3z}{x^2yz^4} \times x^3y^3z$.

- **A.** $3x^8y^6z^2$
- **B.** $\dfrac{3x^4}{z^3}$
- **C.** $\dfrac{3x^3y^2}{z^3}$
- **D.** $\dfrac{3x^6y^5}{z^2}$
- **E.** $\dfrac{3x^9y^6}{z^2}$

18. List $\dfrac{2}{3}$, $\sqrt{2}$, 0.7, $\dfrac{7}{4}$, and 1.5 in order from least to greatest.

- **F.** $\dfrac{2}{3}$, 0.7, $\sqrt{2}$, 1.5, $\dfrac{7}{4}$
- **G.** $\dfrac{2}{3}$, $\sqrt{2}$, 0.7, $\dfrac{7}{4}$, 1.5
- **H.** $\dfrac{2}{3}$, $\sqrt{2}$, 0.7, 1.5, $\dfrac{7}{4}$
- **J.** $\dfrac{2}{3}$, 0.7, $\sqrt{2}$, $\dfrac{7}{4}$, 1.5
- **K.** $\dfrac{2}{3}$, 0.7, $\dfrac{7}{4}$, 1.5, $\sqrt{2}$

19. Find $(2+4i)(3-2i)+(-3i)(5i)$.

- **A.** $-17+8i$
- **B.** $13+8i$
- **C.** $13+16i$
- **D.** $29+8i$
- **E.** $29+16i$

20. The quadratic formula states that

$$x = \frac{-b \pm \sqrt{b^2 - 4ac}}{2a}$$. Find x given that

$a = 2$, $b = 4$, and $c = 2$.

F. $-1 \pm \sqrt{2}$

G. -1

H. 0

J. 1

K. $1 \pm \sqrt{2}$

21. Quadrilateral *ABCD* has point *B* located at
(2, –1). Find the new coordinates of *B* once the
quadrilateral is translated (4, –7).

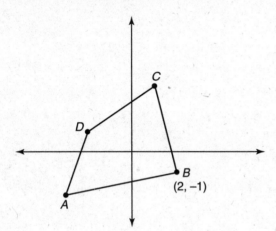

A. (4, –8)

B. (4, –7)

C. (4, 6)

D. (6, 6)

E. (6, –8)

22. Solve $\frac{3}{4}n + \frac{2}{5}n = 46$ for *n*.

F. 2

G. 13.5

H. 16.7

J. 40

K. 184

23. Find the equation of a parabola with maximum at (3, 4) that goes through (5, 2).

DO YOUR FIGURING HERE

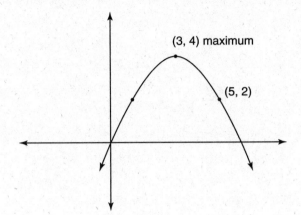

A. $f(x) = -\dfrac{1}{32}(x+3)^2 + 4$

B. $f(x) = \dfrac{3}{32}(x+3)^2 - 4$

C. $f(x) = -\dfrac{1}{2}(x-3)^2 + 4$

D. $f(x) = \dfrac{3}{2}(x-3)^2 - 4$

E. $f(x) = -1(x-3)^2 + 4$

24. Jack is a newborn baby who spends 60% of his time sleeping. Out of the other 40% of his time, 60% is spent either eating, burping, or having his diaper changed. What percent of Jack's total time is left for playing?

F. 0%

G. 16%

H. 20%

J. 24%

K. 40%

25. Solve $\dfrac{-2}{x^2 - 2} = \dfrac{2}{x - 4}$.

A. {−6, 2}

B. {−3, 4}

C. {−3, 2}

D. {−2, 6}

E. {3, 2}

26. Given that $a = b$, which of the following reflects the multiplicative property?

F. $ac = bc$

G. $b = c \Rightarrow a = c$

H. $a + c = b + c$

J. $ab = 1$

K. $a^m = b^m$

27. Determine the volume of a cone with a circular base of area 9π and a height of $7x$.

A. $\dfrac{3}{7}\pi x$

B. $21\pi x$

C. $9\pi \times 7x$

D. $63\pi x$

E. $567\pi x$

28. Express $\sin\theta$ in terms of $\cos\theta$.

F. $\dfrac{1}{\cos\theta}$

G. $\sqrt{\cos\theta}$

H. $1 - \cos\theta$

J. $1 - \cos^2\theta$

K. $\pm\sqrt{1 - \cos^2\theta}$

29. Which expression represents the pattern in the table?

1	2	3	4	5	n
3	0	–3	–6	–9	

A. $-3n$

B. $-3n + 6$

C. $n + 2$

D. $3n$

E. $6n - 3$

30. At Frank's Pizza a medium pizza is priced at $12.95 and a large pizza is priced at $15.95. A medium pizza has a diameter of 6 inches and a large pizza has a diameter of 8 inches. Carlos would like to buy the pizza that costs the least per square inch. Select the expression that represents the difference in areas of the large and medium pizzas.

   F. $\dfrac{15.95}{64\pi} - \dfrac{12.95}{36\pi}$

   G. $\dfrac{15.95}{16\pi} - \dfrac{12.95}{9\pi}$

   H. $8\pi - 6\pi$

   J. $16\pi - 9\pi$

   K. $64\pi - 36\pi$

31. Which of the following is equivalent to $(3x^3y^4)(-2x^2y^5)^3$?

   A. $-216x^{216}y^{729}$
   B. $-24x^9y^{19}$
   C. $-24x^{18}y^{60}$
   D. $-18x^9y^{19}$
   E. $24x^{16}y^{60}$

32. Find the greatest common factor of $116x$ and 128.

   F. 2
   G. 4
   H. 32
   J. $116x$
   K. $128x$

33. Determine the slope of a line perpendicular to $-3x + 5y = 20$.

A. -4

B. $-\dfrac{5}{3}$

C. $-\dfrac{3}{5}$

D. $-\dfrac{1}{4}$

E. $\dfrac{3}{20}$

DO YOUR FIGURING HERE

34. The student council is going to hire a DJ for the winter dance. Each board member is responsible for getting a quote from a DJ and providing an equation that reflects the quote so that the council can select the best quote. Alex talks with Sound Machine and is told that they will charge a set-up fee of $35 and an additional $20 per hour. Which equation represents the cost for x hours?

F. $35 - 20x$

G. $15x$

H. $20x + 35$

J. $35x + 20$

K. $(20 + 35)x$

35. Find the perimeter of

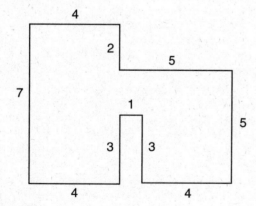

A. 25

B. 32

C. 35

D. 38

E. 63

36. Select the graph of $\dfrac{(x-4)^2}{25} + \dfrac{(y-9)^2}{4} = 1$.

F.

G.

H.

J.

K.

37. A bag contains 4 red marbles, 7 white marbles, and 3 blue marbles. If Sue pulls one marble from the bag, what is the probability that the marble will be blue?

A. $\dfrac{1}{14}$

B. $\dfrac{1}{11}$

C. $\dfrac{3}{14}$

D. $\dfrac{3}{11}$

E. $\dfrac{11}{14}$

38. Which of the following is the solution set of x values for $3x^3 - 15x^2 - 42x = 0$?

F. $\{-2, 21\}$
G. $\{-2, 7\}$
H. $\{-2, 3, 7\}$
J. $\{-2, 0, 7\}$
K. $\{-2, 0, 21\}$

39. Determine the equation of the line that contains the points $(-2.5, 4)$ and $(5, -2)$.

A. $6x + 7.5y = 2$
B. $6x - 7.5y = 2$
C. $12x - 15y = -4$
D. $12x + 15y = -4$
E. $12x + 15y = 30$

40. Find the area of a right triangle with hypotenuse of 10 and side of 8.

F. 5
G. 24
H. 40
J. 48
K. 80

41. Find x, given that $|5x-9|-8=-1$.

   A. no solution

   B. $\dfrac{8}{5}$

   C. $\dfrac{16}{5}$

   D. $\left\{2,\dfrac{8}{5}\right\}$

   E. $\left\{\dfrac{2}{5},\dfrac{16}{5}\right\}$

42. Find the volume of a regular hexagonal pyramid with a base of side length 4 and a height of 9.

   F. $12\sqrt{3}$

   G. $36\sqrt{3}$

   H. $72\sqrt{3}$

   J. $144\sqrt{3}$

   K. $216\sqrt{3}$

43. Find the height a 17-foot ladder can reach on the side of a building when it hits the ground at a 65° angle.

   A. 7.2 ft.

   B. 15.4 ft.

   C. 36.5 ft.

   D. 48 ft.

   E. 224 ft.

44. The diameter of a circle is 34 cm and a chord in that same circle is 30 cm. What is the distance from the center of that circle to the chord?

   F. 4 cm

   G. 8 cm

   H. 8.5 cm

   J. 16 cm

   K. 26 cm

45. Find *x*.

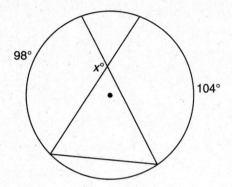

- **A.** 49°
- **B.** 52°
- **C.** 79°
- **D.** 98°
- **E.** 101°

46. If the first term in an arithmetic series is $\frac{8}{3}$ and the last term is $\frac{40}{3}$, and the sum is 72, what are the first four terms?

- **F.** $\frac{8}{3}, \frac{12}{3}, \frac{16}{3}, \frac{20}{3}$

- **G.** $\frac{8}{3}, \frac{14}{3}, \frac{20}{3}, \frac{26}{3}$

- **H.** $\frac{8}{3}, \frac{16}{3}, \frac{24}{3}, \frac{32}{3}$

- **J.** $\frac{8}{3}, \frac{16}{3}, \frac{32}{3}, \frac{40}{3}$

- **K.** $\frac{8}{3}, \frac{20}{3}, \frac{28}{3}, \frac{40}{3}$

47. If $3x\sqrt{50} - \sqrt{32x^2} = \sqrt{18}$, find *x*.

- **A.** $-8\sqrt{2}$
- **B.** 0
- **C.** $\frac{3}{11}$
- **D.** $\frac{1}{3}$
- **E.** $\frac{12}{11}$

48. If $-2(x-7) + (x-6) = 23$, find x.

    F. -31

    G. -15

    H. -5

    J. -3

    K. -1

49. Find the area of an equilateral triangle with a side length of 12.

    A. $6\sqrt{3}$

    B. $18\sqrt{3}$

    C. $36\sqrt{3}$

    D. $72\sqrt{3}$

    E. Cannot be determined from the given information

50. Determine the point of intersection of the following system of equations.

$$y = -\frac{1}{2}x + \frac{13}{4}$$
$$-2x + 3y = 8$$

    F. $(0, -3)$

    G. $(0, 3)$

    H. $(0.5, 3)$

    J. $(8.5, -3)$

    K. $(8.5, 3)$

51. Which of the following is not true for a kite?

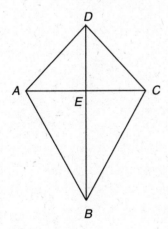

    A. $AE \cong CE$

    B. $DE \cong BE$

    C. $\angle ABE \cong \angle CBE$

    D. $\angle E = 90°$

    E. $\angle ADB \cong \angle CDB$

52. Tony has an A average in his math class and there is one test left. In order to keep the A, he will have to maintain an average test score that is at least 90%. He has completed 5 of the 6 tests and his current average is 91%. Which of the following scores is the lowest he can earn while still maintaining his A?

F. 80%

G. 85%

H. 89%

J. 90%

K. 91%

53. Determine the number of real solutions there are for $9x^2 - 12x + 18 = 0$.

A. no real solutions

B. 1 real solution

C. 2 real solutions

D. 3 real solutions

E. Cannot be determined from the given information

54. Find the perimeter of the quadrilateral that circumscribes this circle.

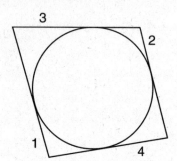

F. 10

G. 12

H. 15

J. 17

K. 20

55. Find $f(-3)$ given that
$f(x) = -2x(x^2 - 8x + 4) - 3x^2 - 2$.
A. -258
B. 31
C. 193
D. 247
E. 258

56. Find point B of segment AB if A is located at
$(-3, 7)$ and the midpoint of AB is located
at $(1, 3)$.
F. $(-2, 10)$
G. $(-1, 5)$
H. $(3, -7)$
J. $(5, -1)$
K. $(10, 2)$

57. Which function has an amplitude of 4 and a
period of 8?
A. $y = -4 \sin \theta$

B. $y = \sin \dfrac{\pi}{8} \theta$

C. $y = 4 \sin \dfrac{\pi}{8} \theta$

D. $y = 4 \sin \dfrac{\pi}{4} \theta$

E. $y = \sin \dfrac{\pi}{4} \theta$

58. Find the measure of the exterior angle of a
regular dodecagon.
F. $15°$
G. $30°$
H. $36°$
J. $144°$
K. $150°$

59. Select the equation that reflects the coordinates in the table.

x	0	1	2	3
y	2	6	18	54

A. $y = 3x + 2$
B. $y = 3x + 3$
C. $y = 2^x$
D. $y = 3^x$
E. $y = 2(3^x)$

60. Find angle x in this isosceles trapezoid.

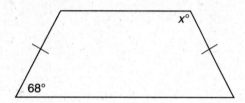

F. 22°
G. 56°
H. 68°
J. 102°
K. 112°

ANSWER KEY
Math Practice Test

1.	E	21.	E	41.	E
2.	J	22.	J	42.	H
3.	E	23.	C	43.	B
4.	G	24.	G	44.	G
5.	A	25.	C	45.	E
6.	H	26.	F	46.	F
7.	A	27.	B	47.	C
8.	J	28.	K	48.	G
9.	C	29.	B	49.	C
10.	J	30.	J	50.	H
11.	B	31.	B	51.	B
12.	H	32.	G	52.	G
13.	D	33.	B	53.	A
14.	J	34.	H	54.	K
15.	A	35.	D	55.	C
16.	G	36.	G	56.	J
17.	D	37.	C	57.	D
18.	F	38.	J	58.	G
19.	D	39.	E	59.	E
20.	G	40.	G	60.	K

Answers Explained

1. **(E)** To determine the radius, use the distance formula to find the distance between the point on the circle and the center point. The distance formula is:

$$d = \sqrt{(x_2 - x_1)^2 + (y_2 - y_1)^2}$$

In this case, it equals $d = \sqrt{(4-1)^2 + (2--2)^2}$, which is $\sqrt{3^2 + 4^2} = \sqrt{9+16} = \sqrt{25} = 5$. Now you have the radius and the center point, which is all you need to write the equation of the circle. The general form of the equation is $(x-h)^2 + (y-k)^2 = r^2$. With the center and radius for this particular circle, we have $(x-4)^2 + (y-2)^2 = 25$.

2. **(J)** The first round through you will have $6x^2 - 3x + 21 + 2x^4 + 2x^2 - 3x + 5$. Then, combining like terms and writing in descending order results in $2x^4 + 8x^2 - 6x + 26$.

3. **(E)** For this problem you can choose to either simplify and then substitute or to substitute and then calculate. Simplifying first results in $2x^2 - 6xy + 2y^2$. With values for x and y substituted into the simplified expression, you have $2(-6)^2 - 6(-6)(3) + 2(3)^2 = 2(36) + 36(3) + 2(9) = 72 + 108 + 18 = 198$.

   Substituting in first is fastest because you can enter the values in parentheses and exponents directly into your calculator. $2 \times -6 \times (-6 - 3 \times 3) + 2 \times (3)^2 = 198$.

4. **(G)** If you set Alissa's age to x, then Bennett is $2x$ and Neal is $x+3$. The sum of x, $2x$, and $x+3$ is 63, so $4x+3 = 63$. Solving for x, you find that Alissa (x) is 15 and so Neal is 18 (3 years older than Alissa).

5. **(A)** Using a proportion to solve, we note that $\dfrac{\text{mistakes}}{\text{minutes}} = \dfrac{2}{3}$. Knowing that she performs for a total of 18 minutes, we can use $\dfrac{2}{3} = \dfrac{x}{18}$. Since 3 times 6 is 18, and 2 times 6 is 12, we find that Corina makes 12 mistakes in 18 minutes.

6. **(H)** Every candy bar earns \$1, so x represents the number of dollars earned from candy bars. Every t-shirt earns \$5.75, so $5.75y$ represents the number of dollars earned from t-shirts. The sum of all money earned ($x + 5.75y$) must be greater than or equal to \$2500 (the amount required to pay for the trip).

7. **(A)** Diagonals of a kite meet at a right angle. Angle 2 and angle CBD are complementary, making $m\angle 2 = 69°$. The two congruency statements are indicated on the diagram. There is not enough information on the diagram to indicate the measure of angle 3.

8. **(J)** In order to have a middle term of $-3x$, there must be an outer and inner product that adds to $-3x$; in this case that is $-3x$ and $3x$. Distributing this answer out will give us the first term of $2x^2$, the middle term of $-6x$, and the last term of -9.

9. **(C)** This is a proportion problem where $\dfrac{\text{students with nickname}}{\text{total students}} = \dfrac{3}{7} = \dfrac{x}{35}$. Since 7 times 5 is 35, we multiply 5 by 3 to find that 15 out of 35 students will go by a nickname.

10. **(J)** Since $|x-7|=5$, we know that $x-7=-5$ OR $x-7=5$. To find all possible solutions, we must solve both cases. The first case, $x-7=-5$, results in $x=2$. The second case, $x-7=5$, results in $x=12$. So the solution is $x=2$ or 12 because either would result in a true statement.

11. **(B)** Distribute $3x$ across $(x+4)$ and then -7 across $(x+4)$ to give $3x^2 + 12x - 7x - 28$, which simplifies to $3x^2 + 5x - 28$.

12. **(H)** A right triangle being rotated around one leg causes the base of the triangle to form a circle and the hypotenuse to slope from the circle to a point that describes a cone.

13. **(D)** With $33 + (4-9) - 24 \div 8$, the parentheses and division come before addition and subtraction, resulting in $33 - 5 - 3 = 33 - 8 = 25$.

14. **(J)** This problem can be solved by isolating the radical, squaring both sides, setting the equation equal to zero, and using the quadratic formula. You will get two real solutions, 8 and 1.5625, and 1.5625 is an extraneous solution. However, this process is much more time-consuming than the one you should use on the exam, which is to plug each value into the equation and find the one that makes the sentence true (the one in which the sides of the equation are equal). The only solution choice that makes the equation true is 8.

15. **(A)** Begin by sketching triangle PQR. Using the law of sines enables you to set $\dfrac{\sin 110°}{9}$ equal to $\dfrac{\sin R}{7}$. Multiplying both sides by 7 gives you $\dfrac{7\sin 110°}{9} = \sin R$. In order to isolate R, you must take the inverse sine of both sides, giving you $R = \sin^{-1}\left(\dfrac{7\sin 110°}{9}\right)$.

16. **(G)** This is determined simply by taking 17% of 39%, or $0.17 \times 0.39 = 0.0663$ (6.6%).

17. **(D)** First simplify $\dfrac{3x^5 y^3 z}{x^2 yz^4}$ by dividing (find the difference of the powers) and you get $\dfrac{3x^3 y^2}{z^3}$. Then multiply that by $x^3 y^3 z$ to get $\dfrac{3x^6 y^5}{z^2}$.

18. **(F)** Use your knowledge of the fractions and the decimals and check the value of $\sqrt{2}$ on your calculator. The value of $\sqrt{2}$ is 1.414, which makes it larger than .7.

19. **(D)** Distribute $(2+4i)$ across $(3-2i)$ to get $6 - 4i + 12i - 8i^2$ and add the product of $-3i$ and $5i$, which is $-15i^2$. Recalling that i^2 is equivalent to -1, you get $6 + 8i + 8 + 15$, which simplifies to $29 + 8i$.

20. **(G)** Substitute the values of a, b, and c into the quadratic formula to get the following:
$$\frac{-4 \pm \sqrt{4^2 - 4(2)(2)}}{2(2)} = \frac{-4 \pm \sqrt[2]{16-16}}{4} = \frac{-4}{4} = -1$$

21. **(E)** Simply add 4 to the x coordinate and -7 to the y coordinate to get $(2+4, -1+-7)$, which simplifies to $(6, -8)$.

22. **(J)** To quickly eliminate all fractions, multiply through both sides of the equation by 20. You will be left with $15n + 8n = 920$. Collecting like terms results in $23n = 920$, and dividing by 23 on both sides reveals that $n = 40$.

23. **(C)** The general equation for a parabola is $f(x) = a(x - h)^2 + k$. You can substitute the coordinates of the maximum for h and k and the coordinates of the point for x and $f(x)$. These substitutions give you $2 = a(5 - 3)^2 + 4$, which simplifies to $2 = 4a + 4$, which simplifies to $-2 = 4a$ and $-\frac{1}{2} = a$. Once you have the value of a, write the equation of the line by leaving $f(x)$ and x variables and replacing a, h, and k with the values specific to this function.

24. **(G)** If 60% of 40% of Jack's time is spent doing anything but playing, then 40% of 40% is left for playing. 40% of 40% is 16%.

25. **(C)** Multiply across the equation by $(x^2 - 2)(x - 4)$ to eliminate denominators. This leaves you with $-2(x - 4) = 2(x^2 - 2)$, which distributes out to $-2x + 8 = 2x^2 - 4$. Bringing all terms to the right and setting the equation equal to zero gives you $0 = 2x^2 + 2x - 12$. By factoring out a 2, you have a quadratic equation with a leading coefficient of one. $0 = 2(x^2 + x - 6)$ factors to $0 = 2(x + 3)(x - 2)$, giving you the solutions of x as -3 and 2. You must check to make sure that neither of these x values would cause the original equation to be undefined. They do not, so the solution is $\{-3, 2\}$.

26. **(F)** The multiplicative property of equality says that when you multiply two equivalent expressions by the same non-zero term, the resulting expressions are also equivalent.

27. **(B)** The volume of a cone is $\frac{1}{3}$ the volume of the cylinder with the equivalent base and height. Since the area of the base is 9π and the height is $7x$, the volume is $\frac{1}{3} \cdot 9\pi \cdot 7x$ or $21\pi x$.

28. **(K)** $\sin^2\theta + \cos^2\theta = 1$, and subtracting $\cos^2\theta$ from both sides leaves you with $\sin^2\theta$ in terms of cosine. The problem states that you are to find the value of sine in terms of cosine, so you must take the square root of both sides, which results in $\sin\theta = \pm\sqrt{1 - \cos^2\theta}$.

29. **(B)** Each term is decreasing at the constant rate of negative 3, which gives you $-3n$. The next step is to determine the value of the rule when n is zero (what we would call the y intercept if we were finding an equation in terms of x and y). To do that, we use any value of n and the corresponding value of the rule. Since $-3(1) +$ zero value $= 3$, we find that the zero value equals 6. Given the constant rate and the value at $n = 0$, we are able to write the rule of $-3n + 6$.

30. **(J)** The problem gives you diameters of the medium and large pizzas. The formula for the area of a circle is πr^2. To find the radius, simply take half of the diameter. The area of the large pizza is 8 divided by 2 squared and multiplied by π, or 16π, and the area of the medium pizza is 6 divided by 2 squared and multiplied by π, or 9π. The difference in the areas is simply $16\pi - 9\pi$.

31. **(B)** Raising a power to a power requires that you raise the coefficient to that power and multiply each power by the power (in this case 3). Raising $-2x^2y^5$ to the 3rd equals $-8x^6y^{15}$. Then multiply that result by $3x^3y^4$ to get $-24x^9y^{19}$.

32. **(G)** The greatest number that divides evenly into both $116x$ and 128 is 4. This can be found by first dividing by two and then dividing by two again. The factors left are $29x$ and

32. Since 29 is prime and is not a factor of 32, you have found that the greatest common factor is 2^2, or 4.

33. **(B)** The slopes of perpendicular lines are negative reciprocals of each other. To find the slope of the line perpendicular to $-3x + 5y = 20$, find the slope of this line either by using $-\dfrac{B}{A}$ or by solving for y. The slope of this line is $\dfrac{3}{5}$, and the negative reciprocal of $\dfrac{3}{5}$ is $-\dfrac{5}{3}$.

34. **(H)** The DJ charges \$35 for showing up regardless of the number of hours and then \$20 per hour of service. $20x$ represents the cost for x hours and $+35$ represents the base charge. $20x + 35$ is the total cost of hiring a DJ for the dance.

35. **(D)** Be sure to write all of the side lengths on the diagram. Once you have done that, add them up to find 38 as the perimeter.

36. **(G)**

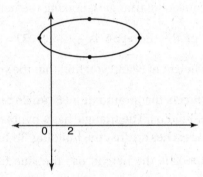

The equation represents an ellipse with the center point at $(4, 9)$ and extended 5 in x and 2 in y. The graph for choice G shows the ellipse translated from the origin to the right 4 and up 9. It extends 5 horizontally in both directions and 2 vertically in both directions.

37. **(C)** There are a total of 14 marbles, and 3 of them are blue. The probability of choosing a blue marble is 3 out of 14.

38. **(J)** Factoring out a $3x$ leaves you with a quadratic with a leading coefficient of 1. Factoring $x^2 - 5x - 14$ gives you $(x - 7)(x + 2)$. So, all together you have $3x(x - 7)(x + 2) = 0$, which means that either $3x$, $(x - 7)$, or $(x + 2)$ must equal zero. Taking them one at a time, x must equal 0, –2, or 7, which is written as $\{-2, 0, 7\}$.

39. **(E)** Use the two points to find the slope, $\dfrac{6}{-7.5}$, and then use one point and the slope in the slope intercept equation to find $b = 2$. Once you have the slope intercept form, multiply through by -7.5 and move x to the left side. Multiply through by -2 to get the equation in standard form (positive x coefficient and no decimals or fractions).

40. **(G)** The area of a triangle is $\dfrac{1}{2}$ base times height. The base and height must meet at a 90° angle. For this problem, you are given the hypotenuse and a leg, which do not meet at a right angle. The first step is to determine the length of the second leg so that you have the

information you need to determine area. Using the Pythagorean theorem, you find that the square root of 100 − 64 is 6. Using the area formula, the area is $\frac{1}{2}(6)(8) = 24$.

41. **(E)** Solving an equation involving absolute value requires that you first isolate the absolute value and then solve for both cases that make the equation true. In this case you have $|5x - 9| = 7$, which means that $5x - 9 = \pm\, 7$. If $5x - 9 = 7$ then $x = \frac{16}{5}$, and if $5x - 9 = -7$ then $x = \frac{2}{5}$.

42. **(H)** The volume of a pyramid is $\frac{1}{3}$ of the area of the base times the height. In this case, the base is a regular hexagon with side length of 4. To find the area of a regular polygon, you can use the formula $A = \frac{1}{2}\, ap$, where a is the apothem (height of an interior triangle) and p is the perimeter. To find the apothem you must consider that a regular hexagon is made up of six equilateral triangles, making the height of each $\frac{1}{2}s\sqrt{3}$. The permimeter is 24. The area of this hexagon is $\frac{1}{2}(24)(2\sqrt{3}) = 24\sqrt{3}$. Take that area and multiply it by 1/3 and the height of 9, and you find that the volume of the pyramid is $72\sqrt{3}$.

43. **(B)** The ladder meets the ground at a 65° angle and is 17 feet long. This forms a right triangle with the building. The triangle has a hypotenuse of 17 feet, and you are asked to find the height it reaches against the building. To find the height, given the hypotenuse and the angle opposite the height, use the sine function. In this case, $\sin 65° = \frac{x}{17}$. Multiplying both sides by 17 will give you the value of x, which is 15.4.

44. **(G)** A diameter of the circle can be drawn to have an endpoint in common with the chord. The distance from the center to the chord is the perpendicular bisector of the chord. Drawing the distance, the chord and the diameter will construct a right triangle with a hypotenuse of 17 cm and a leg that is 15 cm. Finding the distance is as simple as finding the square root of the difference between 17 squared and 15 squared, which is 8.

45. **(E)** The arc lengths of 98° and 104° give you the inscribed angle measures of 49° and 52°. These inscribed angle measures are two angles in a triangle. The third angle is 79°, and $x = 180° - 79° = 101°$. Alternatively, $x = \frac{98 + 104}{2}$ and measures 101°.

46. **(F)** This problem involves two steps. The first is to use the series formula to determine the number of terms included in the sum. Using the formula, you find that $72 = \frac{n}{2}\left(\frac{8}{3} + \frac{40}{3}\right)$, which results in $n = 9$. Once you know that $\frac{40}{3}$ is in fact the 9th term, you can use the sequence formula to determine the common difference. Using the sequence formula, you find that $\frac{40}{3} = \frac{8}{3} + (8)d$ and $d = \frac{4}{3}$. Knowing the common difference and the first term in the sequence, you will simply add $\frac{4}{3}$ to each term to find the next.

47. **(C)** Simplifying each radical, the equation simplifies to $15x\sqrt{2} - 4x\sqrt{2} = 3\sqrt{2}$. Combining like terms on the left side of the equation gives you $11x\sqrt{2} = 3\sqrt{2}$, and dividing both sides by $11\sqrt{2}$ results in the solution $x = \dfrac{3}{11}$.

48. **(G)** Distribute -2 across $(x - 7)$, add like terms, solve for x, and you find that $x = -15$.

49. **(C)** To determine the height of the equilateral triangle, you can remember the special right triangle and know that the height is $6\sqrt{3}$. Or you can drop a segment from the vertex perpendicular to the base and use the Pythagorean theorem to find the height, given that the hypotenuse is 12 and the base in this case would be half that, or 6. Once you have determined the height, use the triangle area formula to find that the area is $\dfrac{1}{2}(12)(6\sqrt{3}) = 36\sqrt{3}$.

50. **(H)** One way to solve is to write each equation in standard form and use elimination. Another way to solve is to substitute the value of y which is $-\dfrac{1}{2}x + \dfrac{13}{4}$ for y in the second equation, solve for x, and then substitute back in for y. The most efficient way to solve this system is to solve the second equation for y, put both equations into the graphing calculator, graph them, and find the point of intersection.

51. **(B)** The diagonals in a kite meet at a perpendicular angle; AC is bisected but DB is not bisected. The diagonals also bisect angles D and B but do not bisect A and C.

52. **(G)** Currently Tony has a total of 455 points (91 times 5), and in order to keep an A he must have a total of 540 points (90 times 6) after the next test. That is a difference of 85 points, so Tony must earn at least 85 points, on the next test to maintain his A average.

53. **(A)** The discriminant of the quadratic formula, $b^2 - 4ac$, tells you the value of the part of the formula that is under the square root symbol. Taking the square root of a negative number will result in imaginary solutions or no real solutions. In this case, $144 - 4(9)(18)$—or if you divide through by 3 first, $16 - 4(3)(6)$—are both negative, resulting in no real solutions.

54. **(K)** From each vertex to the point tangent to the circle, the two segments are congruent. So, the perimeter is $3 + 2 + 2 + 4 + 4 + 1 + 1 + 3 = 20$.

55. **(C)** To find $f(-3)$, substitute -3 in for each x and use order of operations. Doing so will give you $6(9 + 24 + 4) - 27 - 2 = 6(37) - 29 = 193$.

56. **(J)** The midpoint is made up of coordinates that are the average of the coordinates of the endpoints. In this case you can find x and y by using the midpoint formula with one endpoint and using (x, y) as the second endpoint. For instance, $\dfrac{-3+x}{2} = 1$ *and* $\dfrac{7+y}{2} = 3$. Solving each equation for the variable results in an x-value of 5 and a y-value of -1, indicating that the missing endpoint occurs at $(5, -1)$.

57. **(D)** The amplitude change is determined by the coefficient of the function. The period change is determined by the coefficient on the angle. Recall that $\dfrac{2\pi}{b}$ is the period, so setting 8 equal to $\dfrac{2\pi}{b}$ and solving for b gives you $\dfrac{\pi}{4}$.

58. **(G)** A dodecagon has 12 sides and the sum of the interior angles is 1800°, making each interior angle 150°. The interior and exterior angle pairs are supplementary, making the exterior angle measure 30°.

59. **(E)** The pattern is increasing at an exponential rate, in this case meaning that each term is three times the last term. This growth indicates that 3 must be raised to the x power. It does not tell you everything, though. You must still evaluate the expression at $x = 0$ to determine the rest. When $x = 0$, $3^x = 1$, but the value of y is 2, indicating that 3^x must be multiplied by 2, making the equation $y = 2(3^x)$.

60. **(K)** In an isosceles trapezoid, the two angles at each base are congruent to each other. Since a trapezoid has two parallel sides, the side crossing those parallel sides is a transversal and results in consecutive interior angles being supplementary. With those two relationships, the result is that x and 68° are supplementary, making $x = 112°$.

ONLINE PRACTICE TEST

For even more ACT Math practice, remember you can access the online practice test at *barronsbooks.com/tp/ACT36*.

Reading

Balancing Efficiency and Accuracy

13

→ **USE WHAT YOU ALREADY KNOW**

→ **READING STRATEGIES**

→ **QUESTION TYPES**

→ **READING IS THE KEY!**

The ACT reading test is based on a set of 5 passages and will require you to answer 40 questions, all in 35 minutes—a lot to do in little time. If you approach this task appropriately—by seeking the right combination of efficiency and accuracy—you should be able to read all passages and complete all questions. Chapters 13, 14, and 15 of this book offer a series of strategies to help you streamline your approach to this section.

USE WHAT YOU ALREADY KNOW

Relevant background knowledge or "schemas" aid reading comprehension by helping a reader make connections. Good readers are always connecting current reading to prior knowledge, which helps them understand text and remember information. So, it follows that the first thing to consider before reading ACT Passages is how much you *already* know about *every* ACT reading test. Here is a list of ten things you will *always* know about the ACT reading test:

1. There will always be 5 passages, 40 questions, and 35 minutes to complete the task.
2. Passages and questions will always come from one of four categories: prose fiction (short story or excerpt from a novel), social science (mostly history and government), humanities (nonfiction about any topic other than science, history, or government), and natural science (think human interest science as opposed to academic science).
3. All passages will include a citation with a bit of background information.
4. All passages will include 2 to 8 paragraphs. The number of paragraphs will almost always correlate to the density or difficulty of the language: the fewer paragraphs, the more dense the reading.
5. At least 3 of the 5 passages will be structured like a traditional essay: introductory first paragraph, examples and explanations in the middle, and a conclusion at the end.
6. All passages will include an identifiable tone: e.g. cynical, reverent, ironic, didactic, etc.
7. Questions will normally ask you to recall details, make reasonable assumptions about details, define vocabulary in context, or identify the central purpose of the passage. In other words, you will need to be a flexible reader who zooms in to address detail and zooms out to understand the big picture.
8. Questions will often contain easy-to-spot proper nouns and line numbers, which will expedite re-reading when it is necessary.

9. ACT will not present questions in the order that they appear but will skip around.

10. Questions will always contain one answer that is correct, making process of elimination an option every time!

In other words, you actually know a tremendous amount about the test before you have ever seen it. Use the predictability of the test to your advantage.

INSIDE THE ACT 36 MIND

The ACT reading section is about balancing efficiency and accuracy. You don't need to skim, but you also can't luxuriate in the content or style of the passage. Based on clues the test offers, you will know when to look at the big picture and when to focus on details, when to look at the passage and when to look at the questions. Eventually, you'll know how to avoid a useless piece of information without missing something important. That's the key. Eight minutes per passage is not a lot of time, but it's enough if you work wisely.

READING STRATEGIES

The chapters on reading, besides supplying you with lots of practice, will cover the following strategies:

It's All in the Timing

When you're working on a homework assignment or a final exam, you often have as much time as you need to read and answer questions. Not this time. To prepare for the reading test, you'll need to adopt time-saving strategies. More students run out of time on the reading section of the ACT than on any other section. On a very general level, you want to spend about four minutes reading each passage and four minutes answering each set of questions, which leaves you three minutes of leeway at the end of the test. Timing is the key to success.

Before Reading

SEE THE BIG PICTURE

Take a few seconds to look at the passage as a whole. How many paragraphs does it contain? What size are the paragraphs? How many lines long is the passage? Mentally get a picture of the size and even the structure of the passage. Do you notice multiple lines of dialog? Are some of the paragraphs longer than others? By gaining a broader perspective of the passage, you prepare your mind to read in more detail.

CLEAR YOUR MIND AND PREHEAT YOUR BRAIN

These strategies sound simple, but they are easy to overlook when time is a factor. Remove all mental clutter. Think only about your background knowledge of the topic and the words in front of you. Forget about any mental distractions that might cause you to lose focus as you read. Read the passage's citation, thinking briefly about the topic and glancing at key words in the passage. Spend a few seconds identifying what you already know about the topic. Your brain needs to be primed to accept the new information. Skimming the questions for key words, line numbers or dates may also help you focus your reading, but don't spend more than a few seconds doing so. Reading the questions prior to reading the passage is NOT recommended; there is not enough time to do this.

While Reading

IDENTIFY MAIN IDEA AND TONE

Once you've "preheated your brain," use the first paragraph to begin identifying the main idea and tone of the passage. Early on in your reading, consider the purpose of the passage. A first paragraph of a fictional passage may introduce the main character and conflict within a story. A social science passage may begin by exploring the dynamics of Socialist Russia. Think about the author's attitude, the tone of the passage. How does the author feel about the subject or topic? Normally, you'll be able to tell within a paragraph or two. As you continue beyond paragraphs 1 and 2, read to absorb the big ideas, knowing you can look up the details later.

"INDEXING" THE PASSAGE: THE KEY TO BALANCING EFFICIENCY AND ACCURACY!

No strategy will help you identify important details more efficiently than this one. Don't get bogged down in detailed note taking or text marking, but do follow this quick but *invaluable* three-step process, which works best when executed paragraph by paragraph.

Indexing 101:

1. **READ EACH PARAGRAPH**, while trying to focus on its main argument or claim. Nonfiction paragraphs will almost always have one. The main argument will be a combination of the topic *and* the author's opinion on the topic. Avoid getting bogged down in detail as much as you can, but don't skim either—reading for the main argument lies somewhere in between.

2. **SUMMARIZE THE MAIN ARGUMENT** of the paragraph in your head; *in your own words*. Each paragraph will have a central argument or angle. Some might have more than one major idea that feels important, but try your best to narrow your summary.

3. **CHOOSE A KEY WORD OR SHORT PHRASE TO WRITE IN THE MARGIN** before moving on to the next paragraph. The word only needs to make sense to you, as its sole purpose is to trigger your short-term memory if and when a question relates to this paragraph.

Now, try the strategy using a sample paragraph:

1. **READ.**

   Soon the governments of the United States and its allies enthusiastically pursued a "peace dividend," slashing military budgets and manpower levels in order to reduce taxes or divert resources to other pursuits. By the late 1990s, sobering international challenges had taken the bloom off; however, the enduring complexities of national security were apparent to many. Indeed, although the stakes were never as high as they had been during the potential life-or-death struggle with the Soviet Union, American armed forces found their operational tempo of deployment to distant theaters and into harm's way greater than it had been since the Vietnam War.

2. **SUMMARIZE THE MAIN ARGUMENT IN YOUR HEAD.** Once you have sifted through bizarre phrases such as "had taken the bloom off" and "operational tempo," your summary will probably sound something like the following:

   "Governments cut military budgets after the Cold War but eventually realized that they were still deploying forces for other challenges."

3. **WRITE A KEY WORD OR PHRASE IN THE MARGIN.** Your key phrase might be something like *"still deploying,"* but it can be anything as long as it is brief and reminds you of the paragraph's central claim.

Of course, the more you practice this strategy, the more efficient and effective you'll become at it. There are two reasons this strategy works. First, since indexing forces you to focus on the main argument of a paragraph and to quickly commit the argument to memory before you move on, it makes you more efficient when determining answers to questions. Second, indexing helps you break the passage up into manageable sections. By spotlighting one chunk of text at a time, you will feel less overwhelmed and more focused as you move through the test.

TIP

Transitions are the links that hold the essay together, so be sure to note them as you index a passage.

TAKE NOTE OF TRANSITIONS

As you read, consider how the passage is structured. Notice the major transitions. In a traditional essay, an intro will precede the supporting paragraphs, which will precede a conclusion. Many ACT passages fit this mold. As you index the passage, pause to consider (for just a second) how paragraphs connect. After quickly reading the passage in three to four minutes, you should have a good idea about how the entire passage is organized. When it comes to tracking down details, knowing how paragraphs fit together is as important as knowing the contents of each paragraph.

After Reading

GUESS FIRST, THEN FIND THE ANSWER

Especially when questions ask you to infer the main point, the tone, or the definition of a word in context, treating the question as though it were a "short answer" question can help immensely. Guessing the correct answer first may help eliminate some answer options or help identify which options sound similar to your initial response. If none of the answer options are close to your initial guess, then you will probably need to spend more time looking for the answer to that question. These indicators can help you search your index to locate the answer within the text. A key phrase from the question stem probably falls into one of the categories listed in your index. Your understanding of the organizational structure will be helpful as well, as are dates. For example, if you see the year *1938* in the question, chances are it's somewhere in the passage, too. Skip over your index and go directly to the passage to find the date. All of these strategies can get you close to an answer before you even consider the four answer choices.

To find the correct answer look for line numbers, key words, and dates within the question.

QUESTION TYPES

Essentially, the ACT gives you three types of reading questions:

1. Questions that ask you to find a detail in the passage
2. Questions that ask you to make an inference or judgment about the passage
3. Questions that test your knowledge of vocabulary in context (least common)

Knowing that you'll only be required to do three different things when you answer questions can be comforting when you're pressed for time.

READING IS THE KEY!

Whatever you do, master the skills in this section. If you can handle the reading portion of the exam, you will be at a huge advantage when it comes to at least three quarters of the ACT, as science and English—and even mathematics, to a degree—require many of these skills.

Prose Fiction: Are You a Good Judge of Character? 14

→ **STAYING FOCUSED**

→ **COST OR CAPS? APPROACHING A FICTION PASSAGE**

→ **EXERCISES #1-3**

→ **TWO FINAL PRACTICE SETS**

→ **FOUR KEYS TO SUCCESS IN FICTION READING**

Many students find the prose fiction passage to be the easiest passage in the reading section. Why? Because, if you're like many high school students, teachers have fed you a steady diet of fiction for years. You understand its central elements—plot, character, conflict, theme—the way a dog knows its favorite corner. You've circled around and around these elements, settled into them, wandered away, returned. What's more, you likely require very little time with a new piece of imaginative literature before you've become accustomed to its author's particular rhythms and tendencies. In short, you're already a fiction pro. Even if you prefer to read nonfiction, you feel at ease—or at least not totally bewildered—when you sit in front of a work of fiction.

STAYING FOCUSED

For you, the biggest challenge may be to stay focused and, in a sense, not let yourself enjoy or analyze the reading too much.

INSIDE THE ACT 36 MIND

Remember: You are reading prose fiction only to answer multiple-choice questions on the ACT. You are not reading for enjoyment. You are not reading to wow your teacher with your ability to analyze similes, symbols, and syntax. You're reading for points, and points alone!

The purpose of this chapter is to teach you to read fiction in a way that maximizes its value to you as a test-taker. You have 8 minutes to read a 900–1000-word passage (or two 400–500 word passages) and answer 10 questions. You won't have time to luxuriate and enjoy the story, and you won't have time to analyze the significance of the color red as it applies to feminist discourse. If you want to pick up "easy" points on the fiction passage, focus on working as efficiently as possible. Move on as quickly as you can to the nonfiction passages, where you will see 75 percent of the points.

Work Accurately but Efficiently

Know *why* you're reading! Here are two approaches to avoid if you want to save time:

1. ***DON'T* READ FOR ENJOYMENT.** Reading because you love the words will hurt you, as relaxed reading is seldom goal-oriented reading.

   Skilled readers, even when they read with no goal in mind, are constantly making connections. Mostly semiconsciously, they wonder about things, remember other books and events, notice structure, repair confusion, and marvel at expert writing. For now, set aside the expansive mind-wandering that makes reading enjoyable.

2. ***DON'T* READ AS THOUGH YOU'RE EVENTUALLY GOING TO WRITE AN ESSAY.** Although more closely related to your goal, reading the way you've been taught to read in English class doesn't work well either. Reading for the perfect essay topic isn't focused enough. When doing so, you tend to troll the passage for every possible minute detail, analyzing a work of fiction to death in the hope that you'll discover something "original" to say.

   If you enjoy searching for subtle arguments, the ACT is not calibrated for you. It's easier! Focus on four pillars of analysis: characterization, overview, structure, and tone. The first letters of these categories spell "COST," and it will cost you time and accuracy if you fail to focus on these simple tenets.

REMEMBER

Reading fiction on the ACT is very different from reading for your English class or for pleasure. On the exam, you're reading for points only!

COST OR CAPS? APPROACHING A FICTION PASSAGE

A writer of traditional fiction can only develop so much in 75 to100 lines. Fiction passages, therefore, are almost always brief studies in character. Here are two methods that will help you think through a fiction passage efficiently and accurately. Choose the one that makes the most sense to you personally. Then practice your chosen method until it is second nature.

Option 1: "COST"

(Stands for Characters, Overview, Structure, Tone)

CHARACTERS

As almost all fiction passages are character-driven, understanding the subtleties of character will help you immensely. Ask yourself the following questions as you read, and you should know all you need to know to answer even the most challenging ACT question:

- How many central characters are there?
- From whose point of view is the passage told?
- How do the central characters look, think, feel, and act?
- How would you characterize the relationships among central characters?
- What conflicts exist among central characters?
- What conflicts exist within the minds of central characters?

Practice enough and you'll be able to do this kind of simple analysis in the time it takes to read the passage quickly.

OVERVIEW

Read to identify the theme, *big picture*, or main idea—whichever term makes you most comfortable. Having a general sense of the passage will help you answer detail and inference questions and will allow you to answer big-picture questions before you even look at the answer choices.

STRUCTURE

Take note of the paragraph sequence, and determine each paragraph's role in the passage as a whole. Essentially, create a brief index or summary of the passage as you go. The most efficient way to internalize the structure of a passage is to write a one- to three-word summary of each paragraph in the margins. Why one to three words? Anything more takes up too much time, and anything less decreases your ability to recall the paragraph when you refer back to it, which you'll have to do when asked a question about detail.

TIP

Restrict your index to one to three words per paragraph.

TONE AND MOOD

Tone in fiction is the narrator's attitude toward the subject. Mood is the emotion or feeling that you, the reader, are supposed to receive from the passage as a whole. Getting the feel for these "voice" elements will position you for success on many ACT questions.

Option 2: "CAPS"

(Stands for Characters, Attitude, Problem, Solution)

CHARACTERS

Much like you would do when using the "COST" method, get to know characters as well as you can. Note characters' appearances, thoughts, feelings, actions, relationships, conflicts, and realizations. Consider from whose point of view the passage is told. There will be one to three central characters to consider. Characterization should be your primary focus every time you read a fiction passage.

ATTITUDE

Observe how the narrator and other characters come across. What are their attitudes toward the subject they describe or the situation they inhabit?

PROBLEM

Most ACT fiction passages will present a situation or conflict and resolve it in some way by the end. Focus on the central problem or issue in the passage, and track its development as you read.

SOLUTION

Find the solution to the problem. Typically it will come in the concluding paragraph or two. Consider how the resolution to the problem affects what you know about the central characters and their attitudes.

That's it. All ACT fiction questions will be variations on one of these literary elements. No Christ figures, esoteric literary devices, or Freudian analysis, just crisp, clear, focused reading. Let's try a couple of questions about *Dracula* by Bram Stoker.

EXERCISE #1

Read the following text and respond to the questions below. Use this time to practice either COST or CAPS.

What I saw was the Count's head coming out from the window. I did not see the face, but I knew the man by the neck and the movement of his back and arms. In any case I could not mistake the hands, which I had had so many opportunities of studying. I was at first
Line interested and somewhat amused, for it is wonderful how small a matter will interest
(5) and amuse a man when he is a prisoner. But my very feelings changed to repulsion and terror when I saw the whole man slowly emerge from the window and begin to crawl down the castle wall over the dreadful abyss, face down with his cloak spreading out around him like great wings. At first I could not believe my eyes. I thought it was some trick of the moonlight, some weird effect of shadow, but I kept looking, and it could be
(10) no delusion. I saw the fingers and toes grasp the corners of the stones, worn clear of the mortar by the stress of years, and by thus using every projection and inequality move downwards with considerable speed, just as a lizard moves along a wall.

What manner of man is this, or what manner of creature, is it in the semblance of man? I feel the dread of this horrible place overpowering me. I am in fear, in awful fear, and there
(15) is no escape for me. I am encompassed about with terrors that I dare not think of.

PRACTICE QUESTIONS

1. Which of the following details is NOT included in the narrator's description of the Count?
   A. His winglike cloak
   B. His terrifying facial expression
   C. His nimble fingers and toes
   D. His inverted body position

2. It can be inferred from the passage that the narrator witnesses the actions of the Count with a mixture of:
   F. respect and nostalgia.
   G. anxiety and arrogance.
   H. impatience and amusement.
   J. curiosity and fear.

EXPLANATIONS

1. **(B)** This question asks about detail, and you may notice that one of the pillars of fiction is *not* attention to detail. Confused? Don't be. Two strategies are on your side. First, if you paid attention to the characterization of Count Dracula, you know that he is depicted crawling facedown wearing a cloak. Rule out answer A. Now think about structure. In most passages, you'll have several paragraphs with which to contend. If you have a sense of the focus of each paragraph, you know that paragraph 1 contains a detailed description of the Count. Take a few seconds to scan the paragraph, finding references to his fingers and toes and his inverted body position. C and D are out, leaving you with answer B. If you require further proof, note that lines 1 and 2 state clearly that the narrator can't "see the face" and therefore can't read a facial expression.

2. **(J)** A sense of tone and mood is critical to this question. It could be argued that the narrator respects the Count, but nowhere is there proof that he feels a longing for the past. Rule out option F. Next, the narrator feel anxious, but he feels more helpless than arrogant; therefore, option G is incorrect. H and J are the best answers, as it could be said that the narrator feels impatient in the sense that most prisoners feel impatient, and he does mention early in paragraph 1 that he is "amused." But look at the scope of the passage. What's missing? Doesn't the overriding tone have more to do with fear than impatience or amusement? The narrator's amusement is passing, and his impatience has little to do with his observations of the Count. Fear drives the tone of this passage. Be wary of "out of scope" answers such as answer H. These kinds of answer choices are prevalent in the ACT Reading section, and often appear correct, especially when you're pressed for time.

EXERCISE #2

Read the below passage and respond to the following questions. The passage is an excerpt from Lewis Carroll's *Alice in Wonderland*.

"You ought to be ashamed of yourself," said Alice, "a great girl like you," (she might well say this), "to go on crying in this way! Stop this moment, I tell you!" But she went on all the same, shedding gallons of tears, until there was a large pool all round her, about four inches deep and reaching half down the hall.

Line

(5) After a time she heard a little pattering of feet in the distance, and she hastily dried her eyes to see what was coming. It was the White Rabbit returning, splendidly dressed, with a pair of white kid gloves in one hand and a large fan in the other: he came trotting along in a great hurry, muttering to himself as he came, "Oh! the Duchess, the Duchess! Oh! won't she be savage if I've kept her waiting!" Alice felt so desperate that

(10) she was ready to ask help of any one; so, when the Rabbit came near her, she began, in a low, timid voice, "If you please, sir—" The Rabbit started violently, dropped the white kid gloves and the fan and scurried away into the darkness as hard as he could go.

- How many central characters are there?

_____

_____

_____

- From whose point of view is the passage told?

_____

_____

_____

- How would you describe the way central characters look, think, feel, and act?

_____

_____

_____

- How would you characterize the relationships among central characters?

_____

_____

_____

- What conflicts exist among central characters?

_____

_____

_____

- What conflicts exist within the minds of central characters?

_____

_____

_____

Now, answer these multiple-choice questions about the passage.

1. When Alice stops talking to herself and addresses the rabbit, her attitude goes from:
   A. timid about her crying to angry.
   B. nervous about the rabbit to timid.
   C. critical of herself to hesitant.
   D. decisive about her situation to indecisive.

2. All of the following details convey the rabbit's hurried state EXCEPT:
   F. "a little pattering of feet" (line 5).
   G. "The rabbit started violently" (line 11).
   H. "'won't she be savage if I've kept her waiting!'" (line 9).
   J. "scurried away into the darkness" (line 12).

EXPLANATIONS

1. **(C)** Knowledge of both characterization and structure will help you in question 1. Furthermore, this question presents opportunity to employ the "guess first, then answer" strategy. In reading the short passage, it should become clear to you that one central character, from whose point of view the story is told, has a surprise run-in with another character. The change in the central character's attitude—one state before the encounter, another state after the encounter—becomes the focus of the passage. Alice reproaches herself for crying before the rabbit appears and timidly asks for help after he appears, her desperation overpowering her self-reproach for just a moment. So, you might guess that her attitude shifts from self-reproach to cautiousness. Now look at the answer choices. Option A, "timid about her crying to angry," makes little sense given your reading. Alice may seem angry at herself in the first half of the passage, but once the rabbit appears, she focuses on trying to get help. If anything, the attitudes are reversed. Rule out A. The phrase "nervous about the rabbit" should allow you to rule out option B, because nowhere in the text does it suggest that Alice might be nervous about the rabbit before the rabbit appears. In fact, the passage suggests that the rabbit arrives unexpectedly, that Alice hasn't considered his existence until he enters the scene. Option C matches your initial guess fairly well: "self-reproach" sounds like "critical of herself," and "cautiousness" is in the same family as "hesitant." Consider option D: Alice does not seem decisive about her situation at the outset of the passage. If anything, she seems somewhat lost and confused. So, even though she appears somewhat "indecisive" once the rabbit appears, option D can't be correct because she is never decisive in the beginning of the passage.

TIP

Watch for changes in a character's attitude over the course of a passage.

2. **(G)** In order to answer this one correctly, you have to have a sense of how details in fiction convey characterization and mood. You probably realized the rabbit was in a hurry when you read the passage. Now determine which three of the four details make him appear rushed. Option F, "a little pattering of feet," is an auditory image that represents someone in a hurry. Option G, "the rabbit started violently," is in the spirit of the rabbit's jumpy personality but really represents his surprise at meeting Alice more than his rushed state. Option H, a piece of dialog indicating that the rabbit does not want to

keep the duchess waiting, refers directly to his hurried state. Option J, "scurried away into the darkness," again depicts the rabbit in a rush. The rabbit's reaction in option G does not necessarily imply that he is in a hurry.

REMEMBER

For more extra-challenging practice, you can go online for the Challenge Round with 50 difficult questions.

EXERCISE #3

Read the following passage. In the margin next to each paragraph write down a one- to three-word summary. If you see dialog or extremely short paragraphs, it may be in your best interest to "bundle," or summarize several short paragraphs at once.

The following is an excerpt from *The Adventures of Tom Sawyer* by Mark Twain.

"TOM!"

No answer.

"TOM!"

No answer.

Line
(5) "What's gone with that boy, I wonder? You TOM!"

No answer.

The old lady pulled her spectacles down and looked over them about the room; then she put them up and looked out under them. She seldom or never looked THROUGH them for so small a thing as a boy; they were her state pair, the pride of her heart, and
(10) were built for "style," not service—she could have seen through a pair of stove-lids just as well. She looked perplexed for a moment, and then said, not fiercely, but still loud enough for the furniture to hear:

"Well, I lay if I get hold of you I'll—"

She did not finish, for by this time she was bending down and punching under the
(15) bed with the broom, and so she needed breath to punctuate the punches with. She resurrected nothing but the cat.

"I never did see the beat of that boy!"

She went to the open door and stood in it and looked out among the tomato vines and "jimpson" weeds that constituted the garden. No Tom. So she lifted up her voice
(20) at an angle calculated for distance and shouted:

"Y-o-u-u TOM!"

There was a slight noise behind her and she turned just in time to seize a small boy by the slack of his roundabout and arrest his flight.

"There! I might 'a' thought of that closet. What you been doing in there?"

(25) "Nothing."

"Nothing! Look at your hands. And look at your mouth. What IS that truck?"

"I don't know, aunt."

"Well, I know. It's jam—that's what it is. Forty times I've said if you didn't let that jam alone I'd skin you. Hand me that switch."

(30) The switch hovered in the air—the peril was desperate—

"My! Look behind you, aunt!"

The old lady whirled round, and snatched her skirts out of danger. The lad fled on the instant, scrambled up the high board-fence, and disappeared over it.

His aunt Polly stood surprised a moment, and then broke into a gentle laugh.

(35) "Hang the boy, can't I never learn anything? Ain't he played me tricks enough like that for me to be looking out for him by this time? But old fools is the biggest fools there is. Can't learn an old dog new tricks, as the saying is. But my goodness, he never plays them alike, two days, and how is a body to know what's coming? He 'pears to know just how long he can torment me before I get my dander up, and he knows if he can

(40) make out to put me off for a minute or make me laugh, it's all down again and I can't hit him a lick. I ain't doing my duty by that boy, and that's the Lord's truth, goodness knows. Spare the rod and spile the child, as the Good Book says. I'm a laying up sin and suffering for us both, I know. He's full of the Old Scratch, but laws-a-me! he's my own dead sister's boy, poor thing, and I ain't got the heart to lash him, somehow. Every

(45) time I let him off, my conscience does hurt me so, and every time I hit him my old heart most breaks. Well-a-well, man that is born of woman is of few days and full of trouble, as the Scripture says, and I reckon it's so. He'll play hookey this evening,* and I'll just be obleeged to make him work, to-morrow, to punish him. It's mighty hard to make him work Saturdays, when all the boys is having holiday, but he hates work

(50) more than he hates anything else, and I've GOT to do some of my duty by him, or I'll be the ruination of the child."

Tom did play hookey, and he had a very good time. He got back home barely in season to help Jim, the small colored boy, saw next-day's wood and split the kindlings before supper—at least he was there in time to tell his adventures to Jim while Jim did three-

(55) fourths of the work.

> ### POSSIBLE STRUCTURAL INDEX OF THE PASSAGE
>
> Lines 1–6: Woman calls repeatedly for "Tom"—no answer.
>
> Lines 7–12: Description of glasses—woman can't see well.
>
> Lines 13–21: Continues to express frustration while looking for Tom.
>
> Lines 22–31: Woman finds Tom eating jam in the closet and threatens to beat him.
>
> Lines 32–33: Tom escapes.
>
> Lines 35–52: Woman, "Aunt Polly," ponders her parenting skills and her ambivalent feelings about Tom—characterized as a kind, upstanding, concerned parent.
>
> Lines 52–55: Tom is characterized as unabashedly mischievous.

TIP

For passages with dialog or very short paragraphs, try "bundling" several paragraphs together in your index.

The above notes are more developed than yours should be. They have been expanded in order to illustrate this strategy for you. Your notes need only be long enough to trigger your short-term memory—no more than one or two words per section.

---

*Southwestern for "afternoon"

Answer these three questions about the passage. If it's helpful, use your index to help you answer.

1. The line stating that Aunt Polly's spectacles are "built for 'style,' not service—she could have seen through a pair of stove-lids just as well" (lines 10–11) illustrates the idea that Aunt Polly:
   A. doesn't see very well through her glasses.
   B. is not very attractive in her glasses.
   C. is frustrated by Tom's behavior.
   D. is prideful regarding her parenting.

2. In lines 1–21, the narrative is interrupted by brief lines of dialog. It could be argued that this technique serves all of the following purposes EXCEPT:
   F. to highlight Aunt Polly's confusion.
   G. to illustrate that Aunt Polly looks in more than one place for Tom.
   H. to allow the reader to witness Aunt Polly's threatening tone.
   J. to characterize Tom Sawyer as lazy.

3. The primary function of lines 35–51 is to:
   A. characterize Aunt Polly as an angry surrogate parent.
   B. depict Aunt Polly as a caring but confused guardian.
   C. illustrate that Aunt Polly can see again after finding her glasses.
   D. demonstrate Tom's mischievous, playful nature.

EXPLANATIONS

1. **(A)** This question is subtle, because it requires you to sense the narrator's ironic tone. The easiest way to answer a question like this is to translate it into your own words: "Guess, then try to find the answer." Based on your index and the line number reference, you know to focus on a specific section of text. Now translate the passage. The phrase "built for 'style,' not service" indicates that the glasses are more a show item than a functional one. The phrase, "she could have seen through a pair of stove lids just as well" equates Aunt Polly's ability to see through her glasses with her ability to see through a piece of metal, indicating that she can't see through them very well. Scanning the answers, answer A seems to make the most sense. Answer B is not within the scope of the question: Aunt Polly may or may not be attractive, but lines 10–11 neither refute nor support the claim. Aunt Polly is clearly frustrated by Tom, but lines 10–11 don't refer to her frustration, so rule out answer C. Aunt Polly's pride is mentioned just before the quotation, but again, the quotation itself doesn't refer to her pride or her parenting. When the ACT gives you a specific quotation, read it carefully; it will provide you with the answer.

2. **(J)** Here's another subtle question that requires a good deal of analysis. The phrase "it could be argued" is your best friend here; it tells you that you only need to find the one implausible answer. Aunt Polly's repeated attempts to call for Tom could indicate that she is confused, so answer F is *plausible*. At times when Aunt Polly pauses, she seems to be in a different place than she has been previously; therefore, answer G is *plausible*.

Answer H is also reasonable: The choppy rhythm of the passage along with Aunt Polly's dialog allow the reader to sense her irritated tone and frustration with Tom's behavior. Answer J is implausible, based on lines 1–21. We have no clues about Tom's character other than his name and the idea that he frustrates Aunt Polly. There is no evidence to prove or disprove his laziness. Again, it is essential that you base your answers only on the text. Background knowledge of Tom Sawyer and his tendency to laze around and allow others to work for him—as implied in the final section of the passage—is a trap here.

3. **(B)** Because you've indexed the passage, you know the central concern of lines 35–52: Aunt Polly's mixed feelings about taking care of Tom. The monolog in question depicts a woman who wants to raise Tom well but hasn't figured out how to do so. The paragraph depicts her as more exasperated than angry, so disregard option A. Option B matches the index of the paragraph: Aunt Polly's character can be described as caring and confused. Option C is illogical if you read the entire passage and would only tempt a reader who had skimmed so fast that he wasn't able to remember the structure of the passage. Since you've indexed, you know that Twain only mentions Aunt Polly's vision early in the passage—definitely not in lines 35–52. Twain alludes to Tom's devilish nature in this paragraph, but the characterization of Aunt Polly is its "primary function."

TWO FINAL PRACTICE SETS

Using the strategies outlined in this chapter, read the following passages and answer the ten questions that follow each. The first passage comes from *My Antonía* by Willa Cather.

Last summer I happened to be crossing the plains of Iowa in a season of intense heat, and it was my good fortune to have for a traveling companion James Quayle Burden—Jim Burden, as we still call him in the West. He and I are old friends—
Line we grew up together in the same Nebraska town—and we had much to say to each
(5) other. While the train flashed through never-ending miles of ripe wheat, by country towns and bright-flowered pastures and oak groves wilting in the sun, we sat in the observation car, where the woodwork was hot to the touch and red dust lay deep over everything. The dust and heat, the burning wind, reminded us of many things. We were talking about what it is like to spend one's childhood in little towns like these,
(10) buried in wheat and corn, under stimulating extremes of climate: burning summers when the world lies green and billowy beneath a brilliant sky, when one is fairly stifled in vegetation, in the color and smell of strong weeds and heavy harvests; blustery winters with little snow, when the whole country is stripped bare and gray as sheetiron. We agreed that no one who had not grown up in a little prairie town could know
(15) anything about it. It was a kind of freemasonry, we said.

Although Jim Burden and I both live in New York, and are old friends, I do not see much of him there. He is legal counsel for one of the great Western railways, and is sometimes away from his New York office for weeks together. That is one reason why we do not often meet. Another is that I do not like his wife.

(20) When Jim was still an obscure young lawyer, struggling to make his way in New York, his career was suddenly advanced by a brilliant marriage. Genevieve Whitney was the only daughter of a distinguished man. Her marriage with young Burden was the

subject of sharp comment at the time. It was said she had been brutally jilted by her cousin, Rutland Whitney, and that she married this unknown man from the West out (25) of bravado. She was a restless, headstrong girl, even then, who liked to astonish her friends. Later, when I knew her, she was always doing something unexpected. She gave one of her town houses for a Suffrage headquarters, produced one of her own plays at the Princess Theater, was arrested for picketing during a garment-makers' strike, etc. I am never able to believe that she has much feeling for the causes to which she (30) lends her name and her fleeting interest. She is handsome, energetic, executive, but to me she seems unimpressionable and temperamentally incapable of enthusiasm. Her husband's quiet tastes irritate her, I think, and she finds it worth while to play the patroness to a group of young poets and painters of advanced ideas and mediocre ability. She has her own fortune and lives her own life. For some reason, she wishes to (35) remain Mrs. James Burden.

As for Jim, no disappointments have been severe enough to chill his naturally roman- tic and ardent disposition. This disposition, though it often made him seem very funny when he was a boy, has been one of the strongest elements in his success. He loves with a personal passion the great country through which his railway runs and (40) branches. His faith in it and his knowledge of it have played an important part in its development. He is always able to raise capital for new enterprises in Wyoming or Montana, and has helped young men out there to do remarkable things in mines and timber and oil. If a young man with an idea can once get Jim Burden's attention, can manage to accompany him when he goes off into the wilds hunting for lost parks or (45) exploring new canyons, then the money which means action is usually forthcoming. Jim is still able to lose himself in those big Western dreams. Though he is over forty now, he meets new people and new enterprises with the impulsiveness by which his boyhood friends remember him. He never seems to me to grow older. His fresh color and sandy hair and quick-changing blue eyes are those of a young man, and his sym- (50) pathetic, solicitous interest in women is as youthful as it is Western and American.

During that burning day when we were crossing Iowa, our talk kept returning to a central figure, a Bohemian girl whom we had known long ago and whom both of us admired. More than any other person we remembered, this girl seemed to mean to us the country, the conditions, the whole adventure of our childhood. To speak her (55) name was to call up pictures of people and places, to set a quiet drama going in one's brain. I had lost sight of her altogether, but Jim had found her again after long years, had renewed a friendship that meant a great deal to him, and out of his busy life had set apart time enough to enjoy that friendship. His mind was full of her that day. He made me see her again, feel her presence, revived all my old affection for her.

(60) "I can't see," he said impetuously, "why you have never written anything about Antonía."

1. As it is used in the passage, the term "freemasonry" (line 15) refers to:
   A. a trade organization.
   B. a common bond.
   C. an ancient brotherhood.
   D. a set of rituals.

2. All of the following details describing Jim Burden's wife refer to her personal qualities EXCEPT:

F. "she is handsome, energetic, executive" (line 30).

G. "she was a restless, headstrong girl" (line 25).

H. "she had been brutally jilted by her cousin" (lines 23–24).

J. "she was always doing something unexpected" (line 26).

3. A reasonable description of Jim Burden, based on the passage, could contain all of the following adjectives EXCEPT:

A. young-at-heart.

B. impulsive.

C. adventurous.

D. temperamental.

4. The title of the novel, *My Antonia*, probably refers to:

F. the narrator.

G. the Bohemian girl.

H. Jim's Burden's wife.

J. Rutland Whitney.

5. Which of the following choices best describes the narrator's attitude toward Jim Burden and his wife, respectively?

A. Indignant toward him and surprised by her

B. Soothed by him and admiring of her

C. Complimentary of him and critical of her

D. Shocked by him and disapproving of her

6. The passage establishes that the narrator and Jim have all of the following traits in common EXCEPT:

F. an interest in legal matters.

G. an established life in New York City.

H. an intimate knowledge of the Great Plains region.

J. a common fondness for a woman in their past.

7. The central purpose of this passage is to:

A. establish two characters caught in a bad marriage.

B. assess the intelligence of a powerful attorney.

C. provide a vivid description of Nebraska.

D. establish two characters linked by past experiences.

8. The primary function of the first paragraph is to:

F. establish a tone that is later contradicted.

G. lay groundwork for the passage's central conflict.

H. establish setting and mood.

J. describe the pleasures of train travel.

9. The narrator would probably agree with which of the following statements about Jim Burden?
   A. He is a solid husband but a careless businessman.
   B. He has achieved success but has forgotten his past.
   C. He is an amusing man who has planned his life carefully.
   D. He is a romantic individual who has retained his youthfulness.

10. All of the following details suggest that Genevieve and Jim do not have a close marriage EXCEPT:
   F. separate sources of income.
   G. separate interests.
   H. differing levels of enthusiasm for projects.
   J. Jim's interest in other women.

Answers Explained

1. **(B)** This question asks you to define a word given a certain context. While knowledge of the word helps, paying close attention to context and substituting a word of your own may be more efficient. The lines immediately above line 15 establish the context of the word *freemasonry* in the passage: "We agreed that no one who had not grown up in a little prairie town could know anything about it" (lines 14–15). These lines suggest that "growing up in a little prairie town" is a secret understanding that can only be had by people who actually lived the experience. The connection between the narrator and Jim establishes the context for the word *freemasonry*. Next, substitute your own word for the word *freemasonry*. It [growing up in a little prairie town] was a kind of special *connection*. Option A makes little sense unless you associate the word *mason*, which refers to a type of trade, with a trade group. Option B fits well given the idea that the two characters share a common "bond" or understanding of growing up in a small prairie town. Option C refers to the word in its historical sense; the Freemasons are indeed a longstanding fraternal organization. However, the term is not used literally in this context; the narrator uses the term figuratively to emphasize her bond with Jim Burden. Option D alludes to the rituals associated with Freemasons, which, although accurate in a sense, don't relate to the word as it is used here.

2. **(H)** This question really is as easy as it looks. Because you have every line reference in front of you, you may not even need to look back at the passage. Simply determine for yourself which line *does not* seem to represent a personal quality. *Handsome, energetic,* and *executive* do refer to personal qualities, as do *restless* and *headstrong,* so rule out options F and G. Option H refers to the character being jilted by her cousin. Whether or not you can define *jilted* is irrelevant here. Although it helps to know that *jilted* is another word for "dumped," realizing that the action is completed by someone other than Jim Burden's wife is enough to tell you that the phrase does not refer to her personal qualities. Anyone can be jilted, regardless of personality. Option H makes sense. Option J refers to Jim Burden's wife's impulsive nature: a personal characteristic. Rule out J.

3. **(D)** This one is tough because it requires you to prove three separate aspects of Jim's character, just so you can disprove one. Consider saving this question until you have finished all other questions for this passage. Whatever you do, don't spend inordinate amounts of time on it. If your general sense of his character helps you, use it to your advantage. The phrase "he never seems to me to grow older" (line 48) alludes to his being young at heart,

so rule out option A. Lines 46–48 refer to Jim's impulsiveness, and lines 44 and 45 refer to his adventurous spirit by depicting him as he "goes off into the wilds hunting for lost parks or exploring new canyons." These details disprove options B and C. Line 31 refers to Jim's wife as temperamental, but nowhere do we get the idea that Jim shares this quality.

4. **(G)** Two simple inferences should help you narrow this question down in a hurry. First, the narrator mentions the name *Antonía* to Jim immediately following a paragraph where she states her affection for a "bohemian girl." This juxtaposition suggests that the last line of dialog refers to the same girl. Second, the term *My* placed before *Antonía* in the title implies a certain amount of affection for her held by either the narrator, Jim, or both. Option F makes little sense, because the narrator refers to Antonía directly in the final line of the passage. Option G makes sense given the previous inferences. Option H is unlikely: Because Jim Burden's wife is depicted as unsympathetic, it is unlikely that the narrator would attach an affectionate term like *my* when referring to her. Rutland Whitney, option J, has a different name altogether and therefore is an illogical choice.

5. **(C)** This question has two-sided answer choices, so narrow your options by looking at one side first. The left-hand adjectives refer to the narrator's opinion of Jim: *indignant, soothed, complimentary,* and *shocked*. The narrator shows neither angry disbelief nor shock at Jim, so rule out options A and D. Now address the leftover options on the right side, which refer to the narrator's opinion of Jim's wife: *admiring* and *critical*. Because the narrator states that she dislikes Jim's wife and spends nearly two full paragraphs criticizing her, rule out *admiring*.

6. **(F)** This detail question requires you again to prove three options correct in order to disprove one. Option F is shaky: While Jim is an attorney, nowhere does it state that the narrator has an interest in the law. Line 16, which states, "Jim Burden and I both live in New York," helps rule out option G. Lines 8–15 refer to both characters' intimate knowledge of Nebraska, part of the Great Plains, which allows you to rule out option H. The final two paragraphs of the section disprove option J, as both characters clearly feel affectionate toward a woman in their past.

7. **(D)** This "main point" question requires you to have a general sense of the passage, the "O" in the "COST" acronym. Option A is unlikely to be the answer: Although Jim's marriage seems questionable, the narrator mentions nothing of her own. Aside from a slight inkling that the narrator has feelings for Jim, the reader can glean no proof that her marriage is in trouble. While the narrator alludes to Jim's talents as an attorney (option B), this information is merely a character detail and not the main idea. The description of Nebraska (option C) establishes setting and mood but falls short of being a "main point" of the passage. Option D, "establish two characters linked by past experiences," makes sense. The bulk of the passage describes these two characters, their long friendship, and their common interests and affections.

8. **(H)** Understanding the literary elements of tone, conflict, and mood is important when answering this question. Tone in fiction refers to the narrator's attitude. Although her friendly, approving attitude—at least toward Jim—is established in paragraph 1 (option F), it stays consistent throughout the passage. Option G, although it may seem reasonable at first, is not the answer because paragraph 1 does little to set up the central conflict in the passage, which is the narrator's dislike of Jim's wife. Mood refers to the emotional feel of the passage. The detail about the geography of Nebraska in paragraph 1 estab-

lishes the setting. This vivid description also creates mood with phrases such as "burning summers," "stifled in vegetation," "stripped bare," and "gray as sheet-iron." While the passage mentions train travel (option J), describing the pleasures of the train ride is not the primary purpose of the paragraph.

9. **(D)** This question requires you to make an inference based on your understanding of the narrator. Luckily, the entire passage is told from the narrator's point of view, so you have plenty of evidence with which to work. If you can establish that the narrator's attitude toward Jim is positive, that she admires and is even a little smitten with him, then you can assume that her statements about him would fit the same mold. Would she call him *careless* (option A)? Probably not—in fact she clearly admires his business acumen. The first and last paragraphs both disprove option B; the narrator clearly sees Jim as one who reveres and even yearns for his past. The narrator's characterization of Jim as impulsive (line 47) refutes option C. The narrator calls Jim "naturally romantic" (line 36) and also states that he "never seems to me to grow older" (line 48).

10. **(H)** This question also asks you to draw a conclusion based on specific details. Genevieve has "her own fortune" (line 34), which could suggest that their marriage is distant in the financial sense. Rule out option F. Jim and his wife seem to live separate lives, with differing interests and schedules (option G), which could also suggest a marriage that isn't close. Both Jim and Genevieve take on projects with energy and enthusiasm—this trait really doesn't differ in them—which makes option H seem like the answer. Paragraph 4 refers to Jim's "solicitous" interest in women (line 50), a characteristic that could strain his marriage. This tendency, coupled with his demonstrative affection for Antonía, suggests that he might not be completely loyal to his wife. Rule out option J.

Comparative Reading

The ACT Reading test will most likely include at least one set of questions that requires you to consider two passages at once. Passages will be labeled "Passage A" and "Passage B." Questions will begin with a few questions for Passage A, then a few questions for Passage B, and finally a few questions that ask you to compare passages.

Strategically, approach these passages the same way you would approach an individual passage, with one exception: consider reading one passage and answer *its* questions before reading the second passage and addressing the rest.

Sample Comparative Reading Passages

The following passages were adapted from two stories by Pete Carnes, "A Day to Forget" and "A Day to Remember" (2018). Reprinted with permission from the author.

PASSAGE A

Trevor hastily threw his 6'4" swallowtail and wetsuit into the back of his pickup and loaded his twin toddlers into their car seats. Pulling out of his apartment building in Carlsbad, he tore south on the PCH to drop the kids at daycare. On the way, he noticed
Line that Swami's was uncrowded and decided to surf there rather than his original plan,
(5) Turtle's, a reef just to the south. Not as great a wave, but usually free of kooks and grommets. After a tense conversation with Susan, the daycare lady, Trevor headed to Swami's.
"Dang it!" he cursed as he circled the parking lot hunting for a vacant spot. After three

loops, he resigned himself to parking on the highway. Trevor struggled to force his left foot through the tight wetsuit leg, ultimately kicking the asphalt and stubbing the hell

(10) out of his big toe. He dropped a loud series of curses, wiped away the blood with angry hands, and headed down the stairs. A crew of high school kids followed him, eager to catch as many waves as possible during their 90-minute Surf P.E. class. "Spoiled brats," he said aloud as he paddled past them, jealously fuming that his high school hadn't offered such a choice elective when he was there.

(15) When he reached the lineup, Trevor was distracted by three girls, early 20s, laughing gleefully during a lull between sets of waves. *Stupid chicks better not get in my way.* He took off on the first wave that popped up, snaking a few guys who'd been in position before he was. He took waves; others shared. Trevor didn't care. He'd grown up here in North County, and no yuppie transplant was gonna take his waves. Paddling back out

(20) after his first wave, Trevor cut off one of the kids, causing the boy to fall straight into the shallows of the limestone reef. Back in the lineup, the boy approached him. "What was that for, Grandpa? Plenty of room to paddle around wide." Trevor grabbed the kid by the neck and shoved his head under water for a few seconds before pulling it up violently. "Go back to the beach, kook!"

(25) The rest of his session was an exercise in similar frustration. Trevor took more than his fair share of waves, but took no joy in the taking. Nor the riding. Nor the absolute beauty of the day. Nor the pleasant kindness of three pretty ladies trading waves and giggling with the laughter that accompanies a healthy coffee buzz. His mind was elsewhere. Trevor realized that he wouldn't see his wife awake for the next three days thanks to their mismatched

(30) work schedules. He felt the bile of anger rise in his throat. He was always angry.

As Trevor was changing out of his wetsuit and into his official Hilton bartender uniform, the high schoolers slowed down beside his truck and shouted at him, "Have a nice day, jerk!"

PASSAGE B

The drive down Birmingham Road revealed a clean west swell filing in, head-high waves peeling along San Elijo Reef across a perfectly glassy Pacific Ocean. Nathan wiggled his 4Runner through the tiny coastal town of Cardiff-by-the-Sea and headed north on the

Line PCH. After a mile, he turned left into the parking lot at Swami's, his favorite wave in SoCal.
(5) Actually, everybody's favorite wave in SoCal. More than a few times, Nathan had counted over eighty surfers in the water here. It got that good. A 400-yard reef break that broke on any swell direction, handled all swells large and small, and could accommodate a crowd. But this day, a Tuesday, 9:00 A.M. was the perfect time to show up. With the dawn patrollers already gone and the lunch crowd yet to arrive, there were only about fifteen people out.

(10) Nathan didn't have to teach his American Lit class until noon, and UCSD was only a twenty-minute drive south. His students were used to him showing up with his hair still wet, a hint of dried saltwater on his face, and flip-flops slapping the lecture-hall floor as he paced.

After pulling on his wetsuit, Nathan descended the 112 stairs down the cliff and stretched a bit before paddling out. From the entry point, it was a long haul to the lineup

(15) at the top of the headland, but he took his time, feeling the painful joy of each stroke as his lats and deltoids loosened up. *I need to get to yoga more often*, he admonished himself. Once settled in position, Nathan exchanged pleasantries with a few familiar faces. His former boss at Sunset Surfboards paddled over to say hello and ask how the new teaching gig was going. "Well, the money stinks, but I love the hours!" As he turned

(20) to focus his attention on the horizon, Nathan felt completely at peace. The ascending

sun warmed his back, and the reflection on the cool water mesmerized him. Politely
waiting his turn, he hooted happily as his friend Scott dropped into a perfect wave and
immediately pulled in behind the curtain of cascading water, racing through the barrel
for a solid ten seconds before emerging to smack the lip. He felt the spray rain down on
(25) his head as Scott continued down the line.

Nathan's first wave was just as good, as were the nineteen that followed.

Catching twenty waves in two hours was rare at Swami's, but today was a rare day.
Everything felt right; he even got a smiley "Good morning!" from three women as he
passed them on the stairs. Nathan watched them paddle out while he peeled off his wet-
(30) suit in the parking lot. *Maybe I'll see them out here again. And maybe introduce yourself*
next time, dummy.

He strode into class beaming, stoked at the wonders of another day in paradise.

Questions 1–4 pertain to Passage A.

1. It is reasonable to infer from the passage that all of the following aspects of Trevor's life
   have influenced his mood EXCEPT:
   A. the difficulty of preparing to go surfing.
   B. the pressures of raising young children.
   C. a crowded surfing venue.
   D. disagreements with his spouse.

2. Paragraph 1 establishes all of the following EXCEPT:
   F. Trevor's favorite surf spot is called "Swami's."
   G. Trevor has difficulty parking at his surf spot.
   H. Trevor ends up sharing his surf spot with a large group of high school students.
   J. Trevor struggles to dress for surfing.

3. Which of the following statements about people is supported by the passage?
   A. Unrealistic expectations about experiences and interactions can be made better if
      one adopts a positive attitude.
   B. Negative mindsets can often make seemingly enjoyable experiences less enjoyable.
   C. Being surrounded by youthful exuberance can bring out frustrations in people.
   D. Dissatisfying work experiences are often to blame for one's demeanor during lei-
      sure time.

4. The phrase "Trevor didn't care. He'd grown up here..." (line 18) is most likely meant to:
   F. reflect the excitement Trevor feels as he prepares to surf.
   G. illustrate Trevor's disappointment in the quality of surfing on this particular day.
   H. express Trevor's awe that the circumstances of his life allow him to spend time at
      the ocean.
   J. justify in Trevor's mind his inconsiderate behavior toward the other surfers.

Questions 5–7 pertain to Passage B.

5. According to the passage, Nathan shows appreciation for all of the following EXCEPT:
   A. the timing of his arrival at Swami's.
   B. the exercise he gets while warming up to surf.
   C. the wages he earns as a college professor.
   D. the other surfers with whom he gets to share his experience.

6. The line "Well, the money stinks, but I love the hours!" (line 19) characterizes Nathan by showing that he:
   F. values time over money despite not being able to support himself financially.
   G. has a self-deprecating sense of humor that likely endears him to others.
   H. keeps in touch with former co-workers even after he has assumed other jobs.
   J. fails to see the value in seeing his friends accomplish difficult, satisfying tasks.

7. Which of the following phrases most directly illustrates the overall tone of the passage?
   A. "Actually, everybody's favorite wave in SoCal" (line 5).
   B. "... it was a long haul to the lineup at the top of the headland ..." (lines 14–15).
   C. "... Nathan felt completely at peace" (line 20).
   D. "Nathan's first wave was just as good" (line 26).

Questions 8–10 pertain to both passages A and B.

8. Which of the following statements most accurately characterizes the tone of each passage?
   F. Passage A is wistfully sentimental while Passage B is detached and cynical.
   G. Passage A is contemptuous and pessimistic while Passage B is buoyant and serene.
   H. Both passages convey a sense of wonder toward nature but conclude gloomily.
   J. Both passages begin with the narrator anticipating events and conclude with a sense of pride.

9. Above all, reading Passage A and Passage B together creates the sense that:
   A. one's attitude about a series of events is likely to affect how one experiences and remembers those events.
   B. a desire to influence the behavior of others can sometimes allow people to control their environment positively.
   C. if a person decides to participate in a job he loves, he or she is likely to benefit financially over the long term.
   D. if a person stops worrying about the outcome of an event before the event happens, that person is likely to enjoy the event in the end.

10. It can reasonably be inferred that after surfing, Trevor, in contrast to Nathan, feels:
    F. relieved that he had been able to fit in some leisure time before having to go to work.
    G. somehow unsatisfied despite having engaged in one of his favorite activities.
    H. excited to pick up his children from daycare and spend some quality time with his family.
    J. flustered to have to get to work, as he did not have much time to get there.

Answers Explained

1. **(D)** First of all, remember that "EXCEPT" questions often require more effort and patience because it is necessary to eliminate three good options as opposed to finding just one. Although there is some indication of family stress in Trevor's life, no evidence exists to support the idea of conflict with his wife specifically. By contrast, the passage suggests that Trevor wishes he could see his wife more often, making option D the correct answer. Option A is incorrect; clearly Trevor is frustrated after his difficulty parking and struggles to put on his wetsuit. Option B is incorrect, as evidenced by the tense conversation with the day care worker in line 6, which implies the pressures of raising children. Option C is incorrect because Trevor has more than one combative reaction to other surfers sharing the surfing venue with him.

2. **(F)** The passage explicitly states that Swami's is "not as great a wave," (line 5) suggesting that he prefers another spot, making option F the correct answer. Option G is incorrect because of the line ". . . he cursed as he circled the parking lot hunting for a vacant spot" (line 7). Option H is incorrect because of the specific reference of the high school class in paragraph 1. Option J is incorrect because of the specific description in paragraph one of Trevor struggling to get dressed for surfing.

3. **(B)** In order to answer this question correctly, you must make multiple inferences based on events in the story. Option B is the correct answer because a reasonable reader could assume that, through Trevor's bad day, the author is trying to make a point about how one's attitude impacts experience. Trevor's day seems to go from bad to worse, and the reader assumes that his attitude is likely to take almost any experience from pleasant to unenjoyable. Option A is incorrect because of the phrase "can be made better." At no point in the story does the author suggest that Trevor's day will improve. Option C is incorrect because there is no indication that the young people sharing the surf venue with Trevor are actually causing his poor mood; by contrast, they are by all indications minding their own business, except when Trevor confronts them. Option D is incorrect because, although the author alludes to a possibly monotonous job through the description of the bartender's uniform, not enough detail is provided for the reader to reasonably assume that Trevor dislikes his job.

4. **(J)** In order to answer this question correctly, you must have an understanding of both tone and context. Option J is correct because a reader can reasonably assume that Trevor uses his "local" status to rationalize being rude; some part of him feels entitled to surf in this particular spot without being bothered by people who have recently moved to California. Option F is incorrect because it doesn't match the tone of the passage: at no point does Trevor express "excitement" to surf. Option G is incorrect because no details exist in the passage to support the idea that the surfing conditions are subpar. Option H is incorrect because the word "awe" expresses an appreciation or reverence for surfing that Trevor simply does not express. By contrast, he is disappointed and frustrated while surfing.

5. **(C)** Recall that "EXCEPT" questions require more effort since it is necessary to eliminate the three good options before finding the exception. Option C is the correct answer because Nathan suggests while chatting with his friend that he likes his job despite its low pay: "Well, the money stinks, but I love the hours!" (line 19). Option A is proven incorrect by the line "9:00 A.M. was the perfect time to show up" (line 8).

Option B is incorrect because of the line "feeling the painful joy of each stroke as his lats and deltoids loosened up" (lines 15–16). Option D is incorrect because Nathan's exchange of "pleasantries" (line 17) shows that he enjoys sharing the experience with the few other surfers around him.

6. **(G)** In order to answer this question correctly, a reader is required to sense a certain degree of verbal irony in Nathan's tone. Option G is the correct answer because of context and tone: Nathan's obviously friendly relationship with his former boss, coupled with the fact that he tells a joke at his own expense (at least in terms of how much he earns as a college professor). Option F is incorrect because no details in the passage suggest that Nathan struggles financially to the extent that he isn't self-sufficient. Option H is incorrect because, although Nathan has a friendly relationship with his former boss, no evidence exists in the passage to suggest that the two people "keep in touch." Option J is incorrect because the passage describes Nathan watching his friend Scott (line 22) surf and showing appreciation for what he does.

7. **(C)** Answering this question correctly hinges on the phrase "illustrates the overall tone": the correct answer reflects the general attitude of the passage directly. Option C is correct because of its prominence in the passage. In short, this phrase represents the peacefulness within Nathan as reflected in his approach to surfing. Option A is incorrect because, although it has positive connotations, it doesn't directly reflect the overall tone or message of the passage. Option B is incorrect because it simply illustrates the hard work Nathan is willing to put in to achieve a sense of peace. Option D is incorrect because it describes a specific moment in the passage. Although it contributes to the positive tone in the passage, it does not illustrate tone directly.

8. **(G)** In order to answer this question correctly, you are required to sense tone in each passage and to discern the variance in tone between the two. Furthermore, this question tests your vocabulary. Option G is the correct answer because "contemptuous and pessimistic" more or less means "angry and negative," which perfectly describes Trevor's demeanor. By the same token, "buoyant and serene" means "light and peaceful," which describes Nathan's experience perfectly. Option F is incorrect for several reasons, but most obviously because no reasonable reader would describe Nathan in Passage B as "detached and cynical." Quite the opposite, he is connected and optimistic. Option H is incorrect for at least two reasons: Passage A *does not* "convey a sense of wonder" and Passage B *does not* "conclude gloomily." Option J is incorrect because, while a reasonable reader could conclude that both passages begin with a narrator "anticipating events," only Passage B concludes with the protagonist feeling proud of what he has accomplished. You may have been tempted to rule out options H and J without much thought, simply because the passages represent such contrast. In this case, such a gamble would have paid off, but in general make sure to read each answer choice carefully before choosing an answer.

9. **(A)** In order to answer this question correctly, you must rely on your ability to extrapolate "big picture" themes from plot elements. In addition, you need to understand that these passages are intentionally written about the same topic but from wildly different points of view. Option A is correct because when reading these two passages together thoughtfully, it is clear that one character (Trevor) has a bad day because of a bad attitude, and another character (Nathan) has a joyous day because of his optimism. This

contrast suggests the message described in option A. Option B is incorrect because although Trevor does seem to desire control over several aspects of his life, there is no evidence that he succeeds in gaining that desired control. Option C is incorrect because although both passages describe the jobs characters do when they are not surfing, neither goes into enough detail to support the idea that either character is benefitting significantly in a financial sense. Option D is incorrect because, for one, it is mostly illogical and nonsensical. Furthermore, neither character's experience illustrates the idea that worrying leads to enjoyment.

10. **(G)** This question masquerades as a question about both passages while focusing primarily on Passage A. Furthermore, it relies on your ability to interpret tone. Option G is correct because Trevor leaves his surf spot disappointed, his attitude having destroyed his ability to have fun. Option F is incorrect because, although Trevor has engaged in an activity he seems to enjoy, he does not seem relieved or relaxed once he finishes surfing. Option H is incorrect because, although Trevor may indeed be excited to see his children, no direct evidence exists in the text to show that he is. Option J is incorrect because no evidence exists to support the idea that Trevor is late for work.

FOUR KEYS TO SUCCESS IN FICTION READING

1. Remember: It's only eight minutes of the test. Use your time wisely!
2. Read with purpose. Don't lose focus by letting your imagination wander.
3. Stay at the appropriate level of analysis. Don't over-think, and don't read as though you were about to write an essay.
4. Focus on *COST* or *CAPS*.

COST

- Characters: Look for physical or emotional depiction, relationships, and inner and outer conflicts.
- Overview: Think "theme," "main idea," or "generalization."
- Structure: Know how the passage is built, the purpose of each paragraph and each transition.
- Tone and mood: Note the narrator's attitude and the general emotional feel of the passage.

CAPS

- Characters: Note characters' appearances, thoughts, feelings, actions, relationships, and conflicts.
- Attitude: How do characters come across? How do they see things?
- Problem: Focus on the central problem or issue in the passage and track it.
- Solution: Observe how the central issue in the passage gets resolved.

The Nuances of Nonfiction 15

→ **STRATEGIES FOR APPROACHING NONFICTION PASSAGES**
→ **STRATEGIES FOR APPROACHING NONFICTION QUESTIONS**
→ **PRACTICE PASSAGE: SOCIAL SCIENCE**
→ **PRACTICE PASSAGE: NATURAL SCIENCE**
→ **THE HUMANITIES PASSAGE**
→ **EIGHT STRATEGIES FOR READING NONFICTION**

Three of the four passages on the reading test will qualify as nonfiction, chosen from three different disciplines: humanities, social science, and natural science. These passages test your reading ability with texts seen at the college level. Contrary to most high school English curriculums, the world consists mostly of nonfiction.

STRATEGIES FOR APPROACHING NONFICTION PASSAGES
It's All in the Timing

Many students try the same strategy they use when assigned a textbook reading and questions at the end of a chapter: They read the questions first and then hunt for answers as they read. The ACT Reading test does not allow enough time for this strategy. It is more important to gain a solid understanding of the main ideas and structure of the passage *before* reading the questions. Spend about four minutes reading the passage and four minutes answering the questions. This timing strategy will leave you about three minutes of leeway at the end of the test.

With one brief glance at the section, you will gain a sense of which passage will be the most difficult for you. Practice will also reveal which topics make you the most comfortable. Once you determine which subjects you tend to like the most, choose one of two strategies and stick with it. Your first option is to go from easiest to hardest, which might give you a few extra minutes at the end of the test for the passage that you consider the most challenging. This strategy maximizes the amount of time you focus on passages with which you are comfortable; "rushed" time at the end is spent on difficult questions you might have missed anyway. Your other option is to start with the most difficult passage first and get it out of the way. If you begin with the most challenging passage, watch the clock closely. Don't spend more than eight minutes on the passage before moving on to the next one. You can always come back to it at the end.

> **TIP**
>
> In nonfiction passages, the key is to identify the topic, decipher the main idea, understand the passage's structure, and locate supporting details.

> **INSIDE THE ACT 36 MIND**
>
> Don't read the questions before reading the passage—you simply won't have enough time to search for answers as you read the passage.

Regardless of the order you choose, keep these two points in mind.

1. You *do* have the freedom to complete the questions in any order you'd like!
2. A balanced approach maximizes your score. In other words, it is better to guess on a question or two at the end of a passage for the sake of getting to the next one than it is to miss an entire passage or most of it at the end of the testing period.

See the Big Picture

When approaching a nonfiction passage, gain a broad perspective by zooming all the way out. Look at the length of the passage. Prepare to read by counting the number of paragraphs and noting the number of lines. Next, tell yourself, *I have four minutes to read this passage.* Your brain needs to see the passage as a whole before you begin, and it needs to understand the time constraints involved. Because reading doesn't normally involve such ridiculous time limitations, your brain needs to prepare for the challenge of efficient reading. If you don't prepare mentally, your brain will read in the same way it always does. It will take the time to reread the confusing parts, it will decipher confusing vocabulary using context clues, and it will take extra time focusing in on details that, within the confines of the ACT, just aren't important.

Preheat Your Brain

Prepare to read quickly and actively by attuning your mind to the topic. What is the passage about? The brain stores new information by "linking" it to information it already contains. If you are unable to connect the new information to something you already know, then you won't remember any new information. Focus on the citation of the passage and note the title, if there is one; then, read the first few sentences of the passage. What is the passage about? The moon? The Harlem Renaissance? The history of the samurai sword? What do you already know about the topic? Make a connection to what you already know—even if it is incorrect or obscure. You may think, *The only thing I remember about the samurai sword is that my favorite childhood cartoon character used one while fighting evil sorcerers and demons.* Well, that information is enough to "preheat" your brain. The new information about the samurai sword will now be stored in your brain next to your favorite childhood cartoon character. Even though the organizational system sounds odd, the "preheating" process works. (Note: see the list at the beginning of Chapter 13 to remind yourself how much you know about *every* ACT passage.)

Clear Your Mind

This strategy may sound contradictory considering that you were just told to fill your mind with connections to the topic. Keep your connections intact, but clear your mind of tangential topics that might distract you from the task at hand. Mental distractions hinder your ability to remain "in the zone" while reading the passages. Your mind will wander to the baseball game on TV that you aren't watching because you are studying for the ACT. You might think about your new boyfriend and whether or not he wants to date someone smarter than he is. Sometimes more serious and emotional tangents will invade your mental space while you read.

A wandering mind can be your biggest deterrent in achieving the big 36. Commit to the topic at hand. Tell yourself that you are interested in the samurai sword. Your brain is easily manipulated. If you tell it to do something or think a certain way, it usually will. Remember, you only have to be interested in the topic for eight minutes. Also keep in mind that "indexing," as outlined in Chapter 13, can be a great way to focus yourself if a 1,000-word passage makes your mind swim.

Identify Main Idea and Tone

Once you have preheated your brain, move on to the passage. Be careful not to get preoccupied with the details and examples within the passage. As long as you gain an overall understanding of the arguments in the passage, there is no need to remember the details precisely. Getting bogged down by details causes problems for many students when reading nonfiction passages.

Identify the main idea of the entire passage as a whole and the role of each paragraph in expressing it. Identifying the main idea of a passage often stupefies people, but in reality it is fairly simple. Ask yourself the following questions: *What is the topic of the passage? What is the author saying about the topic?* It won't take you long to identify whether the topic is samurai swords or the life cycle of a butterfly. The next step is to decipher what the author is saying about samurai swords or the life cycle of a butterfly. The author may be trying to express the beautiful craftsmanship of the samurai sword. Or, she could be identifying it as one of the deadliest weapons in history. The purpose of the passage may be stated explicitly in either the introduction or the conclusion. In rare cases, you'll have to infer the main idea of the passage once you have read the passage completely.

Deciphering tone is similar to identifying the main idea. Instead of asking yourself what the author is saying about the topic, ask, *What is the author's attitude toward the topic?* Some reading questions may ask you to infer the author's tone. Is it cautionary? Celebratory? Pensive? Critical? Detached? The author may be warning you about a new contagious disease, or he could be celebrating a new astronomical discovery. Identifying the tone of the passage helps you eliminate answer options. If an answer choice doesn't match the tone of the passage, it's almost always wrong.

REMEMBER

Don't get caught up in the details of a passage. Read for the main idea.

Index the Passage!

The process of indexing is outlined in detail in Chapter 13. Learn and practice this process! Observing and briefly noting the purpose of each paragraph will help immensely when it comes to answering questions efficiently and accurately. Don't forget to learn and practice this invaluable technique!

STRATEGIES FOR APPROACHING NONFICTION QUESTIONS

Guess First, Then Find the Answer

Once you have read the passage using the previous six strategies, move on to the questions. Before reading answer options, come up with an answer on your own. If one of the answer options matches your guess, then that answer is probably correct. If there are two or three options that are similar to your initial response, then at least you have narrowed your options. If you are unable to even guess at the answer, the question will likely take you longer than others. Leave the question until you have finished answering the rest of the questions for that passage.

Key Ideas and Details (55–60%) Know the Types of Questions: "Right There," Inferential, and Craft

Use key words within the question stem to help you locate the correct answer. Some questions are "right there" or literal questions, questions that can be answered by looking in the text to find a specific detail. These answers are easy to find; go back to the text and locate them. **The better your index, the easier it is to locate the section of text that addresses the topic in question.** Some "right there" questions are so easy that you won't need to go back to the text. If you are unsure or hesitant about your answer, look it up. There will always be proof.

INFERENTIAL QUESTIONS (13–18%)

Other questions ask you to make an inference or "educated guess" about something not stated directly. ACT inference questions may give you a line from the text and ask you what the line "suggests" about the author's message, the author's attitude, or the topic in general. Key phrases like "it can be inferred that" and "it is most likely that" also indicate an inferential question.

RHETORIC AND LANGUAGE USE (25–30%)

The ACT also tests your knowledge of vocabulary by asking you what a word means based on its context. Vocabulary-in-context questions are also inference questions because you guess about a word's definition based on surrounding information. The ACT may ask you to differentiate between differing perspectives and tones and to generally assess an author's stylistic decisions.

PRACTICE PASSAGE: SOCIAL SCIENCE

The subsequent social science passage and ten questions that follow it are similar to what you will see on the ACT reading test. Read the passage using the strategies outlined in this chapter, and answer each of the questions independently before moving on to the answer explanations. The answer explanations include more specific strategies for responding to questions, so be sure to read them.

Find a watch or a clock. Try not to spend more than eight minutes reading the passage and answering the questions. Remember to take a step back and see the big picture of the passage. Focus on the title, then index the passage itself. Find the topic and the main idea. Be careful not to read too closely; getting bogged down in details slows you down. In the margins, summarize the main point or key ideas within each paragraph in a few words.

The following passage is taken from the United States Department of State's Bureau of Western Hemisphere Affairs.

History of Chile

About 10,000 years ago, migrating Indians settled in fertile valleys and along the coast of what is now Chile. The Incas briefly extended their empire into what is now northern Chile, but the area's barrenness prevented extensive settlement. The first
Line Europeans to arrive in Chile were Diego de Almagro and his band of Spanish con-
(5) quistadors, who came from Peru seeking gold in 1535. The Spanish encountered hundreds of thousands of Indians from various cultures in the area that modern Chile now occupies. These cultures supported themselves principally through slash-and-burn agriculture and hunting. The conquest of Chile began in earnest in 1540 and was carried out by Pedro de Valdivia, one of Francisco Pizarro's lieutenants, who

(10) founded the city of Santiago on February 12, 1541. Although the Spanish did not find the extensive gold and silver they sought, they recognized the agricultural potential of Chile's central valley, and Chile became part of the Viceroyalty of Peru.

The drive for independence from Spain was precipitated by usurpation of the Spanish throne by Napoleon's brother Joseph in 1808. A national junta in the name (15) of Ferdinand—heir to the deposed king—was formed on September 18, 1810. The junta proclaimed Chile an autonomous republic within the Spanish monarchy. A movement for total independence soon won a wide following. Spanish attempts to reimpose arbitrary rule during what was called the "Reconquista" led to a prolonged struggle.

(20) Intermittent warfare continued until 1817, when an army led by Bernardo O'Higgins, Chile's most renowned patriot, and José de San Martín, hero of Argentine independence, crossed the Andes into Chile and defeated the royalists. On February 12, 1818, Chile was proclaimed an independent republic under O'Higgins's leadership. The political revolt brought little social change, however, (25) and 19th-century Chilean society preserved the essence of the stratified colonial social structure, which was greatly influenced by family politics and the Roman Catholic Church. A strong presidency eventually emerged, but wealthy landowners remained extremely powerful. Toward the end of the 19th century, the government in Santiago consolidated its position in the south by ruthlessly suppressing (30) the Mapuche Indians. In 1881, it signed a treaty with Argentina confirming Chilean sovereignty over the Strait of Magellan. As a result of the War of the Pacific with Peru and Bolivia (1879–83), Chile expanded its territory northward by almost one-third and acquired valuable nitrate deposits, the exploitation of which led to an era of national affluence. Chile established a parliamentary democracy in the late 19th cen- (35) tury, but degenerated into a system protecting the interests of the ruling oligarchy. By the 1920s, the emerging middle and working classes were powerful enough to elect a reformist president, whose program was frustrated by a conservative congress. In the 1920s, Marxist groups with strong popular support arose.

Continuing political and economic instability resulted with the rule of the quasi- (40) dictatorial General Carlos Ibañez (1924–32). When constitutional rule was restored in 1932, a strong middle-class party, the Radicals, emerged. It became the key force in coalition governments for the next 20 years. During the period of Radical Party dominance (1932–52), the state increased its role in the economy.

The 1964 presidential election of Christian Democrat Eduardo Frei-Montalva by (45) an absolute majority initiated a period of major reform. Under the slogan "Revolution in Liberty," the Frei administration embarked on far-reaching social and economic programs, particularly in education, housing, and agrarian reform, including rural unionization of agricultural workers. By 1967, however, Frei encountered increasing opposition from leftists, who charged that his reforms were inadequate, and from con- (50) servatives, who found them excessive. At the end of his term, Frei had accomplished many noteworthy objectives, but he had not fully achieved his party's ambitious goals. In 1970, Senator Salvador Allende, a Marxist and member of Chile's Socialist Party, who headed the "Popular Unity" (UP) coalition of socialists, communists, radicals, and dissident Christian Democrats, won a plurality of votes in a three-way contest and (55) was named President by the Chilean Congress. His program included the nationalization of private industries and banks, massive land expropriation, and collectivization.

Allende's program also included the nationalization of U.S. interests in Chile's major copper mines.

(60) Elected with only 36% of the vote and by a plurality of only 36,000 votes, Allende never enjoyed majority support in the Chilean Congress or broad popular support. Domestic production declined; severe shortages of consumer goods, food, and manufactured products were widespread; and inflation reached 1,000% per annum. Mass demonstrations, recurring strikes, violence by both government supporters and opponents, and widespread rural unrest ensued in response to the general deteriora-

(65) tion of the economy. By 1973, Chilean society had split into two hostile camps.

A military coup overthrew Allende on September 11, 1973. As the armed forces bombarded the presidential palace, Allende reportedly committed suicide. A military government, led by General Augusto Pinochet, took over control of the country. The first years of the regime in particular were marked by serious human rights violations.

(70) A new Constitution was approved by a plebiscite on September 11, 1980, and General Pinochet became President of the Republic for an 8-year term. In its later years, the regime gradually permitted greater freedom of assembly, speech, and association, to include trade union activity. In contrast to its authoritarian political rule, the military government pursued decidedly laissez-faire economic policies. During its 16 years in

(75) power, Chile moved away from economic statism toward a largely free market economy that fostered an increase in domestic and foreign private investment. In a plebiscite on October 5, 1988, General Pinochet was denied a second 8-year term as president. Chileans voted for elections to choose a new president and the majority of members of a two-chamber congress. On December 14, 1989, Christian Democrat Patricio Aylwin,

(80) the candidate of a coalition of 17 political parties called the Concertación, was elected president. Aylwin served from 1990 to 1994 and was succeeded by another Christian Democrat, Eduardo Frei Ruiz-Tagle (son of the previous President), leading the same coalition, for a 6-year term. Ricardo Lagos Escobar of the Socialist Party and the Party for Democracy led the Concertación to a narrower victory in the 2000 presidential

(85) elections. His term ended on March 11, 2006, when President Michelle Bachelet Jeria, of the Socialist Party, took office.

1. The author's use of the word *reportedly* in line 67 in reference to Allende's suicide suggests that:
   A. Allende's suicide was witnessed by the military.
   B. Allende's suicide was never confirmed.
   C. Allende's suicide was falsified.
   D. Allende's suicide never happened.

2. The passage states that the Spanish primarily sought which products when initially conquering Chile?

   I. Gold
   II. Land for agriculture
   III. Silver

   F. I only
   G. I and II only
   H. I and III only
   J. I, II, and III

3. The passage suggests that the history of Chile has been:
   A. one-sided.
   B. peaceful.
   C. turbulent.
   D. democratic.

4. Which of the following reforms were included in Salvador Allende's program to improve Chile while he was the President of the Chilean Congress?

   I. Nationalization of private industries and banks
   II. Massive land expropriation
   III. Nationalization of U.S. interests in Chile's major copper mines

   F. I and II only
   G. II and III only
   H. I and III only
   J. I, II, and III

5. According to the passage, during Allende's governance, which of the following did NOT occur?
   A. Mass demonstrations
   B. Inflation reaching 1,000% per annum
   C. Majority support of his policies
   D. Decline of domestic production

6. In the context of this passage, the word *junta* (line 16) most nearly means:
   F. heroic leader.
   G. governmental council.
   H. conquistador.
   J. together.

7. According to the passage, Chile was declared an independent state in 1818. Why did the revolt that led to this independence result in little social change?

   I. Family politics
   II. Raids by the Mapuche Indians
   III. Influence of the Roman Catholic Church

   A. I only
   B. II only
   C. II and III only
   D. I and III only

8. According to the passage, when Chile's border expanded northward the result was:
   F. the discovery of silver and a resulting era of affluence.
   G. sovereignty over the Strait of Magellan.
   H. the acquisition and exploitation of nitrate deposits.
   J. the acquisition of a fertile agricultural area.

9. According to the author, the government's military rule during the 1980s was not typical because it:
   A. was influenced by the Roman Catholic Church.
   B. expanded the territory of Chile northward.
   C. pursued laissez-faire economic policies.
   D. provided a welfare system for the rural poor.

10. According to the passage, which of the following can NOT be proven true of the government of Chile?
    F. The president can be denied a second term in office.
    G. Chile has had an elected president since the time of Diego de Almagro.
    H. Presidential candidates run for office within a multi-party system.
    J. The government has been overthrown by a military coup.

Strategy Review

Before reviewing the answers and explanations, compare your approach to the text with the following strategies for reading this passage.

1. **SEE THE BIG PICTURE.** Note that the passage is 7 paragraphs and 86 lines long. Allow yourself 4 minutes to get through the passage.

2. **FOCUS.** Read the title and realize that the passage will explore the history of Chile.

3. **PREHEAT.** Before reading, ask yourself, *What do I already know about Chile?* Even if you recently realized that Chile isn't just a soup to eat in the depths of winter, your brain will be ready to accept new information.

4. **CLEAR YOUR MIND.** Clearing your mind of outside distractions is critical. Forget about the D you just received on your biology lab. Forget that there is only one week until prom and you have yet to ask your girlfriend to go with you. Think only about Chile and what you can learn about it by reading this passage.

5. **IDENTIFY MAIN IDEA AND TONE.** While reading, identify the main idea and tone of the passage. Within each era of Chile's history there have been disagreements between different parties, ambitious reform efforts that were not always met with support, and turbulent shifts of power between elected individuals and more authoritarian regimes. The tone of this passage is neutral toward any particular group or era; it is merely informative. The straightforward and informative tone matches the main idea of the passage. What is the author saying about the topic? He wants to describe the shifting and volatile nature of Chile's political history by discussing its leaders, from Chile's beginnings as a country of European interest to its more recent political leaders.

6. **INDEX THE PASSAGE.** While identifying the main idea and tone of the passage, index the passage as well. In the margins, mark the content or purpose of each paragraph. For example:

   - Paragraph 1: Early settlers
   - Paragraph 2: Independence from Spain
   - Paragraph 3: Independent republic
   - Paragraph 4: Radical Party dominance
   - Paragraph 5: Frei and Allende reforms
   - Paragraph 6: Allende's downfall
   - Paragraph 7: Pinochet coup and recent leaders

Your summaries for each paragraph don't have to match these examples. Underlining key names or key words, especially within historical passages with multiple historical figures, can also be effective. But don't overdo it. One problem with underlining key information is that you may get a little "highlight happy" and highlight more than necessary. However, because the question stems often include the names of the leaders, underlining the names within the passage may be helpful when searching for answers.

7. **GUESS FIRST, THEN FIND THE ANSWER.** After reading the question stem, try to answer the question before reading the answer options. If one of the answer options resembles the answer in your mind, you have narrowed down the answer options. Indexing the key ideas of each paragraph helps you locate answers quickly. Use key phrases and words within the question stem and the overall gist of the question to lead you to the correct locations within the index.

Answers Explained

1. **(B)** Use your inference skills to answer this question. First, using your personal understanding of how the word *reportedly* is often used, you may have determined the correct answer immediately. Finding the location of the answer to this question is easy because a line reference is given to you in the question stem (line 67). Read the context surrounding the word *reportedly*: "As the armed forces bombarded the presidential palace, Allende reportedly committed suicide." Think about removing the word from the sentence. Without it, the phrase would read, "Allende committed suicide," which is much more factual. Therefore, the word is being used to indicate that Allende may not have committed suicide and that Pinochet's military may have "reported" that he did to hide the fact that they killed him. Options C and D claim that the suicide never happened, and option A claims that the suicide was witnessed and therefore verified. Because the word *reportedly* indicates that the suicide can be neither confirmed nor denied, these three options are incorrect.

2. **(H)** Questions with multiple variables require more time. Make an educated guess before reading the answer options; trust your memory of the passage's content to eliminate some options. This question asks about the first conquistadors in Chile; therefore, the answer will most likely be in paragraph 1. The phrase "primarily sought" is a key in the question stem, because it eliminates other products that they found after arriving in Chile. Paragraph 1 explains that in 1535 the Spanish conquistadors came from Peru "seeking gold" (line 5). Upon reading this, you might rush to choose option A, which offers "gold" as the correct response. Be careful! Later in the paragraph, in lines 11 and 12, the author explains that gold and silver were sought by the Spanish conquistadors, which makes option III a correct response. It wasn't until after the Spanish arrived in Chile that they discovered the profitability of the land; therefore, option G does not work.

3. **(C)** There is no place to "find" any of the answer options explicitly stated within the text; instead, the question relies on your sense of the passage as a whole. First, attempt to eliminate answer options. Option A, "one-sided," logically doesn't make sense because of the many different groups vying for power within Chile. Option B seems unlikely because there are frequent references to violence during Chile's progression as a country. Options C and D make the most sense. Because of the multiple references within the passage to

Chile's democratic process of voting, you may have been tempted to choose option D. However, option C is the best response because of the many ups and downs apparent in Chile's history and because not every era of Chile's history has been democratic.

4. **(J)** The key phrase within the question stem is "Allende's program." Refer to the index and note that the introduction of Allende's program is in paragraph 5. The ACT likes to test your ability to remember details located within a list. Line 71 introduces the details of Allende's program. Three items are included in the list: "nationalization of private industries and banks, massive land expropriation, and collectivization." Two of these items are on the list within the question stem, so you know that at least I and III are correct. When skimming quickly, your brain may stop at the end of that sentence. By continuing on to the next sentence you'll notice that the author adds another detail to the list, "the nationalization of U.S. interests in Chile's major copper mines." I, II, and III are each part of Allende's program; therefore, J is correct. Read the surrounding context to confirm the correct answer.

5. **(C)** Read the question stem carefully. Notice the word *NOT*! Then, by looking at your index, recognize that paragraphs 5 and 6 mention Allende. This question, again, tests your understanding of lists of details. Throughout paragraph 6, an inventory of negative details are given about the results of Allende's governance. One option for answering this question is to comb the details to identify which of the answer options did NOT happen during Allende's regime. Another approach is to look at the answer options again and eliminate some of them. Three of the four options are negative results of Allende's leadership: options A, B, and D. Option C stands out as you review the answer options. Logically, if, according to paragraph 6, the result of Allende's governance is primarily negative, Allende would probably not have gained "majority support of his policies" (option C). Early in the paragraph (line 60) the author introduces the description of Allende's governance by explaining that Allende *did not* enjoy majority support. Because the phrase "majority support" comes directly from the text, this option is distracting. Unless you remember the word *NOT* when reading the phrase "majority support," you might assume that this option is correct as well. Option C is the only response that works.

6. **(G)** Vocabulary-in-context questions are easily answered by replacing the word in question with the answer options and deciding which option works best. The word *junta* appears twice in the passage. Consider the original sentence in lines 14–15: "*A national ___ in the name of Ferdinand—heir to the deposed king—was formed on September 18, 1810.*"

- A national *heroic leader* in the name of Ferdinand . . .

    This option works if you only consider the first half of the sentence. Include the rest of the sentence to make an informed decision: A national *heroic leader* in the name of Ferdinand . . . was formed . . . A national heroic leader can't "be formed" as the rest of the sentence suggests.

- A national *governmental council* . . . was formed . . .

    This option makes the most sense so far and probably fits with your initial assessment of the word's definition. Check the other options just to be certain.

- Option H: A national *conquistador* . . . was formed . . .

- Option J: A national *together* . . . was formed . . .

  Again, you can't "form" a *conquistador* or a *together*, just as you can't "form" a *heroic leader* (option F).

Another strategy is to analyze the function of the original word within the sentence or passage. The word *junta* is used as a noun. Ask yourself: *What actions did the junta perform or what actions did it receive?* First of all, it was "formed" by the government (line 15), and second of all, it made a "proclamation" (line 16). Which of the options can be formed and also make a proclamation? Option G, "a governmental council," is the only option that makes logical sense. Don't be fooled by your understanding of the word *junta* in Spanish, which sounds a little like the word for "together," *juntos.* Context is always more important, because more often than not you will be tested on a word that has multiple possible meanings.

7. **(D)** The most helpful part of the question stem is the date. The passage's chronological order makes it easy to locate 1818 within the passage (paragraph 3, line 23) and quickly read the surrounding area. The passage explains that the "political revolt brought little social change" because of the "stratified colonial social structure." Because "stratified colonial social structure" is not one of the options, keep reading. The "stratified colonial social structure" was "influenced by family politics and the Roman Catholic Church," both of which are options within the question. Option D is the correct response. II is only included as a distraction. Your memory of the passage and your logical thinking might suggest that raids by Indians would certainly cause a society to become stagnant. Within the context of the passage, however, there is no "cause and effect" link between Indian raids and social change. Find the correct answer within the passage if you have any doubts about your initial response.

8. **(H)** If you haven't noticed by now, ACT answer options often contain phrases that can be found word for word in the text, as in option G, "sovereignty over the Strait of Magellan." Your ability to remember a phrase from the text is not enough to give you the correct answer. Make sure the phrase is associated with the question stem. You may be tempted to choose the first response that you remember seeing in the passage. Answer options always include distracting choices that can trick you. Another trick the ACT uses is making one word within the answer option incorrect, as in option F. When Chile's borders expanded northward, its people did not find *silver*, they found *nitrates*. Each incorrect answer option plays on the words used within the text. When you have found the area of the passage that talks about Chile expanding its territory northward, you will notice a few key words that are used in other answer options as distracters: *affluence* and *acquisition.* If you don't read carefully, one of them could trick you into choosing that response because it "sounds" like something that comes directly from the text. Lines 33–36 give you the correct information about Chile's northward expansion, making H the correct response.

9. **(C)** Your background knowledge may help you eliminate a couple of answer options immediately. The phrase "not typical" along with its description of "military rule" can guide your elimination process. Most governments ruled by the military tend to restrict the behavior of their citizens and discourage free thought and action. For this reason, options C, "pursued laissez-faire economic policies," and D, "provided a welfare system for the rural poor," would be more atypical of a militaristic government than the other

options. Also, many governments controlled by a dominant religious group have spent time expanding the territory of the country they govern; therefore, option A, "was influenced by the Roman Catholic Church," and B, "expanded the territory of Chile northward," might actually be typical of a militaristic government. Whether your background knowledge helps you narrow down the options or not, you will still need to find the correct answer within the passage. The date included in the question helps locate the correct response. Skim the passage to find the 1980s, which are mentioned in paragraph 7. In order to answer this question correctly, you have to sift through quite a bit of text. The first half of the paragraph discusses Pinochet's militaristic government and its negative impact on Chile. The phrase "in *contrast* to its authoritarian political rule," located in line 82, identifies any other governmental actions mentioned as not typical of an authoritarian government. Even if you don't know that laissez-faire economic policy means that the government takes a "hands-off" approach, you will still be able to identify option C as the correct response.

10. **(G)** Complicated questions like this one force you to think about the passage as a whole. Sifting through the appropriate details takes time. Read the question stem carefully; don't let that tricky word *NOT* throw you off course. Eliminate answer options that you know are true, and then work on the other options. Options F and J are confirmed true in paragraph 7. Line 66 indicates that a military coup took over the government, which eliminates option J, and lines 76–77 explain that Pinochet was denied a second term as president, eliminating option F. Option H can be proven true as well; throughout the passage, multiple political parties, including Socialists, Communists, and Christian Democrats, are mentioned. The validity of option G is more difficult to determine. The passage refers to multiple presidential elections. The key word in this option is *Diego de Almagro*. Refer to the section of text that discusses Almagro and work your way forward. After Almagro, the passage introduces Valdivia and O'Higgins. The passage does not claim that either figure was president and doesn't mention any elections surrounding their rise to power. Later in the same paragraph, you learn that a parliamentary democracy was established. From that information, you can infer that presidential elections only occurred after Valdivia and O'Higgins. There is not enough information to confirm that option G, "Chile has had an elected president since the time of Diego de Almagro," is true of the Chilean government.

PRACTICE PASSAGE: NATURAL SCIENCE

Natural science passages can be more difficult for many readers because they contain more scientific jargon or technical vocabulary than other passages. Use the context of the passage to figure out the gist of the message. Details may drag you down. Read only to identify the main ideas and the structure of the passage.

STRATEGY REMINDERS

- See the big picture. Notice the length of the passage and look at the number of paragraphs. Prepare mentally to read it in four minutes.
- Focus. Identify the topic by focusing on the title and skimming the first paragraph to look for clues.
- Preheat. What do you already know about this topic?
- Clear your mind. Focus on the topic at hand and only on the topic.
- Identify main idea and tone while indexing the passage. Summarize the focus of each paragraph in the margins. Identify the main idea of the passage by asking yourself, *What is the author saying about the topic*? Identify the tone of the passage by asking yourself, *What is the author's attitude toward the topic*?
- Index the passage by pausing after each paragraph and writing a 2–3 word summary of the paragraph's main point in the margin.

The following passage is adapted from the United States Department of Agriculture Forest Service's report titled "Forest Issues and Disease Conditions in the United States."

Emerald Ash Borer

The emerald ash borer (EAB) (*Agrilus planipennis* Fairmaire) is a nonnative insect originally from Japan, Korea, Taiwan, northeast China, and adjacent parts of Russia. It was unknown on the North American continent until its discovery in the Detroit, Michigan, area in July of 2002. Subsequent surveys showed that a large area of infes-
(5) tation was present, covering at least six counties surrounding Detroit. This "core" area was put under quarantine in the fall of 2002. Infestations were also discovered across the border in Windsor, Ontario, Canada. Following further surveys in 2003, the quarantine was expanded to 13 counties, and by fall 2004 the quarantine included 20 Michigan counties and Lucas County in northwest Ohio. A number of scattered
(10) isolated infestations outside of the quarantine area occur in the lower peninsula of Michigan and northeastern Indiana. It appears that these sites have been present for several years and probably represent introductions via infested ash firewood, logs, or nursery material.

The EAB infests walnuts and elms in its native habitat. In North America, EAB is
(15) found (so far) only on ash (*Fraxinus* spp.), an abundant tree species in urban areas, rural woodlots, and riparian areas.

To contain further spread of EAB in Canada, government officials cut and destroyed all of the ash trees in a 30-km × 10-km zone extending from Lake St. Clair to Lake Erie. This "ash free" zone, in concert with an aggressive regulatory program
(20) to prevent the artificial movement of infested ash material out of the infested area,

is intended to contain the existing infestation so that effective eradication activities can be implemented.

In Michigan and Ohio, EAB infestations are too extensive and numerous to be contained with the kind of "ash free" zones implemented by the Canadians. Instead management efforts have shifted to containment of EAB in the lower peninsula of Michigan and neighboring Lucas County in northwest Ohio by focusing survey, eradication, and ash reduction efforts in key "Gateway Areas." These gateways include northern Michigan south of the Mackinac Straits, St. Clair County just across the river from Canada, and along the borders with Ohio and Indiana.

Initially little was known about EAB biology and habits. Studies and evaluations have been underway since 2002 to investigate host range, biology, trap designs and possible attractants, and control options. Our understanding of EAB is improving but still limited. Control options are also limited; wood-boring insects are notoriously difficult to kill with insecticides once they bore under the bark or into the wood of trees.

The USDA Forest Service is an integral partner, along with the Animal and Plant Health Inspection Service (APHIS) and State authorities, in the EAB containment and eradication effort, providing scientific and technical expertise, including survey, restoration, and public outreach and communications assistance. In 2004, the USDA Forest Service implemented EAB surveys on Federal and State forest lands in Michigan and on public and private forest lands in nearly 20 Eastern States. Special emphasis was placed on areas of known ash decline, around nurseries, and in areas where firewood introductions were likely. EAB detection surveys will continue and be expanded to other States in 2005. The USDA Forest Service also supports and conducts critical technology development activities with university and research cooperators to advance our understanding of EAB biology and dispersal habits, chemical control tactics, management strategies, survey techniques, and monitoring, among others.

Ash trees throughout southern Michigan had exhibited decline and dieback symptoms for years. "Ash yellows," a condition caused by a mycoplasmalike organism (MLO), was prevalent in the area and was one of the presumed causes. Ash yellows and another malady referred to as ash decline were so prevalent that dying ash trees did not draw close scrutiny. EAB has killed millions of ash trees so far and has the potential to decimate the more than 800 million ash trees in Michigan forests. Ash species are common across the Great Lakes region and the Northeastern United States. Ash is also a common roadside, shade, and yard tree. No ash species appear to be resistant to EAB infestation and mortality. EAB appears capable of infesting and killing much of the ash across North America.

Scientists estimate that EAB had been in the United States for perhaps 5–10 years prior to its detection in 2002. EAB was previously unknown outside of Asia and was not on any exotic pest "watch list."

1. According to the passage, which trees does the EAB infest in its native habitat?
   A. Walnut and elm
   B. Oak and ash
   C. Pine and cedar
   D. Ash and walnut

2. According to the passage, the Canadian solution to EAB infestation of an "ash free" zone is not viable in Michigan and Ohio because:
   F. management efforts shifted to the lower peninsula of Michigan.
   G. not enough research has been completed on EAB.
   H. EAB infestations are too extensive and numerous.
   J. U.S. government regulations have prohibited "ash free" zones.

3. Which of the following is NOT true of EAB eradication?
   A. The EAB is difficult to kill with insecticide once it bores under tree bark.
   B. No ash species appear to be resistant to EAB.
   C. Studies and evaluations of EAB within the United States have been underway since 2000.
   D. "Ash free" zones have been declared in Canada.

4. Which infestation area triggered surveys of EAB?
   F. Detroit, Michigan
   G. Windsor, Ontario, Canada
   H. Lucas County, Ohio
   J. lower peninsula of Michigan

5. According to the passage, EAB has been found on ash trees located in which of the following areas?

   I. Urban areas
   II. Rural woodlots
   III. Riparian areas

   A. I only
   B. II only
   C. II and III only
   D. I, II, and III

6. As it is used in the passage, the word *concert* (line 19) most nearly means:
   F. to perform.
   G. to plan or act together.
   H. to arrange by agreement.
   J. to organize by.

7. Which of the following are purposes of the Canadian "ash free" zone?

    I. Prevention of artificial movement of infested ash material out of the infested area
    II. Ash reduction efforts in key "Gateway Areas"
    III. Destruction of all ash trees in a 30-km × 10-km zone

    A. I only
    B. I and II only
    C. II and III only
    D. I and III only

8. Which of the following tree decline and dieback symptoms hindered the discovery that EAB was killing ash trees in southern Michigan?
    F. Ash yellows and ash decline
    G. Ash yellows and ash deterioration
    H. Ash decline and ash flaking
    J. Yellow bark and ash decline

9. According to the passage, which of the following could transfer EAB to other areas?

    I. Purchasing wood chips that were harvested from wood in Michigan and using them in Indiana
    II. Placing extra ash firewood in your vehicle after camping in Michigan and driving to California
    III. Standing near an ash tree in Michigan and then traveling to Florida

    A. I only
    B. II only
    C. I and II only
    D. I and III only

10. According to the passage, which is true of EAB prior to 2002?
    F. EAB was on a watch list.
    G. EAB was not in the United States.
    H. EAB was known outside of Asia.
    J. EAB was previously unknown outside of Asia.

Strategy Review

Preheating: Did you preheat your brain? While focusing on the origins of the passage, the title, and the first paragraph, you should have noticed some key words and phrases: *U.S. Forest Service, disease conditions, emerald ash borer (EAB), infestations, 2002, Michigan,* and *Canada.* You should have thought, *What do I already know about bug infestations?* If you live in Michigan, you may be highly familiar with the EAB. If you live in Colorado or another state with infestations of pine beetles, you may understand the devastation caused by such pests. Even if you are unfamiliar with bothersome bugs, you might connect to an idea you already have about the Forest Service or about other diseases. Your ability to connect to the topic in some form greatly enhances your retention of the material.

Finding the Main Idea and Tone; Indexing the Passage: The main idea and the tone of the passage may be clear within the first paragraph, or you may have to wait until you have read the entire passage to identify them. In the margins, summarize the contents of each paragraph. Your index may not use the same wording as the following one; however, you should have identified similar ideas for each paragraph.

Paragraph 1: Origins of EAB, Canada and U.S.

Paragraph 2: EAB infestation in native habitat and ash trees in U.S.

Paragraph 3: EAB control in Canada

Paragraph 4: EAB control in Michigan and Ohio

Paragraph 5: Current control options

Paragraph 6: Government partnerships and research

Paragraph 7: Late discovery of EAB in Michigan

Paragraph 8: Reasons for no EAB warnings before 2002

Finding the Answer: Did you focus on key words and phrases from the question stems to guide your search? Those key phrases along with your memory of the passage and your notes in the margin should have helped you identify the location of answers within the passage.

Answers Explained

1. **(A)** The key phrase in this question is "native habitat." Your notes for paragraph 2 should have guided you directly to the answer, which is stated word-for-word in line 14: "The EAB infests walnuts and elms in its native habitat." Each of the other options "sounds" correct, so finding the answer is more productive than relying on your memory of the passage's details.

2. **(H)** The question asks you why an "ash free" zone won't work in Michigan and Ohio. Paragraph 4 discusses EAB control in these two states. The first sentence of the paragraph provides the answer: "infestations are too extensive and numerous to be contained with the kind of 'ash free' zones." The answer is "right there" in the passage. Option F is distracting because it contains a phrase used within the passage: "management efforts shifted to the lower peninsula of Michigan" (lines 25–35). The limited research available on EAB infestations (option G) and governmental regulations (option J) sound logical if you can't remember the exact detail. These distracting and even logical answer options are the reason you need to look up the correct response.

TIP

Even if you're not familiar with the topic of a passage, try to make a connection with it on some level.

3. **(C)** Notice the key word in the questions stem—*NOT*. Use "EAB eradication" as the key phrase to find the location of the answer within the index. Think about the passage as a whole and find the areas that specifically address the eradication of the EAB. Because "NOT" questions take more time than others, consider leaving this one until you have finished all other questions for this passage. If your eight-minute passage allowance has ended by the time you get back to this question, make your best guess and move on to the next passage. Option A, "The EAB is difficult to kill with insecticide once it bores under the bark of a tree," is proven true in lines 33–35; option B, "no ash species appear to be resistant to EAB," in lines 56–57, and option D, "ash free zones have been declared in Canada," in paragraph 3. Option C is not true because studies have been underway since 2002, not 2000. Because the dates are so close together, option C may also appear true in your haste to answer the question.

4. **(F)** You may remember from the passage that surveys were conducted upon the initial findings of EAB infestation. The key word in the question stem is actually *triggered*. This word means "started" or "initiated." Locate the section of the passage that discusses the beginning of the EAB infestation. Your index should help you determine that paragraph 1 is the place to look. Lines 3–4 give you the correct answer to this question. Option G is the most distracting because, later in paragraph 1, the word *surveys* is used immediately after a reference to Windsor, Ontario, Canada (line 7). Attending to key words in the question stem helps you choose between two close answers. Options H and J may distract you because they are specifically mentioned within the passage.

5. **(D)** This question may take extra time. Actually, this one is fairly easy once you find the location of the information within the passage. According to the question stem, you are trying to figure out where ash trees are generally located. When referring to your notes, you can predict that the answer will probably be located in paragraph 2 because it mentions ash trees in the United States. Even if you don't have strong notes for each paragraph, you can logically assess that an important detail such as where ash trees are located is in the early part of the passage. Lines 15–16 indicate that ash trees can be found in "urban areas, rural woodlots, and riparian areas." Each of these is an option within the question; therefore option D is correct.

6. **(G)** First, find the word in the passage. Thankfully, the line number (20) is given to you in the question stem. Read the sentence, and before reading any of the answer options, replace the original word with another word that could be used instead. The word *together* fits nicely in the sentence. Sometimes you have to replace the word along with surrounding words to make it make sense: "This ash free zone *together* with an aggressive regulatory program . . . " Go back to the answer options and find the one that most closely resembles the word you have chosen. Option G, "to plan or act together," works best. Option F plays on your initial instincts regarding the definition of the word *concert*. Outside the context of the article, the first definition you would have for *concert* is "a musical performance." Don't allow personal context to distract you. What do you do if you can't think of anything to replace the word in question? A second strategy is to replace the word with each answer choice and decide which option makes the most sense. Options H and J may sound reasonable initially, but if you replace the definitions with the word in the sentence, option G makes the most sense.

7. **(D)** Locate the section of the passage that refers to Canada's "ash free" zone. According to the index, paragraph 3 should contain this information. Also, you could answer this question using logic. You may remember that "ash free" zones require that all ash trees be removed. II indicates that ash trees are only being reduced; therefore, eliminate it as an answer. Now, you only have to choose between answers A and D. In paragraph 3, both I, "prevention of artificial movement of infested ash material out of the infested area;" and III, "destruction of all ash trees in a 30-km × 10-km zone," are identified as part of Canada's "ash free" zone project in lines 19–20 and line 18, respectively, making option D correct.

8. **(F)** The answer to this question is not explicitly stated within the passage; you must infer the correct answer. The following are the key words and phrases in the question stem: *discovery, tree decline and dieback symptoms,* and *hindered.* According to the index, paragraph 7 discusses the late discovery of EAB. The discovery of EAB can only be described as "late" if it was hindered by something. Refer to paragraph 7 for the answer. The first sentence in paragraph 7 contains a key phrase from the question stem—*decline and dieback symptoms.* This paragraph lists two symptoms that "disguised" the underlying problem of EAB: ash yellows and ash decline. The paragraph states that these two problems "were so prevalent that dying ash trees did not draw close scrutiny," which means that they masked or hindered the discovery of the EAB infestation. Each of the incorrect options, G, H, and J, play on the wording of the correct response. They may all sound reasonable, but they do not include the exact wording of the diseases indicated in the passage: ash yellows and ash decline.

9. **(C)** This question asks you to infer based on the passage as a whole. First, figure out how EAB is transferred. Your notes on each paragraph may not be very helpful because multiple paragraphs discuss the spread or control of EAB. Skim each paragraph for ideas about spreading EAB. Lines 10–13 indicate how areas outside of the quarantine area were most likely infested: ash firewood, logs, or nursery materials. The wood chips mentioned in option I are a "nursery material" that could possibly transport EAB. Transferring firewood, as in II, could transport EAB. Nothing in the passage indicates that just standing near an ash tree transports these pests. If EAB could be transferred in this way, people would have to be quarantined as well. I and II make sense; therefore, option C is correct.

10. **(J)** Finding the correct paragraph may be difficult based on the question stem. You could find every reference to 2002 and possibly locate the correct answer, but it may take too long. Look at the answer options to see if they give you a clue where to look. You may remember that the last line of the passage refers to a watch list. Go to the last paragraph and see if it leads you in the right direction. According to the paragraph, EAB was NOT on a watch list or known outside of Asia; therefore, options F and H are not correct. EAB was probably in the United States for 5–10 years prior to 2002, so option G is not correct. Option J, "EAB was previously unknown outside of Asia," is correct. The wording of these options may fool you, so read carefully.

THE HUMANITIES PASSAGE

Look for the Passage "Type"

Every ACT Reading section contains one nonfiction passage labeled *Humanities*. This passage is less predictable in terms of genre than the other three passages. Sometimes you'll see a factual essay, and sometimes you'll come across a narrative passage from a memoir or human-interest story.

You can *still* use the main reading strategies presented in this book to approach the Humanities passage. All it takes is a split-second glance at the passage to determine whether the passage is a factual essay or a narrative.

POSSIBILITY #1: FACTUAL ESSAY

Identifying markers:

1. An academic tone
2. Traditional Essay Structure: Introduction, body paragraphs that provide evidence to support a thesis, conclusion.
3. A focus on abstract ideas and factual information.
4. Point-of-View: Third Person. No personal pronouns.

If it's a factual essay, use the "indexing" strategy outlined in Chapter 13.

POSSIBILITY #2: NARRATIVE

Identifying markers:

1. A more conversational tone
2. Narrative Structure: A speaker who uses storytelling techniques, characters, and imagery to make her point.
3. A focus on people and their interactions with the world.
4. Point-of-View: First Person, or at least an emphasis on personal pronouns.

If it's a narrative passage, use either the COST or CAPS method from Chapter 14, whichever you prefer.

EIGHT STRATEGIES FOR READING NONFICTION

1. **IT'S ALL IN THE TIMING.** Spend no more than eight minutes on one passage, unless it is your last one.

2. **SEE THE BIG PICTURE.** Take in the passage as a whole before you begin reading. Observe how many paragraphs and lines you will be reading. Tell yourself that you only have four minutes to read the passage.

3. **FOCUS.** Look carefully at the citation and the title. Skim the first paragraph for key words to identify the topic.

4. **PREHEAT YOUR BRAIN.** What do you already know about the topic? Make a connection so that the new information you are going to read about has something to attach to inside your brain.

5. **CLEAR YOUR MIND.** Remove all mental clutter. Think only about your background knowledge of the topic. Forget about school, parents, friends, and any other mental distractions that cause you to lose focus as you read. Remain focused on the topic at hand, seeking to learn all you can about it.

6. **IDENTIFY THE MAIN IDEA AND TONE.** Remembering specific details the first time through the passage is not important; you have time to look them up later. Use the following two questions to identify the main idea and tone of the passage: 1) What is the author saying about the topic?, and 2) What is the author's attitude toward the topic? By identifying the main idea and tone of the passage, you will be better prepared to answer inferential questions about certain sections or about the passage as a whole.

7. **INDEX THE PASSAGE.** Summarize the purpose and function of each paragraph. Take brief notes in the margins that give you an index you can refer to while answering the questions.

8. **GUESS FIRST, THEN FIND THE ANSWER.** As soon as you have read the question stem, take a stab at the answer. Doing so helps you eliminate incorrect answer options. Next, identify key words or line numbers within the question stem, and use the index you created to find the answer in the text.

ONLINE PRACTICE TEST

For even more ACT Reading practice, remember you can access the online practice test at *barronsbooks.com/tp/ACT36*.

Science

Overview of the Science Test

16

→ **SPECIFICS OF THE TEST**

→ **SCIENTIFIC REASONING IS TESTED**

→ **KNOWING YOURSELF AS A STUDENT**

→ **BE A SCIENCE SLACKER, NOT A STUDENT**

This chapter will give you a quick refresher course about the ACT science test, introduce you to some general strategies for success on any standardized test, and then explain the format of the rest of this section of the book. Throughout this section you will see various tip boxes, which will give you specific, easily remembered advice about the best ways to approach the test. And be sure to pay special attention to "**Inside the ACT 36 Mind**." These are like getting a backstage pass into the workings of the ACT test writers. They will give you insight into how the test is structured, help you recognize answer choices that are included to distract you into making mistakes, and let you in on some of the tricks that test writers use so that not everyone will score a 36. By learning about how the test is created, you will be better prepared to reach your goals.

Now, take a look at the ACT science test.

> **There are no shortcuts to the ACT Science Test**
>
> Students are often looking for quick fixes to their ACT Science scores. There are none. Like the Reading section, this test is complicated, covers many diverse topics, and does not allow for enough time to analyze the passages. There are strategies you can use to help you be more efficient and boost your chances of getting to the correct answer. There is no substitute for practicing these strategies.

SPECIFICS OF THE TEST

The science section has a similar general format on every ACT test. Knowing this format and the instructions for completing the test beforehand will allow you to spend your time focusing on the passages themselves. The general instructions for the ACT science test look like this:

> **SCIENCE TEST**
>
> 35 Minutes—40 Questions
>
> Directions: There are several passages in this test. Each passage is followed by several questions. After reading a passage, choose the best answer to each question and fill in the corresponding oval on the answer sheet. You may refer to the passage as often as necessary.
>
> You are NOT permitted to use a calculator on this test.

TIP

Now that you have read the instructions, do not waste time reading them again on test day. They will not change.

Passage Types

For many years, the "traditional" ACT science section has had seven passages, each one numbered with Roman numerals, such as "Passage I," "Passage II," etc. The types of passages generally had a set number of questions (5, 6, or 7).

THE "TRADITION" HAS ENDED!

Recently, the Science section has changed. The test has become less structured and the number of passages and questions in each passage can vary. Students have reported different test structures on different dates, and there have been some (unverified) reports of different test structures given at different schools on the same date. Relax. If you can recognize the passage types and know how to approach them, then you will be prepared for any version of the test.

The passages are classified into three different types, each with a range in number of questions. They are:

1. **DATA REPRESENTATION**—12–16 Total Questions. There are 2–3 of these on the test.
2. **RESEARCH SUMMARIES**—18–22 Total Questions. There are 2–3 of these on the test.
3. **CONFLICTING VIEWPOINTS**—6–8 Total Questions. There is 1 of these on the test.

The passages may be single pages or multiple pages, but the test writers avoid making you flip back and forth between pages.

The rest of the science chapters will dissect passages and give you detailed descriptions and strategies for mastering each of the types.

Scoring

Every question on the science test is worth 1 point. There is no penalty for guessing incorrectly, so you should attempt to answer every question. Every 1 to 2 correctly answered questions raises your score by one point, especially in the 30 and over range.

INSIDE THE ACT 36 MIND

You've probably heard the idea that when in doubt on a test, "Guess answer choice C." On the ACT (and almost every other standardized test you may take), this is not true, especially since almost half of the questions do not even have "C" as an option. Also, test makers and test companies have designed the tests to avoid bias. They make sure that, statistically, no answer choice is used more than any other. Also, don't worry if one answer seems to come up several times in a row. If you know, or are pretty sure, that your answer choices are correct, do not change them because there is a weird pattern on your answer sheet. At the end of a section, avoid *blindly* guessing "C" or "H." They come up statistically less often.

TIP

If you are running out of time on the ACT, quickly fill in any blank answers on the answer sheet— even if you have not read the question.

SCIENTIFIC REASONING IS TESTED

TIP

There are few facts to learn for the ACT science section. You are being tested on how science is done, so think like a scientist!

Probably the most important thing to remember about the science section of the ACT is that this is a test of scientific reasoning, not a test of scientific knowledge. Unlike the tests you take in school, you are not expected to come in with much specific prior knowledge about any of the topics presented in the passages. As an ambitious student, you have probably taken several science courses, including some advanced ones, so you are naturally going to be more familiar with the concepts. More important, you will have had more exposure to scientific methods and processes—this is what is being tested.

Because there is no specific content you're expected to know, almost all of the information you need to answer the questions is found in the passages. Make sure to focus on this data, and don't spend time over-thinking topics you may have studied in class. Overanalyzing the content of any passage will only waste valuable time.

What About the Facts?

Although there is no set of defined science facts you need to know, there will be 4–5 questions that require scientific knowledge. They are usually topics covered in your courses: density, scientific naming, units of measurement, gravity, photosynthesis, DNA, scientific methods, concept of depth (fossils/glacial deposits), insulators, cell structure, etc.

Based on a sampling of released tests, students need to have at least a working knowledge of cell biology, genetics, chemical reactions, atomic structure, and basic principles of physics—topics that you should have learned in your science classes. Certain "facts" have been tested repeatedly. Here are 5 concepts that have come up on more than one test:

1. Water freezes at 0° C and boils at 100° C.
2. Acids have a pH of 0–6.99. Bases have a pH of 7.001–14
3. Force = Mass × Acceleration /Gravity is acceleration downward.
4. The independent variable is changed by the experimenter. The dependent variable is the data collected. The controlled variable remains constant.
5. Understand ratios in chemical equations. You are given the following chemical equation:

$$2H_2O + O_2 \rightarrow 2H_2O_2$$

The question asks if 5 molecules of O_2 are consumed, how many molecules of H_2O_2 will be produced? The answer will be 10 because there is a 1 : 2 ratio in the equation.

Looking at a different set of tests would have resulted in a different set of facts, and these are only the ones that have shown up more than once. So, what should you do?

There is no way to accurately predict what topics will be covered on any specific ACT, so do not waste your time trying to cram for the ACT Science section. Hopefully, you've been paying attention in class!

What should you do if a question seems to be factual? First, ask yourself if this is something that you would be expected to know from a basic science class. This may be about specific facts or experimental procedure. If so, then use your reasoning to come up with an answer. If the question seems too specific or complicated, then look for the topic in the Introduction or the experiment descriptions. Content-specific vocabulary is often defined for you.

What About Math?

There *is* some math on the ACT Science section; however, if you think you need a calculator to solve any of the problems, you are working way too hard. The math questions tend to be very basic and involve a few key concepts: calculating a simple percent, finding the average/mean, solving a percent change equation (when the equation is given), or finding a simple rate of reaction. Most of the more complicated looking questions can be solved without math. Look at the units, then match the correct answer—most of the time, you do not need to calculate anything.

Timing and Order

TIP

Use the information the test writers have given you, not what you think you already know.

With 40 questions to answer in only 35 minutes, you have about 52.5 seconds to answer each one. That means you must practice working as quickly and as accurately through the questions as you possibly can. Don't bother sitting with a stopwatch to time yourself, and don't focus on the clock so much during the test that you get distracted. With some general strategies and practice, you can eliminate some of the time pressure.

You will be able to answer some of the passages more quickly, and some will take more time. What many students have found to be a highly effective strategy is to do the passages out of order. That's right—do not go through the test starting at question 1 and finishing with question 40. Go through the test by doing certain passages first and others last. Warning: This is a technique that must be practiced before the actual test.

As explained earlier, the passages are broken down into three types, each with a different number of questions. Because some of these require more intensive reading, while others can be scanned quickly, they should be done in the following order:

1. **DATA REPRESENTATION**—Do these 2–3 passages first/second.
2. **RESEARCH SUMMARIES**—Do these 2–3 passages first/second.
3. **CONFLICTING VIEWPOINTS**—Do this one passage LAST!

The passages are most easily identified by their structure, so remembering to do them by type will help you save time in the long run.

As soon as you open your test booklet to the science section, you should quickly scan through each passage and mark the passages "1st/2nd" or "LAST" on the top of each page. Then start answering the questions.

INSIDE THE ACT 36 MIND

The test writers need a way to separate out students so that not everyone will score a 36. That's one of the reasons there is not really enough time to complete the test. They very often put the Conflicting Viewpoints passage in the first half of the test because most students will slow down to carefully read the passage, creating tremendous time pressure to finish the rest. Many people get so stuck that they never get to two or more passages at the end of the test. If you leave the Conflicting Viewpoints passage and its questions for the end, you will have more time to complete all the passages more accurately. Statistics show that even if you run out of time and don't get to this last passage, you can still score in the high 20s by answering the other passages correctly.

For some students, going out of order is the hardest advice to follow. You may have spent years working methodically through tests from start to finish. If so, jumping around the test is going to feel uncomfortable at first. Rest assured that with practice it will become easier and easier, and your scores should improve as well.

The other issue involving order on the ACT is that the science section always comes last. By the time you get to this part of the test, you have been sitting for a little less than two and a half hours reading questions and filling in circles on an answer sheet. Your hand hurts from writing, your brain hurts from thinking, and your rear end hurts from sitting. You simply want to finish the test. Don't let test fatigue get in the way. Before the science section, give yourself a pep talk that you're in the home stretch and can see the finish line. Remind yourself to keep going strong.

KNOWING YOURSELF AS A STUDENT

The type of student you are and your academic preferences and abilities have a great deal of influence on how you might approach the ACT science section. Recognizing your strengths and weaknesses and using them to your advantage is an important part of your success. For the purpose of the ACT, students tend to classify themselves into three general categories: science students, English students, and math students.

Science Students

Some students see themselves as **science students**. They have taken all the biology, chemistry, earth science, and physics courses that are offered. They do experiments in their basements and enter science fairs and competitions for fun. They do well in both math and English classes, but the science ones are what they enjoy the most. For these students, this section is the one they have been looking forward to throughout the entire test; however, they have to be careful not to read too much into the data sets or to try to understand every aspect of the experiments.

English Students

Students who see themselves as **English students** breeze through the English and reading parts of the ACT and tend to sweat their way through the math. They enjoy reading and writing and see vocabulary as their friend. They often dread the science section because it does not seem to play to their strengths. Making notations in the margins about data and main ideas helps them from being overwhelmed by the numbers. English students are the ones who will have the most difficulty leaving the Conflicting Viewpoints passage to the end, but it is really to their advantage.

Math Students

Math students like numbers in whatever form they appear. They love doing equations and solving problems in their heads. They can do things with calculators that seem to defy logic. They dread the English and reading parts of the ACT, but they like the Data Representation and Research Summaries passages of the science section because they contain charts and graphs. Math students are the ones who are most likely to get stuck in a Conflicting Viewpoints passage and miss the opportunity to answer easier questions later in the test.

TIP

Don't give a half-hearted effort on the science section just because you're tired. When you're physically there taking the test, be mentally there as well.

TIP

For Science Students
Do not over-think the passage content.

TIP

For English Students
Don't panic over the numbers. Write your own notes in the margins to help you stay focused.

TIP

For Math Students
Don't recalculate all of the data or get lost in the numerical details. Focus on the main ideas of the passages.

Which type of student are you? Or do you not fit into any of the types? In reality, being one type or another should not interfere with your ability to do well on the science section. Make sure to use your strengths to your advantage. Work on your weaker areas by using strategies presented in this section, as well as throughout the book. Skills learned in one area are definitely transferable to another.

BE A SCIENCE SLACKER, NOT A SCIENCE STUDENT

Science teachers (myself included) are cringing at the above statement. Almost everything we teach you in our classes about being a good science student—read carefully, pay close attention to details, analyze data, re-read for comprehension, annotate heavily—should be ignored during the ACT science section. You simply do not have the time to understand the information. You need to quickly find an answer that "fits," regardless of whether or not you understand it. This is an "open book" test. You will have the majority of information there if you need it.

True Science Slackers know how to do this. For those of you who are still confused, think of it this way: Have you ever been in Spanish or French class and had a homework assignment that requires you to read in that language and then answer questions in that language? Have you ever been in a position where you did not understand the passage or the questions? What do you do?!? You read the question and find phrases in the passage that seem to "match." Then you write down the information around that question. And, what usually happens? You get that question correct!

This same strategy applies to the science section. You may not understand (or have even read) the topic, but you can find the answer choice that "matches" the best. In the majority of cases, that is the correct answer. Once you have mastered the Science Slacker strategy, you will be amazed about how little information you have to understand to get the questions correct.

However, it is important to note that slacking will not get you to a 36. There will be times when the information is not "right there" in the graphs or tables, and you will have to go back and read parts of the passage or rely on your knowledge of content and scientific method.

Passage Types and Strategies

17

→ **DATA REPRESENTATION**
→ **RESEARCH SUMMARIES**
→ **CONFLICTING VIEWPOINTS**
→ **"SCIeNCE" STRATEGIES**

There are three main types of passages on the science ACT: Data Representation, Research Summaries, and Conflicting Viewpoints. Understanding the basics of each of the three will help you better approach and answer the questions.

DATA REPRESENTATION

Data Representation passages are often referred to as "graphing" passages because the most common thing about them is their use of graphs. There are 2–3 of them on every ACT, and they are followed by a set of 5–8 questions. The graphs, figures, and data tables that are used in these passages can be related to any scientific content. They include types of illustrations you will find in your science textbooks and in journal articles. The questions generally ask you to pick data points off of a graph, interpret data trends on charts or tables, and analyze information presented in figures or equations.

TIP

Spend no more than 3 to 5 minutes on each Data Representation passage.

You should do Data Representation passages first or second because the questions can be answered most quickly. They usually do not have much to read, except for a brief introduction, and many of the questions are factual.

INSIDE THE ACT 36 MIND

The graphs, figures, and data tables throughout the ACT are designed to intimidate the test-taker. Many of them will be arranged in unfamiliar ways, have multiple sets of data plotted in different directions, or show very complex experimental set-ups. Don't be intimidated by their complexity. The more of these you see during your review and practice, the easier they will seem.

RESEARCH SUMMARIES

The second type of passage is called Research Summaries. These passages are sometimes referred to as "experimental" because they generally describe scientific experiments. There are also 2–3 of these on the test, and they are followed by 5–8 questions and should be done first or second. Like Data Representation, these passages are designed to test your graph skills, your ability to interpret trends, and your overall science reasoning ability, but they also focus on proper experimental design, drawing conclusions, and knowledge of the scientific method. Whether you have never even heard of the subject or have actually performed the experiment in one of your own classes, remember: The correct answers to the questions can usually be found quickly using the information in the passage.

Many times, you can recognize these passages because of headings like "Experiment 1," "Experiment 2," and "Experiment 3." They too may seem very complex and maybe a little bit scary, but try to look at this as a challenge, not as an obstacle. Because these are more complex than Data Representation passages, for some people doing these second will help you maximize your time.

The best way to review for these passages is to make sure you understand the steps of the scientific method and the parts of a controlled experiment. If you are able to identify a hypothesis, recognize a control group, and explain independent and dependent variables from any experimental design, then you are prepared to handle Research Summaries passages effectively.

Spend no more than 5 to 6 minutes on each Research Summaries passage.

CONFLICTING VIEWPOINTS

Conflicting Viewpoints passages contain two or more opposing scientific views about some theory or process. Phenomena that occur over a long time period, such as evolution, or on a scale that is difficult to measure, such as global warming, are common topics. There is only one of these on the test, and it is followed by 6–8 questions. As of now, there have only been 7 questions on any of these passages, but the ACT could always change. You are not likely to find many graphs or figures in these, just several paragraphs of reading, but sometimes these do contain data and pictures. Strategies that you have already learned for the reading section of the ACT, especially for the natural science passages, will come in handy here.

Because these passages are so reading-intensive, you should do them last. For students who are strongest in English, the advantage of this is that if they spend too much time on the other passages, their strong reading skills should help them make up the time and get more of these questions correct. For math students, leaving the Conflicting Viewpoints passage until the end will help prevent them from being bogged down earlier in the test, giving them more time to focus on this at the end.

TIP

Spend no more than 5 to 8 minutes on the Conflicting Viewpoints passage.

"SCIeNCE" STRATEGIES

Although every individual will take the ACT in his or her own unique way, there are some general techniques and strategies that you should follow to maximize your score. You may be doing some of these already, or you may not have any kind of system. Regardless, if your goal is to earn a high score, then learning and practicing a systematic approach to the passages will put you closer to achieving a 36.

To help you remember this approach, use the acronym "**SCIeNCE**." It may seem a little bit goofy, but it just might help you focus. It's certainly worth trying, and it just might boost your score.

> **"SCIeNCE" stands for the following:**
> S—Scan the passage.
> C—Check the main idea.
> Ie—Ignore the extras.
> N—Note the reference in the question.
> C—Choose the best answer.
> E—Eliminate the incorrect answers.

The first three, **SCIe**, are used before you even begin answering any of the questions. They will give you an overview and help you focus on what's important.

S—Scan the Passage

This is the first thing you will do once you start looking at a specific passage. Take a brief amount of time to look over the topic, notice what the graphs and tables are presenting, and see how the questions look. Once you've scanned the passage, you'll know where to find some random piece of information you need to answer one of the questions.

TIP

Scanning the passage should take about 10 to 15 seconds.

INSIDE THE ACT 36 MIND

Another main reason to scan is because ACT test writers often seem to "hide" questions and information. There are many examples of the first question of a passage tucked under the graphs, or a description of an experiment separated from the data, or questions with graphs as answer choices that often look like parts of the passage. Students who immediately jump to answering the questions often miss these and then mis-bubble or leave questions blank.

C—Check the Main Idea

Figuring out the main idea is very important for all of the science passage types. What will help you even more is underlining, circling, or marking these in some way. With Conflicting Viewpoints, for example, writing the scientist's argument in the margin is a very helpful for some practice. Drawing trend arrows for data tables and graphs will also help you understand the passage better. More important, these notations will actually be the answer to some of the questions or will serve as signposts telling you where to look for the correct answer.

TIP

Finding the main idea and marking it in the test booklet will help you analyze the questions better.

Ie—Ignore the Extras

Science passages are filled with extra information and jargon that you do not need to understand and that you don't need to answer the questions. There may be three graphs in one passage, but the questions only refer to two of them. Entire data tables and descriptions of experiments may never be used. Complex equations may be included, but they may not be used for an answer. Don't get tied up in them. Remember, be a Science Slacker.

INSIDE THE ACT 36 MIND

Test writers include extra information to confuse and intimidate the average test-taker. Many students are so tired by the time they reach the science section, and so scared of the complex graphs, that they give up and don't focus enough to answer the questions.

The last three letters of the acronym, **NCE**, are strategies that you will use while you're answering the questions themselves.

TIP

If the question refers to a specific experiment, graph, table, look there immediately to find the answer. Don't waste time re-reading other sections of the passage.

N—Note the Reference in the Question

Some of the most common types of questions in the ACT science section start out, "According to Figure 1," or, "Based on the results of Experiment 3." These are like runway lights for a pilot. They tell you exactly where to go to find the answer. Sometimes, the references are less obvious, like, "A scientist who follows the theory of gradualism would most likely agree with . . . ," but for the student who has checked the main idea, this reference will point to the exact place where an answer can be found. In more complicated questions, there may not be a reference at all, or the reference may be found in the answer choices themselves. Often, the question includes data that should be added to a data table or graph.

C—Choose the Best Answer

This is what the science test is all about. Once you read the question stem, you should have an idea of what the correct answer may be, or at least know exactly where to go back and find it. You will find many hints and tips for doing this throughout this section of the book.

E—Eliminate the Incorrect Answers

For the average test-taker, this step often comes before choosing the correct answer, but high-achieving students often pick the best choice and eliminate the others simultaneously. Once you have an answer, make sure to quickly eliminate the others—physically crossing them out is an excellent strategy, especially if you get stuck and need to return to the question later. You will then have fewer items to consider. And don't overanalyze your answer choices, especially for questions that have simple numbers as answers. If you have found the correct one, mark it and move on. Don't waste valuable time. Sometimes the test writers try to distract you with "close" answers. Eliminating incorrect choices will not let you make simple mistakes.

When you select your answer on your answer sheet, make sure to mark clearly. Even more important, if you change an answer, erase the old one completely. Some people find it useful to make very light marks on their answer sheets and then take a minute at the end of the test to darken them the rest of the way.

Now that you've been introduced to the **SCIeNCE** strategies, it's time to really examine the passages themselves and to practice these strategies. In the next few chapters, we embark on a dissection of the passages, exposing all of their inner parts. Once we've done this, you'll get a chance to use what you've learned with some full-length passages and question sets.

Passage Dissection: Introductions

18

→ **APPROACHING INTRODUCTIONS**

All three types of ACT science passages include some reading. Usually, a paragraph or two is used as an introduction to the passage. Data Representation and Research Summaries passages generally start out with a description of the experiment from which the data was collected. Conflicting Viewpoints passages present two different points of view on a scientific theory or topic. Any of these can be about chemistry, biology, physics, earth science, or a related scientific concept.

Sometimes you may be familiar with the subject because you covered it during a course, sometimes you may have actually performed a similar experiment, but most of the time, the test writers pick some pretty obscure information that few high school students would know. This doesn't matter! The test is not an achievement test—how much you've learned—but it is a reasoning one—how well you can solve problems.

TIP

For the introductions, use some of the same strategies that you use on the English and reading sections of the ACT.

APPROACHING INTRODUCTIONS

For Data Representation and Research Summaries passages, the test writers also tend to include lots of specific detail in the introduction. There are often equations, calculations, units, and many numbers. These details are included to show that the experiment is valid, and for the average test-taker, they are intimidating. For the well-prepared student, they should not really be a problem.

There are two general strategies to approaching the Introductions:

1. **S**can and quickly **C**heck the main idea
2. **I**gnore the Introduction entirely

TIP

Science Slackers will skip the Introductions. They will only read the Introduction if the information is not on the graph/data table and they do not know it from science class.

The strategy you use will depend on your own personal style. Some people need to have the "big picture" before attacking the passage; others do not want to be distracted by the topic and do better by heading straight for the data tables and graphs. Science Slackers will be able to do this more effectively.

Remember, this is an "open book" test. The majority of the answers are there if you need them.

How should you approach the introductions to the Data Representation and Research Summaries passages then? Use the **SCIe** of the **SCIeNCE** strategies to quickly **S**can the section, **C**heck the main idea, and **I**gnore the **e**xtras.

For practice with these strategies, approach each example like you would an actual ACT passage. Try to time yourself to see how long it takes to scan, identify the main idea by circling and/or underlining, and skip the extras. Then analyze how you did by filling out the charts after the examples. (Answers follow.)

EXAMPLE 1

Adding heat to a material causes the molecules to increase their molecular motion. Certain substances have the ability to retain this heat longer than other substances. In solids and liquids, this property is described as *specific heat capacity* and is defined as the heat required to raise some unit (usually 1.0 g) of the substance 1.0°C and is calculated using the following formula: $\Delta Q = m \times c \times \Delta T$, where ΔQ = the amount of heat applied (J or Kcal), m = substance mass (g), c = specific heat capacity (J/g °C), and ΔT = change in temperature ($T_{final} - T_{initial}$). The specific heat capacities for various metals are presented in Table 1 (not actually shown). The time course for each of them to return to their previous temperature after being heated to 100°C is graphed in Figure 1 (not actually shown).

Strategy Practice Chart

Scan the passage.
    <u>Time</u>: _____

Check the main idea.
    <u>Main Idea</u>: _____

Ignore the **e**xtras.
    <u>Extras</u>: _____

How did you do? Here are the suggested answers for this strategy practice. If you came up with the same ones (or something close), great! If you're having difficulty, don't worry. Improvement may take a little time and is the reason that you practice.

TIP

Pay attention to the amount of time you spend scanning the paragraph. On the actual ACT, you won't have the luxury of reading slowly.

Scan the passage.
    <u>Time</u>: 5–6 seconds. Remember, you should spend less than 4–6 minutes on the entire passage.

Check the main idea.
    <u>Main Idea</u>: Specific heat capacity = how much heat a substance can retain. Did you circle or underline this?

Ignore the **e**xtras.
    <u>Extras</u>: The equation and its definitions. Don't let yourself be distracted. That's what the test makers want you to do.

Let's try another example on a different topic. Use the same strategies again as you read through the introduction.

EXAMPLE 2

Most earthquakes occur along fault lines between tectonic plates of the Earth's lithosphere—large pieces of the earth's crust that are continually shifting and moving along, above, and below each other. Forces cause the deformation of the crust and overcome the frictional resistance holding the plates in place, causing displacement of the adjacent layers by as much as several meters. When the plates uplift along these weaker faults, such as the San Andreas Fault—a transform fault boundary between the North American plate and the Pacific plate in California—massive amounts of energy are released. Geologists measure this energy with the use of a seismograph, a machine that records the presence of two different types of waves—P (primary) and S (secondary). P waves are compressional waves, like sound waves. They travel between 6 and 13 km/s through both solids and liquids. S waves are transverse waves, traveling more horizontally, and move half as fast as P waves through solids only. S and P intervals can be used to calculate the epicenter of an earthquake. Figures 1 and 2 (not shown) show S and P intervals for two different earthquakes. Table 1 (not actually shown) displays calculated distances from six different monitoring stations.

Strategy Practice Chart

Scan the passage.

   Time: _____

Check the main idea.

   Main Idea: _____

Ignore the **e**xtras.

   Extras: _____

How did this passage go? Were you able to understand how the introduction is written? See if you used the strategies in similar ways.

Scan the passage.

   Time: 5–6 seconds—no more than 4–5 minutes for the entire passage.

Check the main idea.

   Main Idea: Earthquakes are measured using S and P waves. Circling or underlining will help guide you back to this when you're answering the questions.

Ignore the **e**xtras.

   Extras: Description of San Andreas Fault, definitions of S and P waves, and travel rates.

The important thing to remember from scanning the introductions of Data Representation and Research Summaries passages is that the information is there if and when you need it to answer the questions. Because you will scan the entire passage, tables, and questions all at once, you should quickly become aware of what you might need later, and more important, where to find it.

TIP

Don't forget to circle/underline the main idea or to write the viewpoint in the test booklet right next to the passage.

Conflicting Viewpoints passages should be approached in the same way, except this time you may have to use the **SCIe** of the **SCIeNCE** strategies more than once. Each paragraph/section presents a different view, so you need to pay attention to the topic and organize your thoughts very well.

Following is a Conflicting Viewpoints sample. Once again, **S**can the sections, **C**heck the main ideas, and **I**gnore the **e**xtras. Fill out the chart and then check to see how you did.

We will change this strategy later when we look at Conflicting Viewpoint passages and their questions altogether.

EXAMPLE 3

Scientist 1

While studying galaxies in the early 20th century, scientists noticed that some of the stars at the outermost portion of many galaxies were not rotating according to accepted Newtonian laws of gravity, which state that the gravitational force between two bodies decays at a rate of the inverse square of the distance between them. Visible baryonic matter, all matter made up of atoms and their subatomic baryons consisting of three quarks, could not account for this discrepancy, but the presence of dark matter and dark energy can. Dark matter accounts for approximately 23% of the mass in the universe, as compared to the 4% for baryonic matter. The remaining 73% of the universe consists of dark energy and other radiation. By studying the redshift in light waves and determining the velocities of stars and other satellites in thousands of galaxies, scientists have collected evidence supporting the existence of the dark matter. These studies show that the concentrations of mass are many times larger than the visible galaxy itself and must be due to dark matter. Thus, this evidence restores Newton's gravitational law.

Scientist 2

In our solar system, the farther away a planet is from the sun, the slower its orbit. But in other galaxies, the observable change in the expected velocity of distant satellites is due to changes in acceleration, not gravity. Modified Newtonian Dynamics, or MOND, uses Newton's Second Law, $F = ma$ (F = force, m = mass, and a = acceleration); however, it includes a new acceleration constant that helps explain the situation in galaxies where the force of gravitational acceleration is very small. There is virtually no evidence to absolutely support the presence of dark matter. This mysterious substance has been used to help observational data conform to standard laws of physics, but it has not been unequivocally proven. Dark energy, which fills up what is seen as empty space in the universe, is uniform throughout and helps explain MOND behavior of an accelerating, expanding universe. To help understand the bending of light in relation to various forces, MOND has been modified as TeVeS—Tensor-Vector-Scalar. The tensor aspect describes the curvature of the gravitation fields, the vector shows that the strength of gravity differs from place to place, and the scalar expression shows that light is affected by these properties.

Strategy Practice Chart

Scientist 1:
Scan the passage.
    <u>Time:</u> _____

Check the main idea.
    <u>Main Idea:</u> _____

Ignore the **e**xtras.
    <u>Extras:</u> _____

Scientist 2:
Scan the passage.
    <u>Time:</u> _____

Check the main idea.
    <u>Main Idea:</u> _____

Ignore the **e**xtras.
    <u>Extras:</u> _____

As you can see, the Conflicting Viewpoints passages may not be much different than the introductions to the Data Representation and Research Summaries passages—they are usually just longer. The strategies are similar. Check to see if you approached them like a student aiming for a 36 would.

Scientist 1:
Scan the passage.
    <u>Time:</u> 25–30 seconds—no more than 7–8 minutes for the entire passage.

Check the main idea.
    <u>Main Idea:</u> Dark matter and energy fit into Newton's law to explain the unexpected orbiting behavior of stars/satellites in galaxies. Did you circle or underline this? Writing "dark matter/Newton" next to the passage itself will help guide you as you're answering questions.

Ignore the **e**xtras.
    <u>Extras:</u> Definition of Newton's law, baryonic matter, percentages of matter in the universe, etc. You'll know where to find these if you need them.

Scientist 2:
Scan the passage.
    <u>Time:</u> 25–30 seconds—no more than 7–8 minutes for the entire passage.

Check the main idea.
    <u>Main Idea:</u> Newton's laws and dark matter cannot explain the galaxies' behavior. MOND and TeVeS use acceleration to explain it. Hopefully you underlined/circled this or wrote "no dark matter/non-Newton" next to the paragraph.

Ignore the **e**xtras.
    <u>Extras:</u> Newton's law equation, explanation of parts of TeVeS, etc. Again, if you need this information to answer questions, you should be able to quickly find it.

You've now completed the first part of the passage dissection, the introduction. Remember, this part can be different lengths in the Data Representation and Research Summaries passages. Sometimes it has a lot of information you'll need to answer the questions. Other times, it may only be a single sentence. You should be savvy enough not to spend too much time on the introduction, but even Science Slackers should be perceptive enough not to ignore it entirely.

INSIDE THE ACT 36 MIND

Remember, the test writers often include one question that relies on a piece of obscure information that is tucked away in the introduction. If you can't find an answer, it may be there.

We're now ready to move on to dissecting the next part of the ACT science passages—the tables, graphs, and figures. It's like looking at the muscle layer of a frog or fetal pig, but without the mess.

Passage Dissection: Tables, Graphs, and Figures

19

→ **APPROACHING TABLES, GRAPHS, AND FIGURES**

You will find a huge variety of tables, graphs, and figures in the Data Representation and Research Summaries passages. You will see data tables with both numbers and descriptions. Graphs may be oriented vertically or horizontally. Line graphs can be simple linear relationships, have scales on both sides, or even combine several very different data sets. Bar graphs are often stacked with several different data points shown on the same bar. Some graphs are more like figures than graphs themselves. You will need to be prepared for any of these. (See Figure 1 and other examples on page 248.)

Figures may show experimental apparatus, chemical structures, diagrams of ecosystems, or almost any science-related concept. Flip through any science textbook and you'll get an idea of the wide variety of images you may see. Most of them are fairly straightforward if you don't get distracted by the numbers and unfamiliar topics.

Since you may have never seen some of the types of tables, graphs, or figures, and may be unfamiliar with the topic, remind yourself that the information needed to answer the questions is there. Unlike many testers, well-prepared students will calmly use their strategies to their advantage.

APPROACHING TABLES, GRAPHS, AND FIGURES

Approaching tables, graphs, and figures requires the same strategies you tried when looking at introductions. Again, use the **SCIe** of the **SCIeNCE** strategies to quickly **S**can the section, **C**heck the main idea, and **I**gnore the **e**xtras.

When **S**canning, note the data that are presented in each of the figures, graphs, or tables. Don't take too much time—note the main idea and come back to the specific data or number when you need it.

Checking the main idea reveals if there are any general numerical relationships between data sets, if there are trends in the data and graphs, and which directions and sides the scales are on. For graphs or tables with linear relationships, students often find it useful to quickly draw trend arrows, showing the direction of the data. This can be done with both tables and graphs. You should also underline the axes or table labels.

Figure 1

Temperature (°C)	Average Water Intake (ml)	Average Water Loss (ml)	Average PO$_4$ Release (mg/cm^3)	
35	8	12	3	
40	5	17	9	
50	3	28	4	

In the table above, Temperature and Water Loss are proportional—both sets of numbers increase—while Temperature and Water Intake are inverse—an increase in Temperature results in a decrease in Water Intake. PO$_4$ Release does not demonstrate a trend; the sideways arrow is one way of showing that.

Ignoring the **e**xtras is a major stumbling block for the less skilled test-taker. There is often a lot of extra information, and it is presented in ways that are sometimes unfamiliar. There are only 5–8 questions for each of these passages, so they obviously cannot require you to look at every piece of data. For example, in the table above, you may not need to know anything about PO_4 Release to answer any of the questions. Remember, you don't have to understand the concepts, you only have to be able to analyze the data well enough to answer the questions. Use the following examples to practice your strategies.

TIP

It doesn't really matter which way you draw trend arrows as long as you understand the relationships.

EXAMPLE 1

A. altissima Extract Effects on Germination

Strategy Practice Chart

Scan the graph.

Time: _____

Check the main idea (draw trend arrows/show relationship).

Main Idea: _____

Ignore the **e**xtras.

Extras: _____

Hopefully this was not too difficult and the strategies are becoming more familiar to you. Here is an idea of what you should have done with this graph.

Scan the graph.

Time: 4–5 seconds—just enough time to read the title, labels, and note any trends.

Check the main idea (draw trend arrows/show relationship).

Main Idea: Extract effects on germination—for most of the lines, higher concentrations = lower germination rates. Notice the scale on the *x*-axis of the graph goes from 100 to 0.

Ignore the **e**xtras.

Extras: Species names, specific units.

Here's another example on a different topic that uses a data table as a sample. Practice with your strategies to analyze this table.

EXAMPLE 2

TABLE 1

7:00 A.M. Blood Samples

Patient	Volume (ml)	pH	Cholesterol* mg/dl	Bilirubin mg/dl
1	10	7.4	178	0.25
2	10	7.5	205	1.75
3	15	7.3	183	2.11
4	15	7.4	212	0.88

*Note: Cholesterol values are Total: Total/HDL ratios may be calculated from Test 2.

TIP

Usually, data trends are pretty obvious, so if you don't see one, just find the main idea and go on to the questions.

Strategy Practice Chart

Scan the graph.

Time: _____

Check the main idea (draw trend arrows/show relationship).

Main Idea: _____

Ignore the **e**xtras.

Extras: _____

You may be shaking your head and wondering what you missed on this one. If you noticed, there really didn't seem to be any trends here. Hopefully, you didn't spend too much time looking for them. Frequently, there will be another table or graph with this kind of passage that will require you to compare the information with this table. From that you might be able to draw a trend.

Scan the table.

Time: 4–5 seconds—just enough time to read the title, labels, and note any trends.

Check the main idea (draw trend arrows/show relationship).

Main Idea: Patient blood samples for several different tests. There are no trends in this table.

INSIDE THE ACT 36 MIND

Sometimes, the ACT writers include tables, graphs, and figures that you do not need at all. They make the passage look much more complicated and are designed to waste the test-taker's time. Don't get caught in these traps.

Just remember, Data Representation and Research Summaries passages are designed to test your graph skills, your ability to interpret trends, and your overall science reasoning ability. Despite the sometimes confusing diagrams, you will need to understand the big picture, focus on only the relevant details, and work through these sections quickly. Doing these passages first or second will allow you to answer the most questions in the shortest amount of time.

We're now ready to complete our dissection of the passages with a look at the questions. This is the really juicy part because the questions are what need to be exposed to help you understand the workings of the science ACT.

Passage Dissection: Questions

20

→ QUESTION TYPES
→ QUESTION STEMS
→ ANSWER CHOICES
→ STRATEGIES
→ PRACTICE SETS

Okay, now it's time to look at the "guts" of the science ACT—the questions. There are 40 questions in all, but there are really only three major question types. This chapter will examine these and give you some strategies to help you do well on them.

Because this is a reasoning test, the questions will be based on information that is in the passages and not on facts you've learned in science classes. The three types of questions that you are likely to see are: Factual, Inference, and what we'll call Xtreme.

QUESTION TYPES

Factual

Factual questions are based on facts or data that are clearly presented in either the introductions to the question or in tables, charts, and figures. These are the questions that most people get correct, and that you, as a student shooting for a 36, should rarely miss. The number of this type of question varies from passage to passage and from test to test, but there are generally two or three of these in a Data Representation or Research Summaries passage and one or two in a Conflicting Viewpoints passage. These questions can often be answered quickly and should not require much time.

Inference

Questions that require you to think a little bit more and find an answer that may not be a number in a data table or the main idea of the passage are inference questions. These require you to infer the answer based on some given information or draw a conclusion from an experiment. Inference questions often ask you to extrapolate data "off" a graph, to compare the results from two experiments, or to figure out with which statement a scientist would disagree. Most of the questions in each passage are going to be inference because this is what tests your reasoning skills.

The answer choices are usually straightforward and do not include many tricks. They do require you, however, to consider each one before making the correct choice. If you've taken an honors or other advanced science class, these are the types of questions that your teachers ask you in class or when writing up lab reports. You have to take your time with inference questions, but they won't give you too many problems.

Remember:
Spending too
much time
on an Xtreme
question instead
of answering
more of the
easy ones will
hurt your score.

Xtreme

The "X Games" of questions, these are the ones the test writers design to separate out the very top students. Answering the Xtreme questions correctly will help you reach your goal of scoring a 36. These questions are often combinations of factual and inference questions. What makes them so difficult is that they often require you to pick out conflicting information from different experiments or graphs and then analyze them in a totally new way. They may ask you to do math calculations or derive formulas. One or two questions in Data Representation and Research Summaries passages are usually Xtreme. Two or three in a Conflicting Viewpoints passage is usually the norm. Xtreme questions will take the greatest amount of time to answer.

INSIDE THE ACT 36 MIND

Test writers often use their own little tricks to make the questions harder than they need to be. Many data tables have extra lines of information tucked into the bottom. Some introductions contain one sentence that at first seems to be extra information. Often there is a single sentence before one of the experiments that describes an additional variable not presented on the graphs. Depending on how the actual test is written and printed, this information may be a single line at the end of one experiment at the top of the right-hand column of text (see below*).

Why is this there? It's because we generally read from top left to bottom right in a diagonal fashion. If we are reading something fast, we are most likely to miss something that is in the bottom left or top right corner. It doesn't happen in every passage or on every test, but paying attention to hidden information will help you conquer these Xtreme questions.

Now that you know about the three types of questions, you probably wonder if there is a way to recognize them. Obviously they are not going to be labeled, and they are not going to be in order—passages often start with an easy factual question, but from then on they are pretty well mixed. Only by looking at the entire question will you be able to recognize the type.

To continue our dissection, we're now going to cut a little deeper and look at the structure of the questions themselves. We'll start with question stems and then look at the different kinds of answer choices.

TIP

Knowing each question type is not really that important. Being able to answer them correctly is what matters.

QUESTION STEMS

Question stems are what we normally think of as the question itself. In the ACT science section, there are several common question stems that are used over and over. The most basic ones usually start out with "Based on," or "According to," and then refer to one of the tables, graphs, figures, experiments, or scientists. Then they will ask you for some fact directly from the data or passage. The question stems for inference or Xtreme questions are just a variation of this, but they often include more information and are longer, even entire paragraphs.

Wording to Watch For

Here are the question stems that you'll likely see:

Based on . . . which of the following is most consistent . . .

Based on . . . one would conclude that . . .

According to . . . Scientist 1 would most likely argue that . . .

Based on the results . . . if (some condition) is changed, then . . .

According to Scientist 2's explanation, the reason that . . .

Which student would predict . . . based on (some change in the experiment) . . .

Which scientist would most likely agree with . . .

Assume that (some condition). On the basis of Table 2, one would conclude . . .

(A new piece of information) Based on this information and on . . . which of the following predictions is most likely true/false if . . .

If Experiment 2 had been repeated using . . . then which of the following figures best represents this new data?

A scientist hypothesized (some new information). Do the results of . . . support this hypothesis?

Which of the following statements best explains why (some part of the experiment)?

Suppose (some new fact). Which of the following statements about (this new fact) is most consistent with the information presented in the passage?

TIP

One of the surest ways of ensuring a high score is being so familiar with the test format that nothing is a surprise.

The more you familiarize yourself with the types of questions and the types of answer choices that they are often connected to, the better you will do on the test.

Now let's take a look at the kinds of answer choices you'll likely see.

ANSWER CHOICES

Like question stems, answer choices come in a variety of types. Some of them are simply numbers. Others are one or two factual words. There are usually some *if . . . then* statements. In Research Summaries and Data Representation passages, it is not uncommon to see new graphs or figures as part of the answer choices, and there is usually one question with almost an additional paragraph of reading involved in the answer choices—It should not be a surprise that these are often the Xtreme questions.

What to Look For

The following are the most common types of answer choices, but in any one test there can be a wide variety.

SIMPLE NUMBERS

Numbers are almost always given in ascending or descending order. It is rare to find them presented randomly.

A. 0.2
B. 0.3
C. 0.4
D. 0.5

COMBINATIONS OF NUMBERS

Again, there is usually an orderly pattern.

F. A reading of 0.8 mg/ml at a pH of 3
G. A reading of 0.7 mg/ml at a pH of 4
H. A reading of 0.6 mg/ml at a pH of 5
J. A reading of 0.5 mg/ml at a pH of 6

RANGES OF NUMBERS

Numbers ranges may be given by themselves or with other pieces of information.

F. Between 75 dB and 80 dB at 150 meters
G. Between 85 dB and 90 dB at 150 meters
H. Between 75 dB and 80 dB at 250 meters
J. Between 85 dB and 90 dB at 250 meters

SIMPLE WORDS/PHRASES

Most of the time, words and phrases will be in alphabetical order.

    A. Cellular respiration
    B. Fermentation
    C. Glycolysis
    D. Photosynthesis

LONGER PHRASES OR 50/50 ANSWERS

Longer phrases can tell you whether a question is factual, inference, or Xtreme, depending on how they are related to the question and the passage. Many of the choices will be similar, so consider all of the options before choosing one.

    A. Scientist 1, because of the greater effect of electromagnetism
    B. Scientist 2, because of the greater effect of induced forces
    C. Scientist 1, because of the lesser effect of induced forces
    D. Scientist 2, because of the lesser effect of electromagnetism

I call these types of answers 50/50 answers because you can usually eliminate 50% of the answer choices based on the information in them. Many times these refer to information on the graphs and data tables and, quite often, the information in the answers is contradictory or even scientifically wrong. If this is the case, then immediately eliminate the answer choices with the wrong information. In the example above, if the effects could not have been the result of induced forces, then you could quickly eliminate Answers B and C.

INSIDE THE ACT 36 MIND

If information in the answer choices is scientifically incorrect or contradictory, then the answer choice is WRONG! The ACT will never base answer choices on incorrect data or experiments.

To answer
questions with
graphs or figures
as answer
choices, look
back at your
trend arrows on
the data tables.
You may have
already "drawn"
the data.
Matching your
notes up to the
answer choices
should get you
through these
questions in no
time.

GRAPHS OR FIGURES

Probably the "scariest" kind of question for the average test-taker is one where the answer choices contain additional graphs or figures. What already looks like a complicated passage becomes even more challenging when new graphs are added. They require you to first understand the experiment and, often, then apply data from a table to answer the question.

A.

B.

C.

D.

STRATEGIES

Now that you understand the variety of question types, let's take a closer look at the strategies for answering them. We've already used the **SCIe** parts of the **SCIeNCE** strategies, so now it's time to focus in on the **NCE** ones:

> N—Note the reference in the question.
> C—Choose the correct answer.
> E—Eliminate the wrong answer choices.

N—Note the Reference

Many of the question stems will guide you directly to the section of the passage where you will find the answer. You will see "According to Figure 2," or "Based on Scientist 1," etc. As soon as you see these references—go there! They are like GPS directions telling you exactly how to navigate through the passage. Many factual questions include these references, and since they are generally the ones you can answer the quickest, make the most of the opportunity.

References to questions often include data. If the data is found in a data table, you may want to physically write the data where it "fits." This will help you see the trends and quickly answer the question.

PRACTICE QUESTION

If the average water loss for an organism was 13 ml, what would be the average water intake?

> A. 4
> B. 6
> C. 7
> D. 34

Temperature (°C)	Average Water Intake (ml)	Average Water Loss (ml)	Average PO_4 Release (μg/cm³)
35	8	12	3
40	5	17	9
50	3	28	4

EXPLANATION: (C) Using the reference and placing the data in the table shows that the average water loss should be between 8 and 5 ml. Thus you can eliminate A and D—these answer choices are given to confuse people who misread the wrong column of the data table and looked at PO_4 release or temperature.

In order to get to the correct answer, C, you need to see that the water loss of 13 ml puts the water intake closer to 8, rather than to 5.

Sometimes the reference is to a point on a graph or data table, but the answers cannot be found on that table. In this case, find the information and "translate" it to another graph or table in the passage.

INSIDE THE ACT 36 MIND

While most of these questions are straightforward, the test writers will try to trick you on some of them. They will give a reference to one experiment or figure in the question stem and then give an entirely different reference in the answer choices. For example, you might see, "According to the results of Experiment 1 . . ." in the stem and then answers like, "Experiment 2 should be modified . . ." or, "Agrees most with the data presented in Table 2."

Some of the questions will not have obvious references. They may refer indirectly to the ideas of one of the scientists or the concepts of one of the experiments. A question may begin with a reference to punctuated equilibrium or to alluvial deposits. If you remember where in the passage you saw these topics, then you can quickly go back and find the answer. Students who have **S**canned the passage and **C**hecked the main idea will not have a problem.

What about questions without either a direct or indirect reference? Or ones that refer to both experiments? These will most likely be inference or Xtreme questions and where you will probably spend the most time. There are really no shortcuts to success for these questions. The best advice is to approach them methodically and quickly.

If you feel yourself getting stuck and using up too much time, circle or put a star by the question number, skip to the next question, and come back after you have completed the rest of the questions for that passage. Oftentimes, this technique will help you because some other piece of information in one of the other questions may trigger a response. Overall, how you handle these will depend more on the next two strategies—**C**hoose the Best Answer and **E**liminate the Incorrect Choices.

C—Choose the Best Answer, and
E—Eliminate Incorrect Choices

Well, this is it—the final step in our dissection, where you get to see the guts of the ACT. Choosing the correct answer is what this test, and all of your hard work and preparation, is all about. Your goal is to choose all 40 of the correct answers and achieve your perfect score, a 36. Can you do it? By using your strategies and practicing with passages, you will get closer to the ultimate score.

Choosing the best answer and **E**liminating the incorrect choices are almost always done simultaneously by the advanced student. Other students will ponder over all four answers and then keep referring back to the passage to eliminate the wrong ones. While this might be effective on the tests you take in school, this does not work on the ACT—you simply do not have time!

As you read the question stem and answer choices and then refer back to the passage, you already should have an idea about what the correct answer will be. For factual questions, this usually involves picking out one of the numbers from a table or identifying the main idea of one of the scientists. Unlike in school, you are going to have to go back and refer to the passage because you will not know the topics and specific pieces of data. When you eliminate an answer choice, cross it out. Then make sure to carefully mark the correct answer on your answer sheet.

Choosing the best answer and **E**liminating the incorrect ones are more difficult in inference and Xtreme questions and will require more time. Take advantage of your references in the questions, as well as any trend arrows or notes you've made about the passage. If you have an idea about the correct answer even before you read the choices, then picking the right one will be much easier. When you have to analyze conflicting pieces of information, finding one part of an answer choice that is wrong means that the entire answer is wrong as well, and you don't have to spend more time going through it.

PRACTICE QUESTIONS

Figures 1 and 2 show the germination rates over temperature increase and seedling mass under different salt concentrations for two different plant species.

Figure 1

Figure 2

1. Based on the data in Figures 1 and 2, the researchers should make which of the following conclusions about the overall change in germination rates and seedling mass?
   A. Increased temperature causes a decrease in the number germinated, and increased salt concentration causes an increase in mass.
   B. Decreased salt concentration causes a decrease in mass, and decreased temperature causes a decrease in the number germinated.
   C. Increased temperature and salt concentration have the same effects on the number germinated and seedling mass.
   D. Increased temperature and salt concentration have opposite effects on the number germinated and seedling mass.

EXPLANATION: (D) As you examine the answer choices, it is clear that both A and B are incorrect because the first part of each of the choices is false. Figure 1 shows that as temperature increases, the number germinated increases, so you don't even have to look at the second part of A because the answer is clearly wrong. Likewise, Figure 2 contradicts the first part of answer choice B, so don't bother with the rest; just eliminate it quickly and move on to the next choice. Answer choice C is also wrong, so the correct answer must be D.

2. Based on the data in Figure 2, at 2 mg/ml of salt concentration, the seedlings with the lower mass had what percentage of the mass of the other seedlings?
   A. 40
   B. 50
   C. 60
   D. 80

EXPLANATION: (B) If you picked A, you did not **N**ote the reference in the question to the word, "percentage." You just read the # off the graph, which referred to its mass. The correct answer is B because the seedlings with the lower mass had a mass of 40 g, as compared to the other seedlings with a mass of 80 g. 40/80 = 50%.

3. If under a certain temperature increase, exactly 50 seedlings of a particular plant species had germinated and each of those seedlings had a mass of 40 g, then the salt concentration under which they would have been grown is most likely:
   A. 1.0 mg/ml
   B. 1.5 mg/ml
   C. 2.0 mg/ml
   D. 2.5 mg/ml

EXPLANATION: (D) This question is one of those that requires you to pull information from one figure and apply it to the other. In this case, looking at Figure 1 identified the specific plant species (the darker line). You then had to look at that darker line in Figure 2 at 40 g to find the salt concentration, which was 2.5 mg/ml—correct answer D.

INSIDE THE ACT 36 MIND

If the last question in a passage seems really "easy"—all you have to do is pull a number directly off a graph—there is a good chance you have made a mistake. Be careful. The correct answer to the final question in a passage often requires you to perform a simple math calculation or pay attention to some detail in the label of the graph. Don't fall for the test writers' tricks, especially on the last question in a passage.

PRACTICE SETS

Okay, now let's put all of these skills together. Practice your strategies with the following sample sets of questions. Use the **SCIe** of the **SCIeNCE** strategies to quickly **S**can the section, **C**heck the main idea, and **I**gnore the **e**xtras as you read. Then focus on **N**oting the reference, **C**hoosing the best answer, and **E**liminating the incorrect choices. Analyze how you're doing by filling out the Strategy Practice Chart.

REMEMBER

For more extra-challenging practice, you can go online for the Challenge Round with 50 difficult questions.

Practice Set 1

Temperature and precipitation data were collected over a three-month period for a specific region of the United States. Figure 1 shows the actual daily low temperature as compared to the normal high and low temperatures. Figure 2 compares precipitation amounts and averages throughout the month.

Figure 1

Figure 2

1. According to the data provided in Figure 1, the actual low temperature on December 15 was approximately:
   A. 7.5°C.
   B. 10.0°C.
   C. 12.5°C.
   D. 15.0°C.

2. A student trying to analyze this entire three-month period would most accurately summarize it as:
   F. much warmer than average with much more precipitation.
   G. warmer than average with much less precipitation.
   H. average to slightly colder with much more precipitation.
   J. much colder than average with much less precipitation.

3. During which dates in Figure 1 was the actual daily low temperature most different from the normal high temperature for that same time period?
   A. October 5–7
   B. November 5–7
   C. November 28–30
   D. December 12–14

4. Suppose that, in January, scientists recorded actual average temperatures that were 10.1°C, instead of the normal average of 12.4°C. Normal precipitation is 23.7 cm. Normal high and low average temperatures follow the same pattern as December. Based on this information, which of the following is most consistent with the information presented in this passage?
   F. Precipitation will be lower than average because as temperatures get colder, precipitation amounts decrease.
   G. There should be higher amounts of precipitation because as temperatures get colder, precipitation amounts increase.
   H. There will be more days when the actual low temperature is above the average low temperature.
   J. Precipitation amounts may vary because there is not a direct relationship between temperature and precipitation.

Strategy Practice Chart

Note the reference in the question (if any).

Question 1: _____

Question 2: _____

Question 3: _____

Question 4: _____

Choose the best answer (explain your reasoning).

Question 1: _____

Question 2: _____

Question 3: _____

Question 4: _____

Eliminate the incorrect answers (explain your reasoning).

Question 1: _____

Question 2: _____

Question 3: _____

Question 4: _____

Do you think you used the **NCE** strategies well? Let's check your ideas. **N**ote the reference in the question.

Question 1:   Figure 1 only. Ignore Figure 2.

Question 2:   At first, seems to apply to both, but this can be answered using only Figure 2.

Question 3:   Only Figure 1.

Question 4:   No specific reference—the answers refer to information in both figures.

Choose the best answer.—Some of the answers were fairly obvious, especially for the factual questions. The inference and Xtreme questions were probably trickier, but close reading of the graphs should have resulted in success. **E**liminate the incorrect answers.—See the explanations on the next page.

Did the strategies work for you? Did you have an idea of the correct answer even before looking at the choices? Did you eliminate answer choices that contained information that was clearly wrong? Here are the answers to the questions themselves.

Answers Explained

1. **(B)** A **Factual** Question—The average low temperature was 10.0°C.

   Wrong: (A) 7.5°C is the low for October 15. (C) 12.5°C would be reading the scale wrong. (D) 15.0°C is the average high temperature.

2. **(H)** An **Inference** Question—Figure 2 clearly shows that there is much more precipitation than average and that the overall temperature is slightly colder because of the lower temperature in December.

   Wrong: (F) Although both October and November have slightly warmer temperatures, December is significantly colder. (G and J) There is much more precipitation, so these choices are clearly incorrect.

3. **(A)** An **Xtreme** Question—There is the greatest difference—about 17.5°C—between the lowest temperature around October 6 and the normal high temperature.

   Wrong: (B) This time period is when the low temperature is the highest, but it is actually closest to the normal high. (C and D) These dates appear similar to (A), and (D) refers to one of the lowest temperatures on the graph, but the normal high temperature is much lower than in October.

INSIDE THE ACT 36 MIND

Many times, with questions that have three answers that are similar and one that seems to be very different, the "misfit" answer choice is the correct one. Be careful, though. Test writers usually include at least two or three questions that work exactly the opposite, and they put in the obviously different answer just to trick you.

4. **(J)** An **Xtreme** Question—There is no correlation between the two variables. In October and November, there were warmer-than-average temperatures and increased precipitation. December had the coldest temperature but had increased precipitation as well.

   Wrong: (F and G) Some of the data contradicts each of these answers. (H) There should be fewer days when the actual low temperature is above the average low temperature, not more. Although this could be possible, it is not consistent with the data.

   By, now, you should be getting the hang of the strategies and choosing the correct answers. If you are getting the answers wrong or got lucky with the right answer but used faulty reasoning, make sure to re-read the passage and find out where you are making your mistakes. Here's one more practice set to try.

Practice Set 2

Scientists use many methods to determine the identity and quantity of a substance in samples. Spectroscopy is a simple and powerful method for performing both qualitative and quantitative analyses. Light does not go completely through any liquid. Even in water some light is absorbed. The ratio of the amount of light not absorbed by a liquid (solvent) divided by the total amount of light the solvent was exposed to is called the *transmittance* and is represented by the following equation:

$$T = I/I_o$$

The amount of light that a solvent lets through is not nearly as important as the amount of light that something absorbs. The amount of light absorbed by something is called the absorbance, where

$$A = -\log \text{Transmittance} = I_o/I$$

The absorbance is given on a logarithmic scale, where an absorbance of 0 means no light is absorbed, an absorbance of 1 means 10% of light is absorbed, an absorbance of 2 means 1% of light is absorbed, an absorbance of 3 means 0.1% of light is absorbed and so on.

There is a general relationship between the amount of matter dissolved in a solvent and the amount of light that it absorbs. This relationship is called **Beer's Law**. Table 1 shows a Beer's Law standard curve for methylene blue—a substance used to compare absorbance values of other materials.

TABLE 1

Concentration	Absorbance
0	0.003
1	0.233
2	0.479
3	0.719
4	0.897
5	1.099

Experiment 1

When exposed to light, methylene blue turns from blue to colorless. Absorbance levels of various concentrations of methylene blue were measured, and then the samples were exposed to light for a standard amount of time. Final absorbance measurements were taken and are shown in Figure 1.

Figure 1

Experiment 2

Varying concentrations of a light-sensitive pigment are exposed to lights ranging in wavelength from 600 to 700 nm. Absorbance levels are measured at each point as shown in Figure 2.

Figure 2

1. Based on Experiments 1 and 2, which concentration of the light-sensitive pigment at its highest absorbance is most similar in absorbance to the initial absorbance of methylene blue at the same concentration?
   A. 1.0 mg
   B. 2.0 mg
   C. 3.0 mg
   D. 4.0 mg

2. Based on the description in the passage, the relationship between transmittance and absorbance can best be described by which of the following?
   F. Higher absorbance equals higher transmittance.
   G. Lower absorbance equals lower transmittance.
   H. Higher absorbance equals lower transmittance.
   J. There is no relationship between absorbance and transmittance.

3. According to Table 1 and the information presented, which of the following graphs best represents Beer's Law?

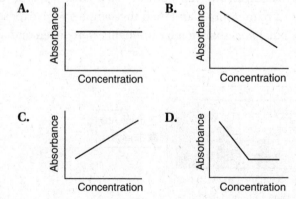

4. According to Figure 1, methylene blue at a concentration of 6.0 mg and exposed to light would have a final absorbance closest to:

F. 1.2.

G. 1.0.

H. 0.8.

J. 0.6.

Strategy Practice Chart

Note the reference in the question (if any).

Question 1: _____

Question 2: _____

Question 3: _____

Question 4: _____

Choose the best answer (explain your reasoning).

Question 1: _____

Question 2: _____

Question 3: _____

Question 4: _____

Eliminate the incorrect answers (explain your reasoning).

Question 1: _____

Question 2: _____

Question 3: _____

Question 4: _____

You should be finding the strategies easier to use every time you practice. Check the descriptions below and see if you're on the right track.

Note the reference in the question.

Question 1: Experiments 1 and 2.

Question 2: Description in the introduction.

Question 3: Table 1 and the introduction.

Question 4: Figure 1 only.

Choose the best answer. As you go through more passages, picking the correct answer should get easier, and you should be getting more questions correct.

Eliminate the incorrect answers. See the explanations on page 268.

TIP

Don't forget to cross out answers that you know are incorrect, especially if you have to come back and reconsider them later. This will save you time.

TIP

When two answer choices mean the same thing but are stated in different ways, they are both wrong. This means you can eliminate them both and have a 50 percent chance of picking the correct answer.

Answers Explained

1. **(B)** An **Inference** Question—The absorbance is 0.4 for both the initial measurement of methylene blue and the light-sensitive pigment at a concentration of 2.0 mg.

    Wrong: (A) The light-sensitive pigment has a higher absorbance than methylene blue at 1.0 mg. (C and D) The light-sensitive pigment has a lower absorbance than methylene blue at 3.0 mg and higher at 4.0 mg concentrations.

2. **(H)** An **Inference** Question—Absorbance is the amount of light not passing through a substance, while transmittance is the amount of light passing through, so there is an inverse (opposite) relationship between the two. The introduction and equations state this.

    Wrong: (F and G) These answers are both wrong because absorbance and transmittance are opposites. (J) There is a relationship between absorbance and transmittance.

3. **(C)** An **Inference** Question—Based on Table 1, as concentration goes up from 0 to 5, absorbance increases from 0.003 to 1.099. Drawing trend arrows should have made this easy.

    Wrong: (A) Absorbance increases. It does not remain constant. (B) This graph shows absorbance decreasing. (D) Graph D shows absorbance decreasing and then leveling off, but Table 1 clearly shows an increase.

4. **(G)** An **Inference** Question—At each higher concentration of methylene blue, absorbance rises. Since at 5.0 mg it is above 0.8, then it should be closest to 1.0 at 6.0 mg.

    Wrong: (F) 1.2 mg is too high, and the question asks about final absorbance. This would be correct for initial absorbance. (H and J) 0.8 and 0.6 are too low based on the trend of the data.

TIP

When a question asks about graphs or tables with more than one data set, underline which one you're looking for in the question. That way, you're less likely to make simple mistakes.

Congratulations! You've finished your dissection and have exposed the inner workings of the ACT science section. You should now be very familiar with the different sections of the passages—introductions; tables, graphs, and figures; and the questions. You have also learned and practiced the **SCIeNCE** strategies for each of them. Now you're ready to put everything you've learned into practice with actual passage examples.

Data Representation Passages

21

→ SAMPLE PASSAGE

Now that you have dissected the science ACT, it's time to practice with an actual Data Representation passage. Don't forget that these passages usually contain multiple graphs, often with different scales on both vertical axes. They are very "number heavy," and contain a large amount of extra information that you do not really need to answer the questions correctly. They sometimes contain a sentence or two either at the beginning of the passage or sandwiched in the middle of several of the diagrams. There is often one question that relies on this information, and many less successful students often miss it.

When approaching the passage, use your **6 SCIeNCE** strategies:

S—Scan the passage
C—Check the main idea
Ie—Ignore the extras
N—Note the reference in the question
C—Choose the best answer
E—Eliminate the incorrect answers.

Before you check your answers, analyze how you used the strategies. Explanations of the problems and tips for answering the questions follow.

> **TIP**
>
> Remember, there are **2–3** Data Representation passages on each test, and they should be done <u>first or second</u>. You can usually recognize them by the set of graphs and data tables.

SAMPLE PASSAGE

Researchers are working to develop nonnatural protein mimics called peptoids. Peptoids differ from proteins in their backbone structure. Typical peptides consist of a central carbon atom, attached to an amino group (NH), a carboxylic acid group (C=O), a hydrogen atom (H), and a side chain called a replacement group (R) (Figure 1).

The structure of a peptoid is different because the replacement groups (R) are attached to the nitrogen atoms, rather than the carbon atoms (Figure 2).

Peptoids have an advantage over peptides in that they form stable, helical structures in solution, are highly resistant to degradation, and might be used to treat pneumonia or other lung infections, including those caused from inhaled biological warfare agents; however, some of them are toxic to cells.

Figure 1: Peptide Structure

Figure 2: Peptoid Structure

Figure 3

Figure 3 shows the effects of two concentrations of peptoids (0.5 mg and 1.0 mg) on two cell types—lung and fibroblast. The optical density (OD) is a measure of the amount of light that is able to pass through the cell cultures and signifies the relative proportion of cells present in a culture. Lethal doses (LD) of a compound are considered to be when at least 50% of the cells have died due to exposure.

1. According to Figures 1 and 2, peptides and peptoids:
    A. contain entirely different atoms.
    B. only differ in the placement of some atoms.
    C. do not differ at all.
    D. behave in the exact same way.

2. At 3 hours, 1.0 mg of peptoid has killed approximately what percent of fibroblast cells?
    F. 20%
    G. 60%
    H. 70%
    J. 80%

3. According to Figure 3, over time, optical density (OD):
   A. increases for both types of cells.
   B. decreases for both types of cells.
   C. increases for fibroblast cells and decreases for lung cells.
   D. decreases for fibroblast cells and increases for lung cells.

4. A scientist trying to examine if there was any correlation between optical density and cell mortality at all peptoid concentrations could correctly draw the following conclusion:
   F. There is no consistent correlation between optical density and cell mortality.
   G. As optical density decreases, cell mortality increases at every peptoid concentration for all cell types.
   H. As optical density increases, cell mortality decreases in lung cells.
   J. Both optical density and cell mortality change throughout a 4-hour time period.

5. By what point in time was a lethal dose (LD) for both cell types first reached due to exposure of the peptoid?
   A. 1 hour
   B. 2 hours
   C. 3 hours
   D. 4 hours

SCIeNCE Strategies

Strategy Practice Chart

Scan the passage.

Time: _____

Check the main idea (draw trend arrows/show relationship).

Main Idea: _____

Ignore the extras. (What information did you skip?)

Extras: _____

Note the reference in the question (if any).

Question 1: _____

Question 2: _____

Question 3: _____

Question 4: _____

Question 5: _____

Choose the best answer (explain your reasoning).

Question 1: _____

Question 2: _____

Question 3: _____

Question 4: _____

Question 5: _____

Eliminate the incorrect answers (explain your reasoning).

Question 1: _____

Question 2: _____

Question 3: _____

Question 4: _____

Question 5: _____

Do you think you used the **SCIeNCE** strategies effectively? Savvy students practice approaching Data Representation passages almost like one of those complicated pictures where you have to find hidden objects—many things look similar, but it takes a keen eye to quickly spot what's correct.

Scan the passage.—Taking 10–15 seconds to look over the passage should have told you that you were dealing with biochemistry concepts and laboratory experiments. Figures 1 and 2 deal with peptide and peptoid structure, while Figure 3 shows two sets of dual experiments.

TIP

Pay attention to graphs with multiple scales on opposite axes or sides. Also be aware that scales from one graph to the next are not always the same.

Check the main idea.—In a Data Representation passage, you must make sure you understand the point of the passage, which is often found in the brief introduction to the passage. In this case, besides peptide and peptoid structure, the third paragraph explains the experiment; "the effects of two concentrations of peptoids (0.5 mg and 1.0 mg) on two cell types" should be circled or underlined. You should also have noted that the graphs have scales on both sides and can be read from either direction. In addition, the scales of the two graphs are not equal. The first graph shows a 1-hour time span, while the second one is 2+ hours.

If the data had been presented in a data table, rather than a graph, drawing a trend arrow to show the relationships would also be appropriate here.

Ignore the **e**xtras.—Data Representation passages are always filled with "extras." You'll need some of them for the tougher questions, but most of the time you can ignore the majority of the extra information. Do you really have to understand the differences in the structure between Figures 1 and 2? Is knowing the definitions of "optical density" and "lethal dose" going to help you? Probably not. The trick is to not get tied up in the details, but to know where they are if you actually need them.

Note the reference in the question.

Question 1: Figures 1 and 2 only. Ignore the graphs when you attempt this question.

Question 2: Only applies to the Fibroblast graph, so don't spend your time on the first one.

Question 3: Both Lung and Fibroblast graphs.

Question 4: No specific reference.

Question 5: Refers back to the introduction.

Choose the Best Answer.—See the answers and explanations below. Data Representation questions often have very obvious correct answers—as long as you've read the graph or data table correctly. Many of these are factual. Inference and Xtreme questions can be trickier, but remember, understanding table or graph trends will often make these pretty apparent as well. Review your trend arrows to see if they give you an easy answer to a question.

Eliminate the incorrect answers.—See the answers and explanations below.

How did it go? Were you able to use the strategies? You have probably used these techniques before and didn't realize it. That's why you're close to achieving your goal of a 36. Perfecting the strategies you already know and learning some new ones should get you even closer. Here are the answers to the questions themselves.

Answers Explained

1. **(B)** A **Factual** Question—Peptides and peptoids differ because the R group is attached to a different atom.

   Wrong: (A) Most of the atoms are the same. (C) The difference is what makes them two separate molecules. (D) The advantages of peptoids, because of their different structure, mean that they behave differently. Remember, the answers to factual questions often are clearly stated in the passage or quickly understood from a figure or graph.

2. **(H)** A **Factual** Question—Reading the Fibroblast graph and looking at the correct point shows that the answer is clearly between 60 and 80%.

   Wrong: (F) 20% is the amount for 2 hours. (G and J) The figures are clearly too low or too high on the Fibroblast graph.

3. **(D)** A **Factual** Question—Optical density increases for lung cells and decreases for fibroblast cells.

   Wrong: (A and B) These answers refer to patterns for other lines on the graphs. (C) This is the reverse of the lines on the graph.

INSIDE THE ACT 36 MIND

When questions have answers that are "reversed," they are often correct. The test makers want you to have to consider all the options, not just make a quick decision and go on with the rest of the test.

TIP

The ACT is filled with questions where the correct answer is "right there" on the graph. Be careful that you don't misread the question and look at the wrong graph, the wrong place on the graph, or the wrong line.

TIP

Although factual questions tend to be easier, they require careful reading of the graphs. The answer choices may be designed to trick you. It is important in questions like these to make sure to eliminate the incorrect answers; on first glance, people sometimes choose an incorrect answer because they're working so quickly. Don't let the lack of time ruin your focus.

4.   **(F)** An **Xtreme** Question—There is no correlation between the two variables. In Lung cells, as optical density increases, cell death increases at 0.5 mg and decreases at 1.0 mg.

   Wrong: (G) This is only true for fibroblast cells. (H) This is not true for 0.5 mg in lung cells. (J) The straight arrows on the end of the lines mean that the data stayed constant after that time. Lung cells only changed over a 1-hour time period.

Xtreme questions are the questions that few students are expected to get correct most of the time. The ACT is designed to separate all the students who take the test into levels. So, if this was one of the first passages on the test, more students would get this correct. Later on, if this were passage 6 or 7, fewer students would get this one because they are tired, rushing, or out of time.

5.   **(C)** An **Inference** Question—By 3 hours more than 50% of the cells had died for both cell types and at all concentrations.

   Wrong: (A and B) The lines are both below 50% for fibroblast cells, and there is not any data for lung cells at either of these times. (D) Although this answer is correct in that >50% of the cells have died, the answer does not agree with the question, which states, "by what point . . . first reached."

Now that you've had the chance to practice your strategies, you should be doing better on Data Representation passages and on the way to reaching your goals. In the next chapter we'll practice with a Research Summaries passage.

Research Summaries Passages

22

→ **SAMPLE PASSAGE**

Research Summaries passages usually consist of two or three experiments about the same concept.

Most of the time, these passages can be recognized by headings such as "Experiment 1," "Experiment 2," "Study 1," "Study 2," etc. However, they sometimes look more like Data Representation passages because they, too, will include graphs and data tables. In a few cases, they may even look like Conflicting Viewpoints passages because they will not have graphs and may have headings that look similar.

Science Slackers will "ignore" the descriptions of the experiments and go right to the information in the graphs and data tables. If questions ask about the experimental procedure, many of them can be answered by looking at the data collected. If the information is not there, then go back and read the descriptions. The one exception to this is if there is no data or graph with the experiment. You will have to read the description of the experiment.

Questions that ask about specific procedures, such as "Why did the student wait 5 minutes after placing the flask in the water bath before attaching the tubing?" or "Which of the factors was not directly controlled in Experiment 1?" or "Why was the mass of the beaker tared [zeroed out on the balance—as defined in the passage] before adding the liquids?" require you to think about how you do experiments and labs in class. They test your knowledge of good procedure and require you to take a step back and think about the experiment itself, not just about the passage.

Don't forget to use your **6 SCIeNCE** strategies:

S—Scan the passage
C—Check the main idea
Ie—Ignore the extras
N—Note the reference in the question
C—Choose the best answer
E—Eliminate the incorrect answers

Once you've gone through the passage and answered the questions, analyze how your strategies worked as well. Explanations of the correct answers, wrong answers, and tips for answering the questions follow.

TIP

There are **2–3 Research Summaries passages on each test, and they should be done first or second.** You can usually recognize them by the separate studies and experiments, as well as graphs and data tables.

TIP

If the question asks you how the design of Experiment 1 was different from Experiment 2, try looking at the information in the data tables and then the description of Experiment 2 first to eliminate some of the easy answer choices.

SAMPLE PASSAGE

When dropped, certain materials tend to bounce higher than others. As an object hits a surface, it becomes deformed to a certain degree and then returns to its original shape. In a sphere or ball, this property is referred to as elasticity. The more elastic a substance is, the more energy of this deformation is retained, the more it will be returned to its original shape, and then the higher and faster the sphere will bounce. The measure of this elasticity is the coefficient of restitution (e), and it can be calculated by several methods:

$$\sqrt{h_b/h_i} = e \qquad h_b = \text{bounce height}$$
$$h_i = \text{initial height}$$
$$v_b/v_a = e \qquad v_b = \text{bounce/separation velocity}$$
$$v_a = \text{approach/impact velocity}$$

Coefficients of restitution have values between 0 and 1.0.

A 2.0 m clear plastic tube was set up on top of a steel plate. A chamber at the top allowed for placement of spheres of varying diameters. An optical, electronic timing device recorded and calculated velocities, while a camera was used to measure the bounce heights. The inside of the tube could be converted into a vacuum chamber to discount the effects of air resistance, as shown in Figure 1.

Figure 1

Experiment 1

Spheres of various substances with the same diameter were dropped from 2.0 meters in the vacuum tube. The bounce height (h_b) was measured and the resulting coefficient of restitution (e) was calculated. Each trial was repeated 10 times and averages were calculated. Results are presented in Table 1.

TABLE 1

Sphere	h_i (m)	h_b (m)	e
Clay	2.0	0.005	.05
Glass	2.0	1.13	.751
Ivory	2.0	1.49	.863
Plastic	2.0	0.78	.624
Rubber	2.0	1.83	.956
Steel	2.0	1.94	.984

Experiment 2

Using the same apparatus, various athletic balls were dropped from 2.0 meters. The approach/impact velocity (v_a) and bounce/separation velocity (v_b) were measured and the coefficient of restitution (e) was calculated. Each trial was repeated 10 times and averages were calculated. Results are presented in Table 2.

TABLE 2

Ball	v_a (m/s)	v_b (m/s)	e
Basketball	2.43	1.94	.798
Bowling Ball	2.58	0.570	.221
Glass Marble	1.49	1.11	.749
Golf Ball	1.78	1.28	.719
Soccer Ball	2.17	1.40	.645
Tennis Ball	2.04	1.83	.897

1. A sphere of unknown material was dropped in the apparatus and the bounce height (h_b) was measured to be 0.84 m. Based on the results of Experiment 1, the coefficient of restitution (e) is closest to:

   A. .547
   B. .613
   C. .648
   D. .871

2. Which of the following factors was NOT directly controlled by the student in Experiment 1?

    F.   The bounce height (h_b)
    G.   The initial height (h_i)
    H.   The type of equipment
    J.   The type of sphere

3. Which of the following types of balls has an elasticity coefficient most similar to ivory?

    A.   Basketball
    B.   Glass marble
    C.   Soccer ball
    D.   Tennis ball

4. Another student repeated Experiment 2 with a newly developed "Super Ball"—a very dense rubber ball that its inventors have made specifically for its incredible bouncing ability. Based on the results of Experiments 1 and 2, the most likely range of coefficients of elasticity for this ball would be:

    F.   between 0.755–0.894.
    G.   between 0.951–0.997.
    H.   between 0.962–1.04.
    J.   between 1.23–1.55.

5. Although the students running Experiment 1 and Experiment 2 used the same equipment and procedures, they collected different data and used different formulas to calculate the coefficient of restitution (e). Which of the following pairs of trials would best confirm that either of the two methods was accurate and consistent?

    A.   Golf ball and glass marble because their e values were extremely close.
    B.   Steel and basketball because their h_b and v_b were both 1.94.
    C.   Ivory and glass marble because their h_b and v_a were both 1.49.
    D.   Glass and glass marble because they were made out of the same material.

6. Based on the results from the two experiments, what is the most likely conclusion that can be drawn about the properties of materials and their elasticity?

    F.   Balls used for sports are more elastic than spheres made of metal.
    G.   Elasticity is always lower in large balls than in small balls.
    H.   Spheres and balls that are softer have higher elasticity than those that are harder.
    J.   Elasticity depends less on the size or softness of the sphere and more on its ability to return to its original shape.

Strategy Practice Chart

Scan the passage.

Time: _____

Check the main idea (draw trend arrows/show relationship).

Main Idea: _____

Ignore the **e**xtras. (what information did you skip?)

Extras: _____

Note the reference in the question (if any).

Question 1: _____

Question 2: _____

Question 3: _____

Question 4: _____

Question 5: _____

Question 6: _____

Choose the best answer (explain your reasoning).

Question 1: _____

Question 2: _____

Question 3: _____

Question 4: _____

Question 5: _____

Question 6: _____

Eliminate the incorrect answers (explain your reasoning).

Question 1: _____

Question 2: _____

Question 3: _____

Question 4: _____

Question 5: _____

Question 6: _____

TIP

For Research Summaries passages, use the same types of strategies you learned for the reading and mathematics sections of the ACT because they rely on the same types of skills.

Were you able to use the **SCIeNCE** strategies for this passage? Research Summaries passages require you to understand an often complex experimental design and interpret diagrams, tables, and graphs quickly and accurately.

Scan the passage.—A quick (10–15 second) scan shows a brief introduction to the concept of elasticity, including several equations. A diagram of the experimental equipment is shown, and two different experiments are described with data presented in a table.

Check the main idea.—Research Summaries passages often contain one main idea and two or three sub-ideas. The concept of elasticity and a value known as a coefficient of elasticity are clearly main ideas. You would be wise to circle/underline these in the passage. For each experiment, you should do the same. Experiment 1 compares spheres and height, while Experiment 2 uses balls and velocity. Since the data is presented in a table, drawing trend arrows to show relationships would be helpful; however, these tables do not show any regular trends.

Ignore the **e**xtras.—Like Data Representation passages, Research Summaries are always filled with "extras." Once again, some of them are necessary, but most are not. Do you really need to compare the difference between numbers that use three decimal places? Most of the time the answers are far more obvious.

Note the reference in the question.

Question 1: Experiment 1.
Question 2: Experiment 1.
Question 3: The stem of Question 3 refers to Experiment 1, but the answer choices require you to look at Experiment 2.
Question 4: Experiments 1 and 2.
Question 5: Experiments 1 and 2.
Question 6: No direct reference at all.

INSIDE THE ACT 36 MIND

Every question is different and may ask you to focus on a different part of the passage. The best advice is to maximize your time by noting the reference and focusing only on that experiment to find the answer.

Choose the best answer.—See the answers and explanations on the next page.

Research Summaries questions contain a variety of answer types. Some involve simply picking out a number from the data. Many others require you to interpret any trends and pick answers that would fit in between other choices. There is usually a combination of fact, inference, and Xtreme questions.

Eliminate the incorrect answers.—See the answers and explanations on the next page.

Eliminating incorrect answers is a key step for the ambitious student. Research Summaries passages may contain three separate experiments and several graphs and data tables. With so much information to consider, you should always try to verify that the answer you picked as correct is the best one. Sometimes the questions contain correct answers—but they are for the wrong experiment. Don't get tricked by the test makers, especially in this section. That will prevent you from achieving your 36!

Hopefully, these strategies are becoming easier to use. With practice they will become second nature. What follows are the correct answers to the questions and explanations to help you understand the nature of the test.

TIP

Be sure to look at the correct column on any table or graph and make sure the relationship between the numbers is clear.

Answers Explained

1. **(C)** A **Factual** Question—A bounce height (h_b) of 0.84 is closest to that of plastic (0.78, e = .624). Higher bounce heights result in higher e values, so the number has to be slightly higher than .624.

   Wrong: (A and B) Too low. (D) Too high.

2. **(F)** A **Factual** Question—The bounce height (h_b) is what the student is measuring and changes based on which type of sphere is dropped.

   Wrong: (G and H) The initial heights (h_i) and the type of equipment are the same for every trial of this experiment. (J) This is the experimental or independent variable in the experiment—what the student is actually testing.

INSIDE THE ACT 36 MIND

Every Research Summaries passage on the ACT includes questions based on experimental design and the scientific method. Remember, this is a test of scientific reasoning. Don't get distracted by the subject of the experiment. Focus on the proper set-up and, regardless of the topic, these questions should be easier.

3. **(D)** A **Factual** Question—A tennis ball has an e value of .897, while ivory has an e value of .863.

   Wrong: (A), (B), and (C) all have e values that are inconsistent with the question. (B) is wrong because the bounce height (h_b) for ivory is the same as the approach velocity (v_a) for the glass marble. The question asks for e values.

   Warning: Although this is a factual question, it requires <u>careful</u> reading of the data tables. As in Data Representation questions, the answer choices are designed to trick you. If you just look for numbers that are close and do not pay attention to the proper column or row on the tables, you are going to miss questions like these—exactly what the test makers want you to do.

TIP

Research Summaries questions are where understanding of experimental design and the scientific method really comes in handy. If you miss questions in these passages, review this topic using your class notes, textbooks, or online resources.

4. **(G)** An **Inference** Question—Super Balls are made of rubber and should have similar coefficients of elasticity as other rubber balls.

   Wrong: (F) This range is too low based on the data. (H) The lower end of the range is fine, but the upper end is >1.0. (J) The entire range is too high.

   This question requires that you look at both of the experiments, but also that you refer back to the introduction. In the middle of the background information, it states, "Coefficients of restitution have values between 0 and 1.0." Consequently, two of the answer choices can easily be eliminated. There are almost always questions like this in the Research Summaries sections, where the correct answer can only be determined by looking at both the description and the data.

ACT test writers seem to love questions like this. They not only test your ability to put together information from various sections of the passage, but they also make you really hunt for that information. Notice that the information you needed was placed right after the equations and right before a description of the equipment—two extra parts of the passage that you can usually ignore. You will also find this kind of information as a single sentence right above a graph or table, at the top of the right-hand column on the actual test, and crammed into additional rows at the bottom of tables or graphs. As you Scan the passage note where these little bits of information are placed and be able to come back to them if needed.

5. **(D)** An **Inference** Question—The glass sphere and glass marble had very similar e values using both methods of data collection and calculation.

    Wrong: (A) The e values were only determined using velocity. (B) There is no direct relationship between bounce height (h_b) and bounce velocity (v_b). (C) There is no direct relationship between bounce height (h_b) and approach velocity (v_a).

6. **(J)** An **Xtreme** Question—Realizing that harder materials sometimes have higher e values than softer ones and that smaller balls sometimes have lower e values than larger ones makes this the only correct answer choice.

    Wrong: (F) Bowling balls are clearly less elastic than almost all of the spheres. (G) Small golf balls have a lower e value than larger balls, like basketballs. (H) Hard steel spheres have higher e values than softer ones like clay.

    This is an **Xtreme** question because it asks you to draw a conclusion from the experiment. It also gives you answer choices with multiple options so that you have to refer back to both experiments and the data. In this case, the correct answer is the last one, but this is often not the case. Eliminating incorrect answer choices is a key step to getting these questions correct.

    Did your strategy practice help? To perform even better, you should continue to work on understanding experiments, whether from passages, journal articles, labs, or textbooks.

    The last chapter of this section features a Conflicting Viewpoints passage, so get ready to read!

Conflicting Viewpoints Passages

23

→ **SAMPLE PASSAGES**

A Conflicting Viewpoints passage is often called a "theory" passage because it relies more heavily on unsupported evidence than on hard data like the Data Representation and Research Summaries passages.

These passages are usually identified by headings, such as "Scientist 1" and "Scientist 2," or topic titles, such as "Darwinism" and "Lamarckism." However, sometimes they will be headed "Experiment 1" and "Experiment 2," exactly like the Research Summaries passage headings. Be careful. These passages may also contain multiple graphs and data tables, so identifying them is not always easy. If it is not clear if a passage is a Conflicting Viewpoint, look at the questions. Are they asking for comparisons between scientists or models? If so, then this is one of these passages. If the questions refer to single pieces of information or contain mostly numbers, then it is probably one of the other types. If you are still not sure, leave it for second to last/last to save time.

TIP

There is **1** Conflicting Viewpoints passage on each test, and it should be done last. You can usually recognize this kind of passage by the comparison questions that follow.

INSIDE THE ACT 36 MIND

Remember, these are the passages designed to waste your time. While they may seem "easier" because there are fewer graphs and numbers, these passages require a great deal of going back and forth between topics. Doing these last and having a strategy to maximize your time will help your score.

Remember, this is the passage designed to test your reading and science reasoning ability. It is also designed to waste time.

The **SCIeNCE** strategies for the Conflicting Viewpoints passage are a little different than for the other passage types.

Scan the passage to see the structure. Do this quickly. Is there an Introduction? Are there comparisons between two hypotheses, four students, three models, etc.? You should put an abbreviation ("I" for Introduction, or "D" for DNA Hypothesis, or "2" for Scientist 2, etc.) in the margins next to these sections.

Check the main idea. This is very different for a Conflicting Viewpoints passage. You are going to use the process of "triage," by figuring out which questions are the most urgent and efficient ones to answer. If you have ever had to go to the emergency room, you have experienced "triage." A child with a broken bone might be seen before an adult with the flu, but someone coming in with the paramedics will be seen before both of the others, regardless of how long they have been waiting.

To "triage" the passage, you will use the abbreviations you marked while scanning. Go to the questions and look at the question stems and answers. If the question is about Scientist 1 only, then mark next to it with a "1." If the answers refer to the difference between Models 2 and 3, then put "2/3." If it refers to both of the hypotheses, then write "B."

Ignore the **e**xtras. Do not read the sections! You want to compartmentalize your thinking, and reading the conflicting ideas will only confuse you and waste valuable time.

Note the reference in the question. This is where the rest of the "triage" process is used. Look at the questions and decide which order you are going to answer them. You need to be strategic. Here's an attack order and strategy:

1ST: Questions about the Introduction only—Read the Introduction and answer these questions. Do this even if there is only one of these questions. This will give you background information about the topic.

2ND: Questions about a single section only—Find the most questions that refer to one of the sections. Read that student/scientist/hypothesis and answer these questions. It does not matter if it is the second (or third or fourth) section.

3RD: Questions about the other single section(s) only—Find the next highest amount of questions that refer to one of the sections. Read that student/scientist/hypothesis and answer these questions.

4TH: Questions about multiple/sections—Do these last. Now that you have read the sections separately, these should be easier.

Choose the best answer. These should be much easier to find (for most of the questions) if you have "triaged" effectively.

Eliminate the incorrect answers. The same holds true if you have used a good strategy.

INSIDE THE ACT 36 MIND

This triage strategy is not foolproof. Sometimes a question that refers to Scientist 1 will have its answer found in the Scientist 2 section, especially if the question asks about evidence that would *contradict* one of the scientist's views. If the question seems to do this, or you are taking too much time, skip it and come back after you have done the other sections.

Use your **6 SCIeNCE** strategies:

S—Scan the passage
C—Check the main idea—Triage the questions
Ie—Ignore the extras
N—Note the reference in the question—Answer single section questions first
C—Choose the best answer
E—Eliminate the incorrect answers

Explanations of the correct answers and the wrong answers and tips for answering the questions follow.

SAMPLE PASSAGES

Sample Passage 1

Silver nanoparticles, which range in diameter from 4–20 nanometers (1 nanometer = 1 billionth of a meter), demonstrate unique properties, especially against various bacteria, viruses, and fungi. Silver has been used to treat infections for centuries, but with the advent of nanotechnology, the use of silver in nanoparticle form has opened new treatment avenues.

Scientist 1

Silver nanoparticles have the potential to revolutionize the medical and consumer products industries. Various researchers have found that silver nanoparticles are effective killers of pathogenic bacteria such as *E. coli*, *B. subtilis*, and *S. aureus*. The antimicrobial mechanism of their action is not completely understood, but they may interact with the bacterial peptido-glycan layer, form pits in the cell wall, change membrane polarity, and/or form free radicals that damage the membrane. One thing that is known is that because the nanoparticles do not act via cell receptors, there is no immune response and thus no antibacterial resistance. Recent studies have also indicated that silver nanoparticles in the range of 1–10 nm attach to HIV proteins and inhibit the virus from binding to cells.

Because of these antimicrobial properties, silver nanoparticle technology has safely been incorporated into surgical instruments, hospital wound dressings, and a wide variety of consumer products, such as washing machines, food storage containers, bandages, and clothing. The possibilities for using the antimicrobial properties of this technology seem boundless.

Scientist 2

While silver nanoparticles may in fact have antimicrobial properties, the risks of their use potentially far outweigh the benefits. The Environmental Protection Agency (EPA) has established regulations for companies that intend to sell products containing silver nanoparticles acting as bacteria killers. Before the products can be sold to consumers, these businesses will have to provide scientific evidence that there is no environmental risk posed by the nanoparticles. Further regulation has since defined the steps that companies would have to undergo before they could incorporate nanotechnology into their products and make claims regarding the antimicrobial properties. Consequently, various companies have dropped references to silver nanoparticles in their literature and packaging, but they have not changed the materials themselves.

Using silver medicinally, usually in the form of nonnanoparticle colloidal silver sold in health food stores as a dietary supplement, has some potential side effects. These include argyria, a permanent incorporation of silver into the skin resulting in a silver skin tone, neurologic problems, kidney damage, stomach distress, headaches, fatigue, skin irritation, and the potential interference with the body's absorption of some drugs. The effects of silver nanoparticles on the soil, air, wastewater, groundwater, and bacteria, algae, protozoa, fungi, plant, and animal life are not at all understood. Consequently, the technology is not without some huge implications, and its further use may result in the opening of a "Pandora's box" of problems.

TIP

Even if reading is your strongest subject, this section should be done at the end of the test because it requires you to go through the most material in the shortest amount of time.

1. According to Scientist 1, silver nanoparticles may be effective against various bacteria because they:
   A. inhibit binding to cells.
   B. cause no immune response.
   C. interfere with the absorption of some drugs.
   D. form pits in the cell walls.

2. The information from Scientist 2 indicates that silver nanoparticles may be hazardous because:
   F. their effects are not completely known.
   G. of their antimicrobial effects.
   H. they can cause neurologic damage.
   J. they may result in permanent skin discoloration.

3. Scientist 2's views differ from Scientist 1's in that only Scientist 2 believes that silver nanoparticles:
   A. have potent antimicrobial properties.
   B. may pose an environmental threat.
   C. can be used safely and effectively in hospital equipment.
   D. are no longer being utilized in consumer products.

4. A company markets its use of silver nanoparticle technology. When the Environmental Protection Agency (EPA) steps in to regulate claims regarding the antibacterial properties of silver nanoparticles, according to Scientist 2, the company may do which of the following and still follow the EPA guidelines?

   I. Nothing and continue to sell its products as designed
   II. Submit to rigorous testing of the properties and safety of the product
   III. Change the packaging and leave the product unchanged

   F. I only
   G. II only
   H. II and III only
   J. I, II, and III

5. Suppose in vitro testing of silver nanoparticles finds that they reduce bacterial concentrations of *E. coli* and *C. botulinum* by 99.9% in petri dish cultures. However, food storage containers, which have silver nanoparticles incorporated into their chemical structure, have a negligible effect on these strains, as compared to similar containers that do not contain this material. Which of the following statements is most consistent with these results and with the information presented in the passage?
   A. Neither scientist would use this as conclusive proof of the antimicrobial properties of the particles.
   B. Scientist 1 would support the incorporation of the nanoparticles into the food storage containers.
   C. Scientist 2 would not support their use because of their apparent safety hazards.
   D. Both Scientist 1 and Scientist 2 would support their use in consumer products because of their strong antimicrobial properties.

6. Based on Scientist 1's explanation, using silver nanoparticles embedded into bandages to treat recurring bacterial infections would be more effective than current antibiotics because:

   F. the bacterial cell walls would be broken down.

   G. the risk of developing argyria would be decreased.

   H. the smaller size (1–10 nm) particles would inhibit growth the most.

   J. the bacteria would not go through natural selection and become resistant to the particles.

7. Which of the following developments would most greatly alleviate Scientist 2's concern about this new technology?

   A. Companies using silver nanoparticles clearly label their packaging.

   B. Testing shows that silver nanoparticles remain embedded in the products and do not have the potential to leak into the environment.

   C. The EPA drops the requirement that companies must prove there is no environmental risk.

   D. Studies on mice show few neurological side effects.

Strategy Practice Chart

Scan the passage.

   Time: _____

Check the main idea. (Triage the questions.)

   Main Idea: _____

Ignore the **e**xtras. (What information did you skip?)

   Extras: _____

Note the reference in the question (if any). Answer the questions by section.

   Question 1: _____

   Question 2: _____

   Question 3: _____

   Question 4: _____

   Question 5: _____

   Question 6: _____

   Question 7: _____

Choose the best answer (explain your reasoning).

   Question 1: _____

   Question 2: _____

   Question 3: _____

   Question 4: _____

   Question 5: _____

   Question 6: _____

   Question 7: _____

TIP

Don't forget to write an abbreviation in the margin for each scientist and question. This will help you answer the questions much more quickly.

Eliminate the incorrect answers (explain your reasoning).

Question 1: _____

Question 2: _____

Question 3: _____

Question 4: _____

Question 5: _____

Question 6: _____

Question 7: _____

Before we look at the answers, let's see how you used the **SCIeNCE** strategies.

Scan the passage. Taking 15–20 seconds to look over the introduction to the passage (7 minutes total) should have told you that the passage was about biology, specifically silver nanoparticles. You should have put in abbreviations in the margins next to these sections: "I" for Introduction, "1" for Scientist 1, and "2" for Scientist 2.

Check the main idea. You should have "triaged" the questions and come up with the following:

Question 1: Scientist 1.
Question 2: Scientist 2.
Question 3: Both.
Question 4: Scientist 2.
Question 5: Both.
Question 6: Scientist 1.
Question 7: Scientist 2.

Ignore the **e**xtras. Hopefully, you did *not* read the sections yet.

Note the reference in the question. Based on your "triage" of the questions, you should have approached the passage in the following order:

1ST: Read Scientist 2: Silver nanoparticles had benefits. Concerned about environmental effects. Answer Questions 2, 4, and 7 first.

2ND: Read Scientist 1: Silver nanoparticles had benefits. Positive feelings toward technology. Answer Questions 1 and 6 second.

3RD: Answer Questions 3 and 5 last.

When you see these signals, make sure to zero in on those sections and those sections only. The test makers will try to distract you with information from the other scientist, but don't be fooled.

Choose the best answer. See the answers and explanations that follow.

Did you pick the best answer? As a good test-taker, your first instincts will often prove correct, but don't get too relaxed. Remember, sometimes the most obvious answer is correct, but for the Xtreme questions, it often is not. If you get stuck, eliminate the wrong answers and move on to a new question.

Eliminate the incorrect answers. See the answers and explanations that follow.

Eliminating incorrect answers in a Conflicting Viewpoints question is often more difficult than in Data Representation or Research Summaries passages because the answers are not obvious. They are rarely numerical, but knowing each scientist's main idea will speed up this process.

How did you do? With practice, these strategies will become second nature and will help you to achieve your goals. Now let's see how you did on the questions themselves.

Answers Explained

TIP

The factual questions should seem easier once you have identified each scientist's idea.

1. **(D)** A **Factual** Question—Scientist 1 lists the ways silver nanoparticles may kill bacteria, including forming pits.

    Wrong: (A) Refers to effect on HIV. (B) Describes a consequence, not a method of killing. (C) From Scientist 2's argument.

2. **(F)** A **Factual** Question—Scientist 2 is the only one to mention hazards, and the main idea is that the overall effects are "not at all understood."

    Wrong: (G) Is a positive effect of silver nanoparticles. (H and J) Refer to other side effects of silver, not necessarily silver nanoparticles.

    Be careful of answers like choice (G), which are clearly wrong. Misreading the question and not paying attention to the word *hazardous* would make this seem to be the most likely answer. Test writers rely on the fact that you are working quickly and skimming some of the material. Missteps like this can keep you from your 36.

3. **(B)** An **Inference** Question—Scientist 2 focuses on the environmental risks of this technology.

    Wrong: (A) Both scientists believe that the nanoparticles are effective against bacteria. (C) Medical use is referred to by Scientist 1 only. (D) Nanoparticles are no longer being advertised as used in consumer products, but the products themselves have not changed. This sounds correct, but requires you to read carefully.

INSIDE THE ACT 36 MIND

Pay close attention to which scientist's views are being discussed. Test writers purposely include multiple references to "Scientist 1" and "Scientist 2" in the question stems to try to confuse the average test-taker.

4. **(H)** An **Xtreme** Question—Options II and III may both be done by companies under the current EPA guidelines.

    Wrong: (F and J) Both of these answers contain option I, which would not be permitted by the EPA. (G) While option II is correct, so is option III, which would eliminate this as the <u>best</u> answer.

    These are Xtreme questions because they rely on you to not only infer what the correct answer is but also to reason the best combination of choices. If you can eliminate one of the options as wrong (in this case option I), then immediately eliminate all answer choices with that option in it (F and J). Then you have fewer choices to make.

5. **(A)** An **Xtreme** Question—Although the nanoparticles are effective in a lab setting, they are not effective in consumer products, so neither scientist would use this as proof.

Wrong: (B) Scientist 1 believes this in general, but it is inconsistent with the results. (C) This is one of Scientist 2's concerns, but the results would not warrant putting the nanoparticles into the containers in the first place. (D) Although this answer is supported by the passage, it contradicts the facts presented in the question stem.

Many Science Reasoning questions on the ACT do not require reading the passage at all to find the correct answer. This is one of them. The tricky part about this question is that the closer you have read, the more likely you are to pick the wrong answer.

6. **(J)** An **Inference** Question—The key word here is *recurring*. The passage implies that bacteria are becoming resistant to various antibacterial chemicals, including antibiotics.

Wrong: (F) This may be one of the ways in which nanoparticles kill bacteria, but it does not explain why they would be more effective than antibiotics. (G) Argyria is referred to by Scientist 2 only. (H) Particles 1–10 nm in size have been shown to be effective against viruses, not bacteria.

Knowing some biology, although not required, definitely helps with this question. Understanding and recognizing the difference between viruses and bacteria, knowing how antibiotics work, and realizing how natural selection plays a role in antibacterial resistance give you an advantage over less advanced science students.

7. **(B)** An **Inference** Question—If silver nanoparticles remain in the materials and do not pose an environmental threat, then this would most alleviate Scientist 2's concern.

Wrong: (A) While this is an issue raised by Scientist 2, it is not the main idea of the argument. (C) Dropping the testing requirement would do nothing to alleviate the overall concerns. (D) Testing in mice would help; however, the neurological side effects are not a primary concern of this scientist.

Answering this question relies just as much on knowing common nonscientific vocabulary—in this case the word *alleviate*—as it does scientific principles.

Another variation of the Conflicting Viewpoints is when there are multiple students or scientists. This type is best approached using "triage." Here's another hint: when you go back to find answers, similar information is often presented in the same order for each viewpoint, so if you can find the information in one place an excellent strategy is to look in the same place for the other viewpoints.

Sample Passage 2

A science teacher brought several of the same species of broadleaf plant to her classroom. She found the mass of each and gave each an equal amount of water. She covered the pots with bags so that only the stem and leaves of the plant were exposed to the atmosphere. She put one on the counter away from any windows. She put one by a running fan, and she put one in a closed cabinet. She asked her students to predict which plant would look the healthiest and to predict whether they would gain or lose mass at the end of 5 days if given no additional water and left in these same conditions.

Four students give their viewpoints about the condition and mass of the plants and provide an explanation for their predictions.

Student 1

The plant on the counter will look the healthiest. The plant will be exposed to light during the day and therefore be able to undergo photosynthesis. In order to accomplish this, water will have to be moved from the roots to the leaves and out to the atmosphere by the process of transpiration. At night, when the classroom lights are off, the plant will go through cellular respiration.

All three plants will lose mass. The plant by the running fan will have the greatest change in mass, followed by the plant on the counter. The plant in the cabinet will have the least change in mass. This is because the effects of transpiration and loss of water mass from the soil are greater than the effects of photosynthesis and gain of mass from glucose production. Transpiration compounds the mass loss from cellular respiration.

Student 2

Student 1 is correct except that the plant in the cabinet will have the greatest change in mass. This is because the effects of cellular respiration, in which the plant consumes glucose, are greater than the loss of water mass from the soil through transpiration.

Student 3

The plant by the fan will look the healthiest. This plant will be exposed to light during the day and therefore be able to undergo photosynthesis. The increased air circulation will result in more transpiration because more water can to be moved to the leaves. This will also allow for more photosynthesis because more CO_2 can be moved into the leaves and more O_2 can be released.

The plants by the fan and on the counter will gain mass, while the mass of the plant by the cabinet will remain constant. The plant by the running fan will have the greatest change in mass, followed by the plant on the counter. This is because photosynthesis produces glucose, which is turned into new plant mass. Since the plant in the cabinet is not going through photosynthesis, there will be no mass change.

Student 4

All of the plants will look equally healthy. The plants on the counter and by the running fan will be exposed to light during the day and therefore be able to undergo photosynthesis. The plant in the cabinet will get its energy through cellular respiration. Both of these process will keep the plants alive and looking equally healthy. Transpiration will occur in all three plants, so water will be lost to the atmosphere. At night, when the classroom lights are off, all the plants will go through cellular respiration.

The plant on the counter will gain mass. The plant by the fan will remain constant, but the plant in the cabinet will lose mass. The effects of photosynthesis will be greater than the effects of transpiration in the plant near the fan. By the fan, the effects of transpiration and loss of water mass from the soil are equal to the glucose added through photosynthesis. Cellular respiration and transpiration will cause the plant in the cabinet to lose the most mass.

1. Which of the students, if any, claim(s) that when the mass is measured after 5 days that the plant in the cabinet will lose mass?
   A. Student 2 only
   B. Student 4 only
   C. Students 1, 2, and 4 only
   D. Students 2, 3, and 4 only

2. Based on Student 1's argument, does photosynthesis require the process of transpiration in order for the plant to gain mass?
   F. Yes, transpiration brings water from the roots to the leaves, but it is not required for the production of glucose.
   G. Yes, transpiration brings water from the roots to the leaves, and it is required for the production of glucose.
   H. No, transpiration brings water from the roots to the leaves, but it is not required for the production of glucose.
   J. No, transpiration brings water from the roots to the leaves, and it is required for the production of glucose.

3. Which of the following unbalanced equations for the process of photosynthesis is most consistent with the viewpoint of Student 3?
   A. $CO_2 + O_2 \rightarrow$ glucose $+ H_2O$
   B. $CO_2 +$ glucose $\rightarrow O_2 + H_2O$
   C. $H_2O + O_2 \rightarrow$ glucose $+ CO_2$
   D. $CO_2 + H_2O \rightarrow$ glucose $+ O_2$

4. Repeated field observations of the effects of photosynthesis, transpiration, and cellular respiration on the plant mass of *Plantago major*, a broadleaf flowering plant found in wide distribution in many natural areas, show that exposure to consistent sunny and windy conditions results in decreased leaf surface area and overall smaller plant height. These results are *inconsistent* with the viewpoints of which student(s)?
   F. Student 2 only
   G. Student 3 only
   H. Students 1 and 3 only
   J. Students 3 and 4 only

5. The most scientifically accurate viewpoint is given by:
   A. Student 1
   B. Student 2
   C. Student 3
   D. Student 4

6. Based on Student 4's viewpoint, the mass changes due to each of the three processes for the plant in the cabinet include:

	Cellular Respiration	Photosynthesis	Transpiration
F.	increase	decrease	increase
G.	increase	no change	decrease
H.	decrease	no change	decrease
J.	decrease	decrease	increase

7. After 5 days, the students measured the mass of each of the plants and found that the plant by the counter lost 50.5 g. Its initial mass was 200.5 g and its final mass was 150.0 g. The intital mass of the plant by the fan was 150.0 g and its final mass was 104.5 g—a loss of 45.5 g. Student 1 thought that his prediction was incorrect and that the plant by the counter had the greatest decrease in mass. The teacher pointed out that the student needed to calculate the percent change in mass, using the formula: [(Final mass (g) – Initial mass (g)) / Initial mass (g)] × 100%. Using that formula, the student found that the plant by the fan had a percent change in mass of:
   A. 25.2%
   B. 30.3%
   C. –25.2%
   D. –30.3%

Answers Explained

TIP

In a question with multiple viewpoints, when you eliminate a viewpoint as incorrect, immediately cross out other answer choices containing that viewpoint.

1. **(C)** A **Factual** Question—Students 1, 2, and 4 all state that the plant in the cabinet will lose mass.

   Wrong: (A) Student 2 agrees with Student 1, so it can't be Student 1 only. (B and D) do not include Student 1, so they are incorrect.

2. **(G)** An **Inference** Question—Transpiration is required for photosynthesis, which uses the water to produce glucose. Student 1 states that there is a gain in mass from the glucose produced by photosynthesis, and that the plant requires water from transpiration to accomplish photosynthesis.

   Wrong: (F and H) State that water is not required to produce glucose. (J) States that transpiration is required for glucose production, but it does not recognize that the glucose production results in a mass increase.

   This is a 50/50 question. Eliminate answers based on the explanations and then figure out the Yes/No.

3. **(D)** An **Inference** Question—The viewpoint states that CO_2 and H_2O are being used, while glucose is being produced and O_2 is being released. This is also a content knowledge question and does not require referring back to the passage.

   Wrong: (A, B, and C) The equations do not match up with either the passage description or with the correct biological process.

4. **(J)** An **Xtreme** Question—The question is looking for an answer that is *inconsistent* with the reported research. Student 3 claims the plant by the fan will gain mass, and Student 4 claims that the plant by the fan will remain constant. Decreased leaf surface area and height would imply a reduced mass.

Wrong: (F) Refers back to Student 1 who argues that windy conditions will cause a decrease in mass. (G) The answer is partially correct, but it is a distracter answer. (H) Student 1's view is consistent with the findings, which makes this entire answer wrong.

5. **(A)** A **Factual** Question—Student 1 makes overall correct arguments about the effects of photosynthesis, transpiration, and cellular respiration. These topics are generally included in biology courses, and this demonstration is a fairly common one in science classrooms.

Wrong: (B) The loss of mass from cellular respiration is not greater than the combined loss from transpiration and respiration. (C and D) State that the plant on the counter will gain mass. Without any additional water, these plants will lose more mass through transpiration and cellular respiration than they will gain from photosynthesis.

6. **(H)** An **Inference** Question—Student 4 claims that the plant in the cabinet will lose mass through cellular respiration and transpiration. Although not explicitly stated, the student implies that photosynthesis will not change the plant's mass.

Wrong: (F and G) State that cellular respiration results in a mass increase.

(J) Contradicts the idea that transpiration results in a mass decrease.

7. **(D)** An **Xtreme** Question—The percent change in mass must be a negative (–) change. For the plant by the fan: (–45.5 g /150 g) $\times$ 100% is –30.3%.

Wrong: (A) This is the calculation for the plant by the counter (–50.5 g /200 g) $\times$ 100% is –25.2% , so (A) is wrong because it shows a positive (+) change in mass. (B) This is a positive (+) change in mass. (C) This is the calculation for the plant by the counter.

INSIDE THE ACT 36 MIND

Remember that the last question in a passage is often more "tricky." If the answer seems really obvious, be careful that you are not making a simple mistake, such as misreading graph labels. Also, whenever a question seems to require a lot of math or includes equations, look at the units first and then "eyeball" the quantities. They are usually pretty obvious.

After working through these practice passages, you should feel even more comfortable with Conflicting Viewpoints passages. Reading scientific articles and texts will expose you to more possible topics and help you out with this section, especially if this is the one that gives you the most problems. Keep practicing!

Tips for Boosting Your Science Score

24

→ **SUGGESTIONS FOR SUCCESS**

Now that you've had a chance to study different kinds of passages, practice your strategies, and analyze your strengths and weaknesses, where do you go from here? You probably have already registered for the test and wonder what else you should be doing to better prepare yourself. Depending on your time frame, here are some reminders and suggestions to help you achieve your 36.

SUGGESTIONS FOR SUCCESS

Experience More Science

Students who have taken the most science classes in high school and have actively participated in their classes perform better on tests like the ACT. Scientific reasoning is a part of any good science curriculum, no matter what the subject. So go through your texts, notes, lab reports, journal articles, etc. and expose yourself to more topics from different sources. Here are some specific ideas for how to do this:

TIP

The more you practice making graphs by hand, the better your overall understanding of the concepts will be. Also, some other advanced science courses require this skill on their standardized exams, so you will be preparing for these tests as well.

READ GRAPHS AND TABLES

Look at a graph or table without reading the caption and see if you can figure out the relationship with the data. Check the caption or description to see if you are correct.

MAKE GRAPHS AND TABLES

Take a complex data table and construct a graph from it. Do not use a calculator or computer to do it for you. Or, try constructing a data table from a graph.

SUMMARIZE SCIENTIFIC JOURNAL ARTICLES

Find a journal article or even an abstract of an article. Write a phrase summarizing the main idea. Or, find scientific articles in the newspaper or online from a source such as Science Daily (*www.sciencedaily.com*), where hundreds of articles are posted every week, and write a one-sentence summary. Besides helping you to identify the main idea of a passage, reading these will expose you to a wider variety of topics.

RUN SCIENTIFIC EXPERIMENTS

Take a lab activity that you've done or are doing in school and modify it. By changing a variable, collecting data, graphing results, and drawing conclusions, you will be using the same skills that the ACT requires in the passages. Your experiments do not have to be extensive or complicated at all. Ask your science teacher for some simple suggestions.

Use Scientific Vocabulary

Analysis of science textbooks has shown that there is often as much new vocabulary in a science course, especially biology, as there is in a first-year language course. Understanding the terminology is very important. What can you do? Here are a few suggestions:

USE ROOT WORDS

You have probably been given a list of Greek and Latin root words that are commonly used in science. Now would be a good time to look them over, as well as some of the terms that commonly use them.

TIP

Don't spend time memorizing vocabulary for this test. The use of the terms might be different, and it would be rare to find the exact definitions used. Understand the concepts—don't memorize the words.

LOOK UP WORDS

When you come across unfamiliar terms, either in an ACT passage, while reading a text or journal, or when reviewing experiments, look up the terms and make sure you understand them in context.

KEEP A LIST

After finding and looking up unfamiliar terms, write them down in your own words on a list somewhere. The processes of putting them into your own words and writing them down will help you understand and remember them easier.

REVIEW PUBLISHED VOCABULARY LISTS

People have surveyed the ACT science section and put together lists of the most commonly used vocabulary terms. Use guides, such as *Barron's ACT*, or online sources to review these lists. Many of your teachers may also have quizzes that you could use to practice with these terms.

TIP

Always try to practice passages under test-like conditions, especially when it comes to timing. Remember, you should spend only three to six minutes per Data Representation and Research Summaries passages, and no more than seven or eight minutes for a Conflicting Viewpoints passage.

PRACTICE, PRACTICE, PRACTICE

There is no substitute for being as familiar with the test as you can and for practicing the strategies. You probably own other guides that contain practice tests. Use the strategies that you learned from this guide to take the practice tests and then to analyze your performance.

Advice from High-Scoring Students

Now you're ready for the actual test. You have a sound knowledge base from your high school classes and from any outside studying you've done. You are familiar with the structure of the science section of the ACT and have become skilled at using **SCIeNCE** strategies. You have spent time practicing with passages so that there are few surprises. So, what else do you need to know? Can you reach your goal?

How about some advice from students just like you? These are people who've been in your shoes and have figured out a method to master the test. Here are four successful students' views of their "secret" to doing well on the ACT science section.

APPROACHING THE SCIENCE TEST

Look over all the information in the passage (graphs, explanations, etc.) once—but thoroughly. Then go through the questions. The information should be fresh in your mind. If it isn't, then where you saw the information should be. Don't second-guess your answers, and most importantly, try to relax!

—Mark

FOUR STRATEGIES THAT WORK

1. *Make sure to do Conflicting Viewpoints passages last, especially if you are more of a math person than an English person—they can take too long and use up valuable time.*
2. *Graph trends are your friends, so make good use of them.*
3. *Don't be scared of unfamiliar vocabulary, or skip words that you think are too big. Most of the important terms are explained in the passages.*
4. *Background knowledge can be helpful. Use what you've learned in your science classes.*

—Rudy

HANDLING THE EXTRAS AND AVOIDING PANIC

When you take the test and feel that you are rushing to complete all of the questions, you tend to overlook very basic information. Look for words that are important, take out most of the little details, and focus on words that are being repeated. Trust what you know, and do not second-guess yourself. Calm down, even if you mess up. There is almost always another chance to take the test again.

—Carly

WHAT TO DO IF YOU GET STUCK

If one passage is taking up too much time, move to the next one and come back at the end. Sometimes seeing a brand new passage can clear your head a bit, so when you get back to the one you skipped, you're not as tired of the topic, and you'll be able to think through it better.
—Bianca

*　　*　　*　　*　　*

These students have all experienced success on the ACT science test. They come from different backgrounds, have different academic strengths, and even approach the tests differently. What they have in common is their ability to use test-taking strategies to achieve their goals. What worked for each of them was slightly different, just like what will work for you will not be exactly the same as what works for anyone else. Despite this fact, what all of these (and other) high-scoring ACT students agreed on was that trying basic strategies, such as **SCIeNCE**, and adapting them in ways that worked for each of them individually was the key to their good performance. Prepare well!

ONLINE PRACTICE TEST

For even more ACT Science practice, remember you can access the online practice test at *barronsbooks.com/tp/ACT36*.

Writing

Writing

Writing an Effective Essay

25

- → **YOUR WRITING GOAL: SOLID, NOT PERFECT**
- → **ACT WRITING CRITERIA**
- → **SPECIFICS ABOUT THE FOUR RUBRIC SECTIONS**
- → **THE RUBRIC DECONSTRUCTED**
- → **SAMPLE ESSAYS**
- → **MORE PROMPT PRACTICE**

Should you choose to complete the optional Writing section of the ACT, you will have just 40 minutes to plan and write a coherent essay that establishes a perspective on an issue and also compares your own perspective to at least one other perspective.

For the sake of fairness and uniformity, all ACT graders will use the same rubric to score essay responses. Two graders will score your essay between 1 and 6, with 6 being the best possible score. ACT then combines those two scores to give you a writing score between 2 and 12. Please note that your performance on the essay will not affect your composite score at all. As of September, 2016, ACT will give you a separate English Language Arts (ELA) score only if you complete the essay. This separate score is an average of your English, Reading, and Writing sections.

More specifically, ACT will evaluate your essay based on your ability to:

1. clearly state your perspective on an issue and compare your perspective to at least one other perspective.
2. develop and support your perspective using sound valid reasoning and evidence.
3. write clear, logical, well-organized prose.
4. use standard written English effectively to communicate your ideas.

Subsequent sections of this chapter will allow you to examine some of these requirements in more detail and decide how you might best prepare to tackle the essay based on your own strengths and weaknesses.

Rarely will you be asked to write an essay in forty minutes—except on the ACT. The time allotted for this particular test dictates how you approach the process. Because you hardly ever have to craft an essay in such a brief time period, practicing this skill is essential.

Using the topics outlined in this chapter, set aside forty minutes whenever you can to practice drafting an essay. Share your responses with your friends and analyze each other's work. Ask teachers to give you feedback. Do whatever it takes to get as much practice on and reaction to your essays as possible. Your peers and teachers will be able to tell you if the essay is comprehensible, logical, and persuasive. Besides writing your own essays, reading professional persuasive pieces helps you identify how solid arguments are developed and organized. Consider reading newspaper editorials and letters to the editor; mimicking the style of an effective writer can be good practice.

YOUR WRITING GOAL: SOLID, NOT PERFECT

An organized, purposeful, logical essay, free of distracting conventional errors, will achieve a high score. Forty minutes is not enough time to spruce up your sentence fluency by combining sentences and adding transitions. It is also not enough time to review your word choice and beef up vocabulary. Although sentence fluency and word choice are factors, the ACT looks primarily for a solid writing sample that proves to potential colleges that you are strong enough to walk their hallways. Colleges want to see that you can handle the basics of writing: choosing a perspective, staying focused, organizing your ideas, providing solid evidence and support for your ideas, maintaining a fluid style, and manipulating the conventional standards of written English.

INSIDE THE ACT 36 MIND

Because ACT essay graders spend only about one minute scoring each paper, your essay has to be solid, not perfect.

As in the other ACT sections, timing is everything. Memorize the following breakdown: 5–30–5. Spend 5 minutes choosing a perspective and preparing your main points and examples. Develop an outline that puts forth your side and also refutes the other side. Once you have a solid outline, stick with it. With only 30 minutes to write the essay, don't stray from your plan of action. Use the last 5 minutes to edit the essay for conventional errors.

First Impressions Count

TIP

Ideas must be thoughtful, clear, and focused. And your writing must be legible.

The first thing anyone notices about a handwritten essay is its appearance: It's either tidy, a mess, or somewhere in between. The same is true for your ACT essay. You must write legibly. The chicken scratch that your English teacher can read only because he has had you in class for an entire year is not going to cut it. Even though, currently, your main mode of communication might be digital, you will again have to reestablish handwriting basics. Remember, ACT essay graders spend approximately one minute reading your essay. If they have to spend the first thirty seconds deciphering whether you have written a "t" or a "d," they may not care to read much more. So take out your pencil and practice good penmanship.

ACT WRITING CRITERIA

Assuming you have mastered the basics of English writing and are seeking an ACT essay score of 4, 5, or 6 out of 6, it may help you to consider some of the subtleties within the higher echelons of ACT's writing rubric. This section attempts to deconstruct some of the thinking behind ACT's writing rubric so that you can set some specific writing goals. In addition, this chapter offers "Hints for success" within each rubric category so that you may further focus your personal goals for improvement. Read the explanations all the way through, or skip to the section where you need the most work. The ACT rubric can seem overwhelming when presented this way. Try to remember that, if you're aiming for the perfect score, you probably employ many of these skills instinctively and may just need to remind yourself of the specific criteria graders look for when they assess your work.

ACT graders are trained to consider four categories when assessing student responses: Ideas and Analysis, Development and Support, Organization, and Language Use. In other words, you will need to present and develop a position in an organized fashion, support your position with evidence, and use language skillfully. Academic writing in high school has no doubt prepared you to understand these best practices in a general way. Students who either fail to understand or fail to execute the basics of these categories will likely score in the bottom half of the rubric (1, 2, or 3). If you are interested in looking at sample essays in the 1, 2, or 3 range, *ACT.org* offers representative examples. In this section, we focus solely on "upper-half" scores so that you can begin to consider what distinguishes *high* scores from *really high* scores. With any luck, this section may also serve a practical purpose by helping you figure out why your AP English teacher keeps nailing you for a "lack of development," or why he or she keeps giving you a B grade for analysis.

"Adequate," "Well-Developed," or "Effective"

These three adjectives summarize scores of 4, 5, and 6, respectively. For a moment, think about the connotations of these words:

- "Adequate" (4) may carry a mildly insulting tone, especially to a high-achieving student, but it actually implies that you have done a satisfactory job. In other words, if you score a 4, you answered the prompt in its entirety, developed your ideas acceptably, organized your thoughts clearly, and used language appropriately. Not bad! That's why it's a 4, not a 3, 2, or 1.

- "Well-developed" (5) is ACT's code phrase for *going beyond* adequate. If you receive a 5, you argued skillfully, developed evidence and reasoning beyond obvious explanations, organized effectively, and used language skillfully.

- "Effective" (6) means you were truly successful, even based on the toughest standards. You addressed the most subtle nuances of multiple perspectives. You developed evidence in insightful ways, organizing your prose seamlessly and purposefully. You made your language sing, writing with purpose, voice, and flow! Though the bulk of this chapter attempts to break down and operationalize some of the specifics of the ACT writing rubric, any experienced academic writer (in other words, almost anyone reading this book) has some sense about the essay he or she submits. By your own standards, think about writing you have submitted that is either "good enough," "pretty darn solid," or "through-the-roof exceptional!" That's your best gauge of the differences among these 3 scores.

SPECIFICS ABOUT THE FOUR RUBRIC SECTIONS

First, consider the following essay prompt, which will provide the basis for subsequent discussion of rubric elements and sample essays:

Role of News Media

In an era when consumers expect information to be delivered around the clock on a minute-to-minute basis, the news media has developed into a powerful cultural force. News outlets that span a wide range of perspectives and ideologies can now deliver the news instantaneously to a targeted audience via a wide range of media technologies. No longer do consumers of the news rely on one newspaper as truth; today's avid media consumer likely considers multiple sources and digests news more rapidly using multiple modes and outlets. Given that most people rely on news media in some form or another for awareness of their world, it is important to consider how this trend has changed the media's influence on the public.

Carefully consider the following perspectives about the role of news media in daily life:

Perspective 1

Bias in the media has manipulated consumers of news to the point that there is no way to understand the actual truth of events. The government should regulate news outlets more carefully and should not hesitate to shut down media companies that deal in inaccurate or biased information.

Perspective 2

Diversity of news coverage is essential to the functioning of a republic. The greater variety of news offered, the more opportunities a citizen has in determining how he or she thinks about a given event. An abundance of media is essential to the decision-making of individuals.

Perspective 3

News media is self-serving and mostly seeks to perpetuate its own business model. Though it is important to be aware of what is happening in the world, it is also essential to understand the role capitalism plays in how news is delivered and to understand that business may affect how information is conveyed.

Write a unified, coherent essay about the role of news media in daily life. In your essay, be sure to:

- clearly state your own perspective on the issue and analyze the relationship between your perspective and at least one other perspective.

- develop and support your ideas with reasoning and examples.

- organize your ideas clearly and logically.

- communicate your ideas effectively in standard written English.

Your perspective may be in full agreement with any of those given, in partial agreement, or completely different.

Take a Breath, and Prepare for 5 Minutes

Spend the first two minutes of your five-minute preparation time reading the prompt carefully, choosing a perspective to defend, and maybe considering how the topic has become debatable in the first place. Explore the nuances of the prompt—its implications and complications. Spend the next three minutes of the preparation time organizing your ideas. Outline the main arguments and counterarguments in support of the perspective you have chosen. Then do the same for the second perspective you must address. Finally, consider examples and ideas that will act as support for your arguments.

The 5-minute Preparation Method

- Read the prompt carefully.

- Identify the issue: (Asking Who, What, Why, and How questions of the prompt might be useful.)

- Brainstorm possible arguments and support for all three perspectives.

- Based on your personal opinions as well as realistic considerations of which perspective you can support, decide on an angle.

- Establish two to three main arguments to support your perspective.

- Identify another perspective as well as possible counterclaims against your perspective, which you will then either concede or refute in defense of your own position.

- Brainstorm examples and ideas that will support your side and disprove counterarguments, or support the second perspective.

THE RUBRIC DECONSTRUCTED

To view the rubric in its entirety, go to *http://www.act.org/content/act/en/products-and-services/the-act/scores/writing-test-scores.html*, or simply search for "*ACT.org writing test scores*" in your browser. There you will find a link to the complete rubric along with other resources. This section of the book examines and analyzes the specifics of the rubric, phrase by phrase. By understanding the mindset of graders, you should be able to set personal goals. While reading the following sections, consider the specific language of the rubric as it applies to *Ideas and Analysis* scores of 4, 5, and 6, and consider the "Hints for success" based on each rubric element.

Section 1: Ideas and Analysis

The first thing to keep in mind is that ACT expects you to "demonstrate effective skill in writing an argumentative essay." In fact, scoring higher than a 1 out of 6 in this category requires you to "generate an argument." Students are sometimes perplexed by this English-teacher-y language, but at its core, writing an argumentative essay requires you to take a position on a topic and then support your position using reason and evidence. The ACT *does not* expect you to pull a detailed research paper out of your head in 40 minutes. Instead, you are expected to consider all three perspectives offered on the issue, then thoughtfully defend your own position on the topic and its "implications, complexities, tensions, values, and assumptions." In short, the Ideas and Analysis section of the rubric assesses your analytical abilities and critical thinking skills more than your technique or style as a writer.

IDEAS AND ANALYSIS #1

The writer:

4. *engages* with multiple perspectives on the given issue.

5. *productively engages* with multiple perspectives on the given issue.

6. *critically engages* with multiple perspectives on the given issue.

HINTS FOR SUCCESS

- **HINT FOR AT LEAST A 4:** Make sure you *engage* with *multiple* perspectives on the issue, which means *at least 2 perspectives*. Even the most skilled writer in the world will score a 3 in this section if he or she only addresses one perspective. Avoid this *major* potential pitfall by developing at least two angles in response to your issue.

- **HINT FOR AT LEAST A 5:** *Productively* engaging multiple perspectives means that you have examined at least 2 perspectives more significantly and profoundly (in the eyes of the scorer) than attempts that receive a 4. Admittedly, the words *productively* and *significantly* are subjective and difficult to define. For a specific hint, think about evaluating multiple perspectives for their strengths *and* weaknesses before stating your opinions about them.

- **HINT FOR A 6:** *Critically* engaging multiple perspectives means breaking down different points of view, analyzing their parts, and evaluating them in ways that show nuanced understanding. Critical thinking skills are developed over the course of a lifetime; you won't learn them by reading this paragraph. For a specific hint, while discussing one perspective on an issue, consider what someone would say if he or she was arguing against you. Address that opposing point of view, and then come back to your own. This process is called *qualifying or refuting an argument* and is an essential component of critical thinking. You might also consider the idea of synthesis, essentially weaving multiple "mini" perspectives seamlessly into one position you consider your own.

IDEAS AND ANALYSIS #2

The thesis (or central argument):

4. reflects *clarity* in thought and purpose.
5. reflects *precision* in thought and purpose.
6. reflects *nuance* and *precision* in thought and purpose.

HINTS FOR SUCCESS

- **HINT FOR AT LEAST A 4:** You need to state your main argument *clearly* and directly. A provable, debatable, opinionated argument about your topic needs to appear prominently in paragraph one of your essay. As a litmus test for a solid thesis, ask yourself these questions: 1. Is my thesis clear and easy to understand? 2. Is my thesis debatable (as opposed to an obvious statement of fact)? 3. Is my thesis provable using reason and evidence? 4. Is my thesis a statement (and not a rhetorical question)?

- **HINT FOR AT LEAST A 5:** Being *precise* with your thesis means stripping away all but what is essential, which can be difficult in a timed writing situation. Check your first paragraph for accuracy and exactness. Specific words matter; slow down and be sure that you are saying exactly what you mean. Attention to the details of language and ideas will take a 4 thesis and make it a 5.

- **HINT FOR A 6:** A *nuanced, precise* argument is difficult to define but easy to spot. It is clear, debatable, and accurate but goes further by acknowledging subtle shades of meaning. For a hint, if you read over your thesis and your response is "Well, duh . . .," then you don't have a nuanced thesis. For a more specific hint, consider an "although" statement in your thesis: "Although___(contrasting view)_____, ___(your view)_____." Acknowledging another perspective within your thesis proves to the reader that you are considering some degree of subtlety and nuance.

IDEAS AND ANALYSIS #3

The (overall) argument (think about the above definition of "argumentative essay"):

4. establishes and employs a *relevant* context for analysis of the issue and its perspectives.

5. establishes and employs a *thoughtful* context for analysis of the issue and its perspectives.

6. establishes and employs an *insightful* context for analysis of the issue and its perspectives.

HINTS FOR SUCCESS

- **NOTE FOR ALL "UPPER-HALF" ESSAYS:** Don't overlook the portion of this rubric element that mentions "the issue *and* its perspectives." You have a tough task here: You *must* consider the context of *at least two* perspectives on the issue, *plus* integrate your own opinion throughout.

- **HINT FOR AT LEAST A 4:** The *context for analysis* means the circumstances, conditions and factors that contribute to your perspective. It might also refer to the causes, complexities, and assumptions surrounding an issue. To ensure that you are addressing *relevant* contextual ideas, think about your issue in the real world. Where do you see it occurring? What do varied opinions about the issue say about the thoughts, backgrounds, or biases of people who hold such opinions? No issue develops in a vacuum, so it is essential that you acknowledge specifically where the issue comes from and why it matters.

- **HINT FOR AT LEAST A 5:** To be *relevant (4)*, all you need to do is provide context that is connected to the issue in some way. To be *thoughtful (5)*, you need to make the reader believe you have considered context carefully, even given the tough time constraints. Consider tossing out the first contextual idea or two that you consider, as there's a good chance thousands of other students will think of the same one. Thirty seconds spent coming up with a more provocative or subtle angle on context can make the difference.

- **HINT FOR A 6:** *Insightful* means deeply perceptive or imaginative, so take some risks. Hold fast to the idea that all contextual elements must be relevant. In other words, don't sacrifice logical connections in the name of looking like a deep thinker. Even so, to score a 6 on this element you'll need to prove to your reader that you've considered context in depth.

HINTS FOR SUCCESS

- **HINT FOR AT LEAST A 4:** This element represents the flip side of the last one. While *context* means "everything surrounding the issue and its perspectives," *implications* refers to effects, consequences, or conclusions one might draw from an issue. Relax, though. You only need to show that you *recognize* implications, complexities, etc. for a 4. If you have acknowledged those elements in any way at all, you have earned a 4 here.

- **HINT FOR AT LEAST A 5:** This element is where graders assess how you've done articulating why the issue should matter, the "so what?" factor. For a specific hint, ask yourself *Who cares?* each time you make a statement about a topic or perspective. If you can't answer your own question easily, you probably need to consider complexity, tension, or underlying meaning more carefully. To *address* these elements means that, beyond showing recognition of complexities, you begin to consider or deal with them in some specific way, usually by developing some thinking about what is "beneath the surface" or beyond obvious elements of the issue or perspective.

- **HINT FOR A 6:** *Examine* is a curious word here, but it may help to think about what a doctor does. Essentially, *examine* means to *inspect methodically and in detail* for the purposes of deeper understanding. Essentially, the more detailed and developed your consideration of the complexities and significance of an issue or perspective is (again, think "so what?"), the higher your score will be.

Section 2: Development and Support

This section of the rubric assesses how you reason through and support your position. Besides assuming you have analyzed multiple perspectives, contexts and implications (see the *Ideas and Analysis* section above), ACT also expects you to develop support for your opinions or "claims" reasonably and logically. If you are unfamiliar with the word *claim*, just think of it as a synonym for argument, thesis, contention, proposal, or opinion statement—whichever term you're used to using.

SHOWING VS. TELLING

Your support paragraphs should always begin with a claim. For example: "The availability of a wide range of news options is essential if media consumers are to expose themselves to different perspectives." While this first sentence represents a strong start, your paragraph will only persuade a reader if it leaves the realm of the abstract and offers specific examples.

Maybe a friend of yours looks only at her own Twitter feed for news and sees mostly the opinions of people she has chosen to see. On the other hand, maybe you know someone who watches several different news channels, reads newspapers like *The New York Times* and *The Wall Street Journal*, listens to news podcasts, and receives regular updates for the purpose of receiving a wider range of opinions. Personal examples like these are perfectly acceptable; what is essential here is that you deepen insights by illustrating your points. Examples from classes you have taken or books you have read are also appropriate and encouraged. *Tell* the reader your claim. Then use effective examples to *show* the reader the problem and ultimately why your perspective is a rational one.

DEVELOPMENT AND SUPPORT #1

Development of ideas and support of claims:

4. clarify meaning.

5. deepen understanding.

6. deepen insight and broaden context.

HINTS FOR SUCCESS

- **HINT FOR AT LEAST A 4:** You've written support paragraphs before and likely have a method with which you are comfortable. To ensure a 4 for development and support, you will need to prove to the reader that you can develop ideas clearly and logically. One helpful method involves thinking of support paragraphs in three, ordered stages: 1) state claim; 2) describe evidence/support/context/implications (whichever is relevant); 3) explain relevance of evidence/support/context/implications. This method should be pretty much foolproof when it comes to *clarifying meaning* for your reader. Remember to always start support paragraphs with an opinionated statement. Avoid the potential pitfall of presenting facts or evidence prior to claims, which tends to make an essay sound as though the writer is reaching for ideas rather than presenting her perspective with poise and confidence.

- **HINT FOR AT LEAST A 5:** To show the reader your ability to *deepen understanding* during a support paragraph, consider one of three strategies: *Strategy 1—refute a counterclaim:* Imagine what someone would say if he or she disagreed with you. Present the opposing view, and then convince your reader why your point of view is superior. *Strategy 2—qualify your claim:* Generally, it helps to qualify or temper all claims. For a simple example, it makes more sense to say, "More people oppose murder than support it" rather than, "All people oppose murder." The latter statement by definition is impossible to defend using reason, so avoid it. All claims, and especially your major ones, should be qualified to show you understand the complexity of the issue. *Strategy 3—offer a concession:* To concede a point means to accept a part of an opposing argument, only to end up bolstering your own perspective by showing that you have anticipated the other side. Again, it might help to think of an "although" statement here: "Although one could reasonably argue that time is too short to examine all news outlets for their varied opinions . . . ." Any of these three strategies will help show a grader that you have a deep understanding of an idea.

- **HINT FOR A 6:** Like most distinctions between a 5 and a 6 in this rubric, proving your abilities to a reader will be subtle. In general, *deepening insight and broadening context* means providing more ideas, claims, qualifications, contexts, or implications that support your claim—and examining them with detail and depth—while staying focused on whichever issue or perspective you offer. Developing ideas insightfully is not easy. For a specific hint, try outlining opinionated articles written by reputable newspaper columnists. First, see if you can identify all claims, qualifying statements, refutations, supporting points, and explanations. Then, look carefully at how the writer weaves together these elements to provide insight artfully. The adage "all great writers are great readers" holds here, so don't hesitate to study and even mimic persuasive authors.

DEVELOPMENT AND SUPPORT #2

Reasoning and Illustration (evidence/defense of your argument):

4. *Lines* of *clear reasoning* and illustration *adequately* convey the significance of the argument.

5. A *mostly integrated* line of *purposeful* reasoning and illustration *capably* conveys the significance of the argument.

6. An *integrated* line of *skillful* reasoning and illustration *effectively* conveys the significance of the argument.

HINTS FOR SUCCESS

- **HINT FOR AT LEAST A 4:** This rubric element assesses your ability to argue logically or, as the ACT suggests, in a *line*. For a moment, picture the actual shape of your writing. Prose, by definition, presents itself in a straight line of words and punctuation, which isn't how most of us think. To *adequately* show *clear reasoning*, make sure you think logically through how to defend your point for a moment before you write a support paragraph. Then, make an effort to place ideas in your paragraph in a way that creates logical flow. If you find yourself heading out on a tangent, make a note and save that point for a new paragraph.

- **HINT FOR AT LEAST A 5:** Reasoning *purposefully* and *capably* means setting specific goals for writing and then proving to your reader that you can reach those goals with ease. For this essay, you'll have at least four or five separate goals: A central claim or thesis that integrates at least two perspectives, discussions of both perspectives and their complexities, contexts, and implications, and probably a section that synthesizes some of these varied ideas into your own perspective. In short, it's a lot to think about in 40 minutes! For a specific hint, make sure that, whichever direction you go, a central, unifying thesis statement holds your essay together. Lots of problems with development come from weak thesis statements. Start strong and your points will be easier to argue in depth.

- **HINT FOR A 6:** *Integrated, skillful reasoning* that *effectively conveys significance* is again the logical extension of the first two hints in this category. The more slick your essay feels to the reader in terms of its clarity, understanding, and insight, the higher you'll score. Practice is the only way to improve. If your school offers one, enroll in an Advanced Placement English course. Teachers of these courses often ask their students to write multiple timed essays in preparation for their AP exams. Many of these students swear that the more they practice this pressure-packed task, the better they get at developing arguments clearly, presenting supports seamlessly, and organizing essays purposefully.

DEVELOPMENT AND SUPPORT #3

Qualifications and complications:

4. *extend* ideas and analysis.

5. *enrich* ideas and analysis.

6. *enrich* and *bolster* ideas and analysis.

HINTS FOR SUCCESS

- **HINT FOR AT LEAST A 4:** This section might seem somewhat simple, but don't overlook it. *Qualifications* and *complications* have come up in other sections of the rubric because addressing them is essential to showing an understanding of the complexity of any issue. *ACT readers want to know that you have moved beyond the standard 8th grade argument*, in which you write 5 paragraphs that go something like this:

  Paragraph 1: My opinion is right

  Paragraph 2: 1st reason my opinion is right

  Paragraph 3: 2nd reason my opinion is right

  Paragraph 4: 3rd reason my opinion is right

  Paragraph 5: Clearly you see that my opinion is right!

If you've gone to school beyond third grade, you've written these essays. Such exercises are useful in training students to begin to argue logically, but they ignore complexity, mostly because most 10 to 14 year-olds struggle to understand complexity. *(By the way, the above outline would likely earn you a 2 or a 3 on this task.)* Now that you're older and probably have plans to become a college writer, you need to examine multiple perspectives on the issue, address alternate points of view, qualify statements, refute counterclaims, and concede valid opposing points. Don't expect an "upper half" score for development unless you do at least some of these things.

- **HINT FOR AT LEAST A 5:** Rubrics can be frustrating. For one, it can be hard to draw distinctions between words like *extend* and *enrich*. Consider the definitions of these words. "Extend" means to "make bigger or longer." To a certain extent, getting a 4 in this category just means developing support paragraphs that are long enough to pass the reader's "eyeball test." "Enrich" means to "improve quality or value." So, to prove to your reader that you've earned a 5 in this category, you'll need to make your argument stronger by getting in there and addressing the complexity of an issue. It's not enough to just explain your original point in a sentence or two and move on. Enriching your claim means proving you've thought through and explained your position by considering questionable details, opposing views, and reasonable counterclaims.

- **HINT FOR A 6:** So, now that you've enriched your analysis, how do you bolster it? This confusing distinction just means your analysis is both high quality *and* well supported. It's propped up, stable, and strong. It might help to think of an analogy here. Picture a house. A house built of the finest materials will still only stand if its foundation and frame are also of high quality. You don't see the frame or foundation of this house, but you'd probably agree that it's at least as important as the expensive quartz countertop in the kitchen. To score a 6 in this category, your essay integrates within its framework an understanding of complexity that feels unified as a whole.

Section 3: Organization

Think about the shape of the essay. A superb ACT essay will have a streamlined structure that is easy to see and understand. An unfinished essay, as you might guess, won't score highly. One trap that higher level students fall into is overdoing the essay. You are accustomed to spending hours drafting, revising, and editing your work. You know what you can do when you have the time. You may have delusions that your forty-minute essay has the potential to sound like something you took a week or more to complete. Don't fall into this trap. Keep the structure simple and clean with separate supports for each argument, designated in advance.

Organize your essay efficiently. In one paragraph, state minimal background and a nuanced, qualified thesis. Create separate paragraphs for separate claims. Within each paragraph, state your own claims, provide examples, refute counterclaims, and concede valid opposing points of view. Finally, conclude your essay by restating some key points and tying it somehow to your lead paragraph. If you practice keeping your writing within a manageable framework, you should have time to finish and even revise for obvious errors during the last five minutes.

ACT's readers will assess your overall organizational strategy as the byproduct of three central elements: your ability to unify all ideas into a coherent whole, your ability to sequence ideas logically, and your ability to craft purposeful transitions. To pull off a 6 in this category, you will need to organize your ideas logically around a strong central statement, staying focused on the big picture as well as the sequence of details that help that central idea emerge. Finally, you'll need to transition seamlessly from point to point.

ORGANIZATION #1

The response exhibits a:

4. clear organizational strategy.
5. productive organizational strategy.
6. skillful organizational strategy.

HINTS FOR SUCCESS

- **HINT FOR AT LEAST A 4:** Ask yourself whether or not you are a natural organizer. Typically, high-achieving student writers fall into one of two categories: those who write and think in terms of organized structures already and those who "brain dump" and *then* work to make their thoughts coherent. If you naturally keep things clear and linear, you need not worry about this category. If you tend to splash thoughts on the page and then organize them, write a quick outline of your thoughts about issues, perspectives, contexts, and implications before you start writing. Five minutes of planning will be worth your time.

- **HINT FOR AT LEAST A 5:** Organizing *productively* as opposed to just *clearly* means that everything—among paragraphs and within them—plays a crucial role. ACT does not expect you to submit publishable work after just 40 minutes, but they do expect you to use words, sentences, and paragraphs productively. Productive organization creates unity and produces a more convincing result. Ask yourself periodically if your writing serves the ultimate purpose of answering the prompt and does so in a logical fashion. If not, you might be writing something *clear* but not necessarily *productive*.

- **HINT FOR A 6:** *Skillful* is ACT reader's way of suggesting that a writer's use of time and space has not only produced the desired result but that the writer has done so in a way that impresses them. Remember that organizational strategies worthy of a 4 are easy to spot; a reader can glance at your essay and see that it is *clearly* organized. Level 6 organization is achieved more subtly and is more difficult to teach. It involves unity, logical sequencing, and clear movement from one element to another. To use an analogy, it would be easy to tell people, skillful or not, to go play soccer. It would be *clear* to most what they were doing. In contrast, it would be difficult to expect good results by simply telling someone how to become a *skillful* soccer player. Only thousands of hours of practice would make that person truly skillful. Writing works the same way, and there are no shortcuts. Read as much as you can, practice your craft, and study the work of superior wordsmiths.

ORGANIZATION #2

4. The overall shape of the response reflects an emergent controlling idea or purpose.

5. The response is mostly unified by a controlling idea or purpose.

6. The response is unified by a controlling idea or purpose.

HINTS FOR SUCCESS

- **HINT FOR AT LEAST A 4:** *Overall shape* says it all here: you can obtain a 4 in this category by using paragraphs properly. That's about all you need to know. When you come to a new idea, indent. Even a skilled writer operating under time constraints will occasionally overlook simple strategies that aid clarity. Paragraphs are your friend. Don't get in a hurry and forget to use them.

- **HINT FOR AT LEAST A 5:** *Unity* is a tricky thing to achieve under time constraints. While the *Ideas and Analysis* section of the rubric asks you to dig deep into multiple perspectives, this section asks you to keep your goal in mind. Make no mistake, your purpose is to answer a complex question about an issue while incorporating at least two perspectives. That said, you must also do so in a way in which all pieces fit together logically. Again, for those who don't organize naturally, starting with a brief outline will help. As you write, periodically check your own focus. Your essay will move from topic to topic, but ultimately it should answer only one, complex question.

- **HINT FOR A 6:** Keep two ideas in mind. 1. You need to construct a controlling idea or purpose that is strong enough to sustain you for the whole essay. (See Ideas and Analysis #2 for more details on how to write a precise, nuanced thesis.) 2. Practicing timed responses will help you maintain control of an argument. In short, get used to timed writing. This point may sound repetitive, but practice and extensive reading are the best ways to improve at writing unified essays quickly. As has been stated before, classes such as Advanced Placement English are typically good environments in which to hone your craft.

ORGANIZATION #3

4. Ideas are logically grouped and sequenced.

5. A logical sequence of ideas contributes to the effectiveness of the argument.

6. A logical progression of ideas increases the effectiveness of the writer's argument.

HINTS FOR SUCCESS

- **HINT FOR AT LEAST A 4:** Refer to section above entitled Development and Support #3. You will see a basic essay structure, probably one you've used before, presented for a different purpose. As long as you use a logical structure, overall and within paragraphs, you should be able to obtain a 4 in this category. Again, if you're not a natural organizer, use a brief outline to keep yourself on target.

- **HINT FOR AT LEAST A 5:** Think for a second about how organization *contributes to the effectiveness* of an essay. To some degree, the topic or task will dictate your structure. Will you work chronologically? Sequentially? Will you move toward a climactic ending, or will you start with your strongest point and work downwards? Your sequencing is up to you, but you'll need to show some purpose in your organization, not just an ability to write 5 separate paragraphs, to obtain a 5 in this category.

- **HINT FOR A 6:** To *increase the effectiveness* of your essay through organization, you'll need to make it clear that you have been purposeful with all organizational strategies. One obvious way to do so is by attempting to "hook" your reader. If you like catchy lead sentences or paragraphs, that's fine but not essential. (Note: make sure you avoid hook cliches such as quotes, dictionary definitions, rhetorical questions, and sweeping statements like "Throughout history. . . .") Repetitive strategies such as motifs can also show a reader that you seek to increase your essay's effectiveness through organization. One trick that can also serve to unify an essay is the strategy of mentioning your lead idea again at the end of your essay. This may sound corny, but given that your reader will be assessing your work quickly, obvious, eye-catching strategies can sometimes work to your advantage.

HINTS FOR SUCCESS

- **HINT FOR AT LEAST A 4:** Before you worry too much about transitions, remember that a new paragraph is a transition. Even a period signals to the reader that you are moving from one thought to another. There is no need to be fancy when moving from sentence to sentence or from topic to topic. As long as you maintain logical sequencing (*within paragraphs: point → evidence → explanation within paragraphs and overall: beginning → middle →end*), you will likely include *clear* transitions.

- **HINT FOR AT LEAST A 5:** Before you start another paragraph, think about its purpose. Are you moving into a contrasting thought? If so, you'll likely transition using a phrase such as "whereas" or "yet." Are you continuing to another aspect of the same basic perspective? You'll probably use "in addition" or "moreover." Cause-effect relationships will necessitate transitions such as "as a result" and "because." *Consistently clarifying* relationships among sentences or among ideas is often about finding the right word or phrase that helps you do so concisely and clearly. Don't get caught using "and" and "then" all the time. Show your poise and sophistication as a writer by getting beyond elementary transitions like "first," "second," "third," and "last."

- **HINT FOR A 6:** Simply put, *strengthening relationships* through transitions means creating flow. If your essay is a song, transitions are the build-ups from the verse to the chorus or the rests between the middle section and the big finish. Transitions will strengthen your writing if they make it more fluent and less choppy. Meaningful transition sentences also show a progression of thought. Don't jar your reader each time you change topics, unless you're going for the element of surprise.

Section 4: Language Use

Finally, ACT judges your skill as a writing stylist. The well-known novelist Tim O'Brien puts it this way: "There are twenty-six letters in our alphabet. And there are some punctuation marks, and that's it." The last section of the rubric attempts to enumerate your use of these letters and punctuation by evaluating word choice, sentence fluency, stylistic and "register" choices (discussed later on), voice, tone, as well as the basics of grammar, mechanics, and usage.

As these rubric categories are more self-explanatory in some ways than the others, one general hint for success is offered in each category. This book does not attempt to teach sound writing style but rather attempts to remind you of some of the fundamentals. Ultimately, it will be up to you to choose your best words, craft your best sentences, and present ideas in a tone and register appropriate to the task.

LANGUAGE USE #1

The use of language:

4. conveys the argument with clarity.

5. works in service of the argument.

6. enhances the argument.

HINT FOR SUCCESS

Each essay has its own style and flair—that's what makes your essay unique. Sometimes, high-achieving students want to decorate their essays with a lot of fluff in order to sound smart. This tendency, as was mentioned during the English chapters, is no substitute for clarity and precision. Keep the style of your essay sophisticated and functional. Dispense with the fanfare and focus on crafting a comprehensible essay that sounds like you wrote it.

LANGUAGE USE #2

Word choice is:

4. adequate and sometimes precise.

5. precise.

6. skillful and precise.

HINT FOR SUCCESS

Word choice must be specific and accurate. Demonstrate that you understand how words function—don't use an adverb when you should be using an adjective, and don't use a sophisticated-sounding word unless you are utterly clear on its meaning. Chapter 4 addresses ACT's expectations on word use, which apply to your essay just as they apply to your editing skills during the multiple-choice section.

LANGUAGE USE #3

Sentence structures are:

4. clear and demonstrate some variety.

5. clear and varied often.

6. consistently varied and clear.

HINT FOR SUCCESS

Sentence structure can inhibit or enhance the flow and clarity of your essay. Too many short sentences will make your essay feel choppy and boring. Too many long, complex sentences will make your essay feel endless and cause confusion for your reader. Consciously mix sentence lengths. Varied sentence structure is something a grader *can* notice in less than a minute. Making it obvious that you use different sentence styles and lengths is an easy way to demonstrate to a grader that you are competent with the written word.

HINT FOR SUCCESS

"Voice" is simply the specific ways your writing sounds like you. "Tone" is the attitude you convey. "Register" is the appropriateness of both tone and voice to the writing task in question, the "formality scale" of language as it applies to writing. (It might help to think of the register you would use when conversing with a boss or a teacher versus the one you might use with your best friend at a party.) For this task, keep in mind that you are writing a formal, academic essay. That said, it is okay to sound like yourself. A strategically placed first person account might be appropriate when illustrating a point, for example. Tone and register that are too loose or informal will be off-putting to a grader, as will language that is overly formal or pompous. Finding the *effective* middle ground can be difficult, but you likely have dealt with this dilemma before in school. Trust your academic instincts and you will be fine.

HINT FOR SUCCESS

Are your commas thrown around sloppily, or do you actually know how to use them? Do you capitalize when you need to, or has social media rendered you proper noun-challenged? An essay that isn't well proofread or fails to follow the standards of written English shows poor craftsmanship, and it only takes a second to sense it. In the last few minutes of your time period, check for your most common spelling problems. Do you always confuse *there, their,* and *they're?* Do you forget to add *ing* to the end of a word? Figure out your personal tendencies and memorize how to correct them. Go back through the essay looking for your most common mistakes. In a grader's eyes, an essay that lacks attention to detail at the level of grammar, usage, capitalization, or spelling is at a disadvantage from the outset. Consistent and flagrant grammatical errors will distract your reader, probably causing him or her to maintain a negative bias throughout the rest of your essay. No matter how wonderful your ideas, frequent errors make an essay challenging to read. Once you have built, furnished, and decorated your house, make sure it's clean and organized before submitting it.

SAMPLE ESSAYS

All sample essays have been written in response to the "Role of News Media" prompt previously listed on pages 303–304.

Example #1 (Score: 6)

Today's news media play a prodigious, daily role in creating and shaping public opinion and strengthening society; news media are the sword arm of democracy and freedom. Therefore, it is crucial that the media serve as society's "watchdog" to protect public interest against malpractice by appropriately informing, engaging, and entertaining the public.

One common argument against news media's role is that bias manipulates consumers to extents so extreme that they are brainwashed of reality, unable to understand the actual truth. This argument's supporters believe that the government should regulate news outlets to prevent the distribution of inaccurate or biased news (Perspective 1). Indeed, bias and inaccuracy in news coverage poses ethical concerns. The government should not regulate news outlets in a democracy, particularly American democracy, because it violates the First Amendment freedoms of speech and press. Also, history infamously proves that governments are no more reliable than public news media in delivering accurate information. An example would be Nazi Germany during the Third Reich. The government quickly became corrupt under the rule of Adolf Hitler, who regulated the press and strictly limited or falsified the people's knowledge of what went on in the government through propaganda. As a result, Hitler lost his accountability with the German people and led their government down the wrong path. Therefore, Perspective 1's argument is unreasonable because it is the role of news media to share coverage without government regulation to freely inform the public of governments' actions.

Despite the news media's efforts to report and reveal the government's actions, others argue that news media industry is self-serving. This belief claims that the media seek to perpetuate their own business model as a result of capitalism, which means the public is required to consume news with caution and consideration (Perspective 3). As evidenced by the gun-jumping of the 2000 Bush versus Gore election, breaking a story first is an irresistible prize in news media. The information presented to the public was and continues to be based on the assumption that viewers will tune into the program that has the latest "breaking" news, even if the difference is seconds. I agree with Perspective 3, as profits, ratings, and clicks increasingly determine a news story's significance in the eyes of media companies as opposed to the quality of content and relevance to the public's needs. When information and public interest are abused and degraded, so is democracy. Therefore, as the news media industry grows, it is increasingly important for it to maintain its role as "watchdog" of the government to preserve the quality and educational value of news.

Furthermore, in the age of "news bias," Perspective 2 argues that it is the role of news media to report diverse perspectives to dilute the influences of mass media malpractice. This argument suggests that an abundance of media opens up more opportunities to diversify individuals' decision-making foundations. Public interest is best protected against mass media's excessive manipulation when local, non-mainstream news services help offset mass media corporations' political biases. As much as people will preach that the diversification of news media has "greatly improved" and "come so far," there is still much to be done. We live in a diverse and multicultural world, and it is the media's ethical role to represent that global culture. Mass news media would rightfully come alongside more local newscasts to be representative of the public's views on the local, national, and international levels, thus protecting public interest against malpractice by encouraging unique coverage, diverse audience engagement, and opinion-provoking empowerment among the public.

The news media industry is a socially, politically, and economically powerful sector of modern civilization. It is a tool that is shared to maintain a balanced society characterized by well-informed people, effective democracy, and social justice. Even though news media have had an equally negative influence on aspects of human life, at its core, the role of news media is to eliminate the boundaries of information, therefore acting as a "watchdog" to protect the public's rights to interpret and share information around the world.

Example #2 (Score: 5)

The news media is vital to the success of a democratic republic. It is the main vehicle for the spread of information and ideas, even if those ideas contradict one's own. Although it has caused conflict, the news media allows citizens to learn about a variety of events and viewpoints as well as to develop their own opinions enriching daily life.

Having a variety of news sources allows readers to understand the events and perspectives of people from different walks of life. For many, the news is an integral part of their daily routine, as it is the most convenient method of exploring the world. While a single media source can give basic facts, it is limited. Each news source reports what it feels is important and, in accordance with perspective three, what makes money. In a capitalist society, it is vital for businesses including the media industry to make money. It can be easy to think that this is degrading the quality of the news one reads. However, it further diversifies the information shared. Some new media organizations will portray news events in a different light compared to other organizations. While news sources can greatly vary in how they report news events, they all have their respective places in society. In order to have a functioning democracy, citizens need to be aware of and understand a variety of perspectives on the issues of the day. Political literacy is essential for a functioning democracy, a principle that is just as true with international policy. One efficient way to understand other nations is to read their news. Sources such as BBC or Al Jazeera allow citizens in the U.S. and around the world to comprehend the issues other nations face on a deeper level. It may seem like a waste of time for average citizens to understand these issues, but they do have the responsibility to vote. In order to make the best decisions possible on domestic policy, citizens must understand how policies affect foreign affairs and therefore must understand foreign dilemmas. Not only does this improve the function of a republic, it allows for globally-minded citizens, a necessity in an increasingly interconnected world. The variety of news sources allows for an improved government, enriched daily life, and well-informed citizen choice.

Diversity in news coverage also allows people to develop their own opinions. Average citizens can be involved in their government despite not being a government official through news media. This idea is explored in perspective two. The author of perspective two is likely a consumer of many different types of news, open to new ideas, and active in politics. The variety of opinions and perspectives idealized in perspective two strengthens their argument but could also cause conflict. Although conflict seems negative, it is the basis of progress and is evident in the countries with multiple news outlets. Countries with more freedoms of press usually develop faster than those with only one source.

For example, South Korea has newer technology, better foreign relations, and greater quality of life compared to North Korea, which only allows state media. Varied news allows for increased speed in advancement. On a more specific level for example, access to scientific journals spreads the news of new discoveries, allowing other researchers to provide input. This process expedites the rate of research and the expansion of knowledge. Varied news develops ideas, people, technology, countries, and in turn the globe, accelerating the improvement of daily life around the world.

Daily life is expanded and improved upon through varied news media. Providing an assortment of perspectives allows unlimited development of ideas and opinions. News media is vital to success and progress. Perhaps if it were free throughout the world, it would improve progress in global relations.

Example #3 (Score: 4)

In the modern age we know everything instantly. Whether it's through social media, newspapers, or major news networks, it's very easy to obtain information. However, with so many outlets that have their own perspective, it's hard to know the truth. As I have grown up, I've realized that every news outlet has their own personal agenda. They often want to push their agendas so much that they'll twist stories to their liking. Because of this, it is crucial that citizens listen to multiple news stations so that they can make informed decisions in their daily lives.

Whether it's CNN, Fox News, or MSNBC, every media outlet has its own social, economic, and political views. Therefore, it's no surprise that each station will report the news (at least) slightly differently. A great example was the divisive 2016 United States presidential campaign, where media outlets portrayed news events in different lights and ultimately played a large role in the presidential outcome. This phenomenon has roots that can be traced back to the 1960 presidential election, the first presidential election in which television is said to have swayed voters in favor of John F. Kennedy. Interestingly, this 1960 election also led to the birth of more biased, party-affiliated news channels. This is why Perspective 3 is so important. It is essential for viewers to be able to recognize truth and bias in news reporting. Media outlets can and will manipulate information to their own liking. With this comes a responsibility to at least attempt to learn as much as one can before making decisions.

Since people view the news every single day, it will undoubtedly affect them in their daily lives. Because of the conflicting viewpoints of many media outlets, it's a citizen's duty to draw information from multiple news sources. If citizens only receive information from one source how can they possibly know if they are receiving the correct information? Whereas if someone is able to look at a news story from many different perspectives, then they are much more likely to make informed decisions. Perspective 2 states that diversity of news coverage is essential to the workings of a Republic. This is very true, especially in a Republic democracy like the U.S., where the people elect representatives. In order to decide on who you want representing you, you must decide on if you like them, not on whether the media outlet likes them.

There are dozens of mainstream media sources all with their own perspective. In order to make well-informed decisions in everyday life, I believe that is it essential for citizens to be aware of media outlets' conflicting viewpoints and pull from multiple media sources. If our society can achieve this, then we will have a very intelligent and informed populous.

MORE PROMPT PRACTICE

Use the following prompt to write your own essay. Refer back to the prompt and sample essays from earlier. Set aside forty minutes; find a pencil and some paper. Spend five minutes preparing, thirty-five minutes writing, and five minutes reviewing and editing your essay. Share your essay with a parent, teacher, or friend. Ask him or her to critique your essay using the writing criteria outlined in this chapter.

bullies@everywhere.com

Human interaction has been plagued by intimidation throughout history, but access to the internet has exacerbated the issue significantly during the past two decades. Cyber-bullying exists in social situations, the workplace, and especially schools. Often hiding behind a wall of anonymity, cyber-bullies damage and destroy lives.

Carefully examine the following perspectives about the issue of bullying.

Perspective 1

Bullying is, in many cases, a time-honored tradition used to build character through adversity. This practice has been carried on in the military, in the classroom, between siblings, and on the athletic field. It only makes sense that as technology advances, bullying enters the online world. Of course, it should do so without violent acts or criminal activity, but bullying isn't going anywhere, in person or online.

Perspective 2

Bullying for the purpose of motivation is wrong. The practice is demeaning for the victim, often leading him or her to diminished self-esteem, emotional trauma, and suicidal ideations. Those who seek to motivate should do so in a more constructive, positive manner, and those in charge should assert their authority when they encounter bullying in any form.

Perspective 3

Bullying, especially online, should be treated as the crime it is. Authorities must hold those accountable who engage in bullying. Laws pertaining to bullying need to be enforced, with the criminals who commit these offenses punished to the fullest extent of the law.

Write a unified, coherent essay addressing the problem of bullying. Be sure to:

- clearly state your own perspective on the issue and analyze the relationship between your perspective and at least one of those provided.

- develop and support your ideas with reasoning and examples.

- organize your ideas clearly and logically.

- communicate your ideas effectively and in standard written English.

Your perspective may be in full agreement with any of those given, in partial agreement, or completely different.

ONLINE PRACTICE TEST

For even more ACT Writing practice, remember you can access the online practice test at *barronsbooks.com/tp/ACT36.*
